Classic Fantasy Writers

Writers of English: Lives and Works

Classic Fantasy Writers

Edited and with an Introduction by

Harold Bloom

CHELSEA HOUSE PUBLISHERS
New York   Philadelphia

Jacket illustration: Edward Burne-Jones (1833–1898), *The Baleful Head* (courtesy of Bridgeman/Art Resource).

CHELSEA HOUSE PUBLISHERS

Editorial Director Richard Rennert
Executive Managing Editor Karyn Gullen Browne
Picture Editor Adrian G. Allen
Copy Chief Robin James
Art Director Robert Mitchell
Manufacturing Director Gerald Levine
Production Coordinator Marie Claire Cebrián-Ume

Writers of English: Lives and Works

Senior Editor S. T. Joshi
Series Design Rae Grant

Staff for CLASSIC FANTASY WRITERS

Research Peter Cannon, Robert Green
Editorial Assistant Mary Sisson
Picture Researcher Pat Burns

First Printing

1 3 5 7 9 8 6 4 2

Library of Congress Cataloging-in-Publication Data

Classic fantasy writers / edited and with an introduction by Harold Bloom.
    p.   cm.—(Writers of English)
    Includes bibliographical references.
    ISBN 0-7910-2204-8.—ISBN 0-7910-2229-3 (pbk.)
    1. Fantastic fiction, English—Bio-bibliography. 2. Fantastic fiction, American—Bio-bibliography. 3. Novelists, American—Biography—Dictionaries. 4. Novelists, English—Biography—Dictionaries. 5. Fantastic fiction, American—Dictionaries. 6. Fantastic fiction, English—Dictionaries. I. Bloom, Harold. II. Series.
PR830.F3C53 1994   93-8346
823'.0876609'03—dc20   CIP

◈ Contents

◈ User's Guide

THIS VOLUME PROVIDES biographical, critical, and bibliographical information on the fourteen most significant fantasy writers up to the early twentieth century. Each chapter consists of three parts: a biography of the author; a selection of brief critical extracts about the author; and a bibliography of the author's published books.

The biography supplies a detailed outline of the important events in the author's life, including his or her major writings. The critical extracts are taken from a wide array of books and periodicals, from the author's lifetime to the present, and range in content from biographical to critical to historical. The extracts are arranged in chronological order by date of writing or publication, and a full bibliographical citation is provided at the end of each extract. Editorial additions or deletions are indicated within carets.

The author bibliographies list every separate publication—including books, pamphlets, broadsides, collaborations, and works edited or translated by the author—for works published in the author's lifetime; selected important posthumous publications are also listed. Titles are those of the first edition; if a work has subsequently come to be known under a variant title, this title is supplied within carets. In selected instances dates of revised editions are given where these are significant. Pseudonymous works are listed, but the pseudonyms under which these works were published are not. Periodicals edited by the author are listed only when the author has written most or all of the contents. For plays we have listed date of publication, not date of production; unpublished plays are not listed. Titles enclosed in square brackets are of doubtful authenticity. All works by the author, whether in English or in other languages, have been listed; English translations of foreign-language works are not listed unless the author has done the translation.

The Life of the Author
Harold Bloom

NIETZSCHE, WITH EXULTANT ANGUISH, famously proclaimed that God was dead. Whatever the consequences of this for the ethical life, its ultimate literary effect certainly would have surprised the author Nietzsche. His French disciples, Foucault most prominent among them, developed the Nietzschean proclamation into the dogma that all authors, God included, were dead. The death of the author, which is no more than a Parisian trope, another metaphor for fashion's setting of skirt-lengths, is now accepted as literal truth by most of our current apostles of what should be called French Nietzsche, to distinguish it from the merely original Nietzsche. We also have French Freud or Lacan, which has little to do with the actual thought of Sigmund Freud, and even French Joyce, which interprets *Finnegans Wake* as the major work of Jacques Derrida. But all this is as nothing compared to the final triumph of the doctrine of the death of the author: French Shakespeare. That delicious absurdity is given us by the New Historicism, which blends Foucault and California fruit juice to give us the Word that Renaissance "social energies," and not William Shakespeare, composed *Hamlet* and *King Lear*. It seems a proper moment to murmur "enough" and to return to a study of the life of the author.

Sometimes it troubles me that there are so few masterpieces in the vast ocean of literary biography that stretches between James Boswell's great *Life* of Dr. Samuel Johnson and the late Richard Ellmann's wonderful *Oscar Wilde*. Literary biography is a crucial genre, and clearly a difficult one in which to excel. The actual nature of the lives of the poets seems to have little effect upon the quality of their biographies. Everything happened to Lord Byron and nothing at all to Wallace Stevens, and yet their biographers seem equally daunted by them. But even inadequate biographies of strong writers, or of weak ones, are of immense use. I have never read a literary biography from which I have not profited, a statement I cannot make about any other genre whatsoever. And when it comes to figures who are central to us—Dante, Shakespeare, Cervantes, Montaigne, Goethe, Whitman, Tolstoi, Freud, Joyce, Kafka among them—we reach out eagerly for every scrap that the biographers have gleaned. Concerning Dante and Shakespeare we know much too little, yet when we come to Goethe and Freud, where we seem to know more

vii

his joining in the lunacy that argued for the Earl of Oxford as the author of than everything, we still want to know more. The death of tne author, despite our current resentniks, clearly was only a momentary fad. Something vital in every authentic lover of literature responds to Emerson's battle-cry sentence: "There is no history, only biography." Beyond that there is a deeper truth, difficult to come at and requiring a lifetime to understand, which is that there is no literature, only autobiography, however mediated, however veiled, however transformed. The events of Shakespeare's life included the composition of *Hamlet*, and that act of writing was itself a crucial act of living, though we do not yet know altogether how to read so doubled an act. When an author takes up a more overtly autobiographical stance, as so many do in their youth, again we still do not know precisely how to accommodate the vexed relation between life and work. T. S. Eliot, meditating upon James Joyce, made a classic statement as to such accommodation:

> We want to know who are the originals of his characters, and what
> were the origins of his episodes, so that we may unravel the web of memory
> and invention and discover how far and in what ways the crude material
> has been transformed.

When a writer is not even covertly autobiographical, the web of memory and invention is still there, but so subtly woven that we may never unravel it. And yet we want deeply never to stop trying, and not merely because we are curious, but because each of us is caught in her own network of memory and invention. We do not always recall our inventions, and long before we age we cease to be certain of the extent to which we have invented our memories. Perhaps one motive for reading is our need to unravel our own webs. If our masters could make, from their lives, what we read, then we can be moved by them to ask: What have we made or lived in relation to what we have read? The answers may be sad, or confused, but the question is likely, implicitly, to go on being asked as long as we read. In Freudian terms, we are asking: What is it that we have repressed? What have we forgotten, unconsciously but purposively: What is it that we flee? Art, literature necessarily included, is regression in the service of the ego, according to a famous Freudian formula. I doubt the Freudian wisdom here, but indubitably it is profoundly suggestive. When we read, something in us keeps asking the equivalent of the Freudian questions: From what or whom is the author in flight, and to what earlier stages in her life is she returning, and why?

Reading, whether as an art or a pastime, has been damaged by the visual media, television in particular, and might be in some danger of extinction in the age of the computer, except that the psychic need for it continues to endure, presumably because it alone can assuage a central loneliness in elitist society. Despite all sophisticated or resentful denials, the reading of imaginative literature remains a quest to overcome the isolation of the individual consciousness. We can read for information, or entertainment, or for love of the language, but in the end we seek, so that reading, even in childhood, is rarely free of hidden anxieties. And yet it remains one of the few activities not contaminated by an entropy of spirit. We read in hope, because we lack companionship, and the author can become the object of the most idealistic elements in our search for the wit and inventiveness we so desperately require. We read biography, not as a supplement to reading the author, but as a second, fresh attempt to understand what always seems to evade us in the work, our drive towards a kind of identity with the author.

This will-to-identity, though recently much deprecated, is a prime basis for the experience of sublimity in reading. *Hamlet* retains its unique position in the Western canon not because most readers and playgoers identify themselves with the prince, who clearly is beyond them, but rather because they find themselves again in the power of the language that represents him with such immediacy and force. Yet we know that neither language nor social energy created Hamlet. Our curiosity about Shakespeare is endless, and never will be appeased. That curiosity itself is a value, and cannot be separated from the value of *Hamlet* the tragedy, or Hamlet the literary character. It provokes us that Shakespeare the man seems so unknowable, at once everyone and no one as Borges shrewdly observes. Critics keep telling us otherwise, yet something valid in us keeps believing that we would know Hamlet better if Shakespeare's life were as fully known as the lives of Goethe and Freud, Byron and Oscar Wilde, or best of all, Dr. Samuel Johnson. Shakespeare never will have his Boswell, and Dante never will have his Richard Ellmann. How much one would give for a detailed and candid *Life of Dante* by Petrarch, or an outspoken memoir of Shakespeare by Ben Jonson! Or, in the age just past, how superb would be rival studies of one another by Hemingway and Scott Fitzgerald! But the list is endless: think of *Oscar Wilde* by Lord Alfred Douglas, or a joint biography of Shelley by Mary Godwin, Emilia Viviani, and Jane Williams. More than our insatiable desire for scandal would be satisfied. The literary rivals and the lovers of the great writers possessed perspectives we will never enjoy, and without those perspectives we dwell in some poverty in regard to the writers with whom we ourselves never can be done.

There is a sense in which imaginative literature *is* perspectivism, so that the reader is likely to be overwhelmed by the work's difficulty unless its multiple perspectives are mastered. Literary biography matters most because it is a storehouse of perspectives, frequently far surpassing any that are grasped by the particular biographer. There are relations between authors' lives and their works of kinds we have yet to discover, because our analytical instruments are not yet advanced enough to perform the necessary labor. Perhaps a novel, poem, or play is not so much a regression in the service of the ego, as it is an amalgam of *all* the Freudian mechanisms of defense, all working together for the apotheosis of the ego. Freud valued art highly, but thought that the aesthetic enterprise was no rival for psycho-analysis, unlike religion and philosophy. Clearly Freud was mistaken; his own anxieties about his indebtedness to Shakespeare helped produce the weirdness of in the author, the person whom we have not found, whether in ourselves or in others. In that quest, there always are elements at once aggressive and defensive, Shakespeare's plays. It was Shakespeare, and not "the poets," who was there before Freud arrived at his depth psychology, and it is Shakespeare who is there still, well out ahead of psychoanalysis. We see what Freud would not see, that psychoanalysis is Shakespeare prosified and systematized. Freud is part of literature, not of "science," and the biography of Freud has the same relations to psychoanalysis as the biography of Shakespeare has to *Hamlet* and *King Lear*, if only we knew more of the life of Shakespeare.

Western literature, particularly since Shakespeare, is marked by the representation of internalized change in its characters. A literature of the ever-growing inner self is in itself a large form of biography, even though this is the biography of imaginary beings, from Hamlet to the sometimes nameless protagonists of Kafka and Beckett. Skeptics might want to argue that all literary biography concerns imaginary beings, since authors make themselves up, and every biographer gives us a creation curiously different from the same author as seen by the writer of a rival *Life*. Boswell's Johnson is not quite anyone else's Johnson, though it is now very difficult for us to disentangle the great Doctor from his gifted Scottish friend and follower. The life of the author is not merely a metaphor or a fiction, as is "the Death of the Author," but it always does contain metaphorical or fictive elements. Those elements are a part of the value of literary biography, but not the largest or the crucial part, which is the separation of the mask from the man or woman who hid behind it. James Joyce and Samuel Beckett, master and sometime disciple, were both of them enigmatic personalities, and their biographers have not, as yet, fully expounded the mystery of these contrasting natures. Beckett seems very nearly to have been a secular saint: personally disinterested, heroic in the French Resistance, as humane a person ever to have composed major fictions and dramas. Joyce, self-obsessed even as Beckett was preternaturally selfless, was the Milton of the twentieth century. Beckett was perhaps the least egoistic post-Joycean, post-Proustian, post-Kafkan of writers. Does that illuminate the problematical nature of his work, or does it simply constitute another problem? Whatever the cause, the question matters. The only death of the author that is other than literal, and that matters, is the fate only of weak writers. The strong, who become canonical, never die, which is what the canon truly is about. To be read forever is the Life of the Author.

◈ Introduction

LITERARY PROSE FANTASY in the nineteenth century results from the displacement of the genre of romance, which moves from center to periphery under the pressure of the naturalistic novel. This process of the archaic parent, romance, being thrust aside by the realistic child, the novel, culminated a usurpation well under way throughout the eighteenth century. Nineteenth-century prose romance preserved itself through a new role as children's literature, as in the sequence that goes from Lewis Carroll on to *The Wind in the Willows*, Oscar Wilde's fairy tales, and Kipling's animal stories. Another route of prose romance towards survival, more prophetic of modern fantasy, was in the religious fantasies of George MacDonald, the matrix out of which C. S. Lewis, J. R. R. Tolkien, and Charles Williams were to emerge. The socialist, mythological prose romances of William Morris, with their curiously effective blending of Pre-Raphaelite sensibility and Nonconformist radicalism, seem more archaic now than MacDonald's fascinatingly unhealthy mixture of Neo-Christianity and sadomasochism.

The classic fantasy writers rely upon the archetypal patterns of romance, which are all too susceptible to the rival analyses of Freudians and of Jungians. Aesthetically such reductions are peculiarly tiresome when applied to the mode of fantasy, since they work even better for Rider Haggard's *She* than they do for Lewis Carroll's *Through the Looking-Glass*, the still unmatched masterpiece of prose fantasy in English. Carroll has the strength to destroy nearly all modern and contemporary methods of criticism, so astonishing is his originality and his command of a disciplined inventiveness. Prose fantasy, as the belated form of romance, tends to feature a dialectical alternation of Promethean and narcissistic tendencies in our nature; Carroll playfully exploits both, while gliding over the destructive elements in each. Borges, the modern fantasist with the most critical insight into the genre, charmingly regarded both onto-theology and speculative metaphysics as being forms of fantastic literature:

> I compiled at one time an anthology of fantastic literature. I have to admit that the book is one of the few that a second Noah should save from a second flood, but I denounce the guilty omission of the

major and unexpected masters of the genre: Parmenides, Plato,
John Scotus Erigena, Albertus Magnus, Spinoza, Leibniz, Kant, Francis
Bradley. In fact, to what do the prodigies of Wells or Edgar Allan Poe
amount—a flower that comes to us from the future, a corpse subjected
to hypnosis—confronted with the creation of God, with the
laborious theory of a being that in some way can be three and solitarily
endures everlastingly *without time?* What is the bezoar compared
to the notion of a pre-established harmony? What is the unicorn before
the Trinity? Who is Lucius Apuleius before the Great Vehicle's
proliferators of Buddhas? What are all the Arabian nights of
Scheherazade paired with a Berkeley argument? I have venerated
the gradual invention of God; also of Heaven and Hell (an immortal
remuneration, an immortal punishment). They are admirable and
curious designs of man's imagination.

Borges goes a long way towards explaining the effectiveness of George MacDonald
and his Neo-Christian descendants, and also the even more powerful achievements
of such modern Gnostic masterpieces as David Lindsay's A *Voyage to Arcturus,*
Ursula K. Le Guin's *The Left Hand of Darkness,* and John Crowley's *Ægypt* and
Little, Big. Theology, whether orthodox or heretical, finds its last literary refuge in
classic and in modern fantasy, again in flight from the now aged and dying child
of romance, the realistic novel.

                                                                      —H. B.

L. Frank Baum
1856–1919

LYMAN FRANK BAUM was born in Chittenango, New York, on May 15, 1856. A sickly youth, he attended and dropped out of Peekskill Military Academy before working at jobs ranging from acting and theatrical management to newspaper reporting to chicken farming (the subject of his second book, *The Book of the Hamburgs* [1886]). In 1882 he married Maud Gage, the daughter of a prominent suffragette, with whom he had four sons. They moved to the Dakota Territory in 1888 and to Chicago in 1893 as Baum continued to run through jobs: storekeeper, axle-grease salesman, department store buyer and window dresser, and finally writer of children's books.

Baum's first book for children, *Mother Goose in Prose* (1897), was also the book debut for illustrator Maxfield Parrish. Baum would continue to work with talented illustrators throughout his career, most notably William W. Denslow and John R. Neill. Baum's early children's books met with moderate success, but he and Denslow had difficulty finding a publisher for their 1900 collaboration, *The Wonderful Wizard of Oz*, and had to absorb the printing costs themselves. *The Wizard of Oz* (as it was called in later editions) was an instant success and has never been out of print. The book became a Broadway musical hit in 1902, and was filmed in 1910, 1920 (with Oliver Hardy as the Tin Woodman), and by MGM in 1939. Demand for sequels was immediate, but Baum wrote several other books—notably *American Fairy Tales* (1901)—before producing *The Marvelous Land of Oz* (1904). In 1905 Baum adapted it into a musical. Four Oz books later, in *The Emerald City of Oz* (1910), he announced the end of the series, but hundreds of protesting letters from children convinced him to relent.

Besides his fourteen Oz tales, Baum wrote scores of other children's books, including adventure books for boys, works for older children, and fantasies that he eventually tied into his complex Oz mythology. He also wrote four unsuccessful novels for adults, under one of his many pseudonyms.

After 1902 Baum lived with his family in California, where he raised songbirds and chrysanthemums at "Ozcot," a house built with Oz earnings.

He worked on a number of plays, most of which were never completed, and toured the country with his "Radio-plays," which used a combination of live actors and slides. Although popular, his "Radio-plays" were expensive to produce and Baum went bankrupt in 1909. The success of *The Patchwork Girl of Oz* in 1913 returned Baum to solvency, but his fascination with the motion picture industry led him to run a financially disastrous studio, the Oz Film Manufacturing Company, in 1914–15. The Oz books grew increasingly dark in tone before his death on May 6, 1919; the last, *Glinda of Oz*, was published posthumously in 1920. Up to 1963 a number of other authors—especially Ruth Plumly Thompson—continued the Oz series, but none of these met with anything near the success of Baum's originals.

▨ *Critical Extracts*

UNSIGNED   ⟨. . .⟩ *The Wizard* is ingeniously woven out of commonplace material. It is of course an extravaganza, but will surely be found to appeal strongly to child readers as well as to the younger children, to whom it will be read by mothers or those having charge of the entertaining of children. There seems to be an inborn love of stories in child minds, and one of the most familiar and pleading requests of children is to be told another story.

The drawing as well as the introduced color work vies with the texts drawn, and the result has been a book that rises far above the average children's book of today, high as is the present standard. Dorothy, the little girl, and her strangely assorted companions, whose adventures are many and whose dangers are often very great, have experiences that seem in some respects like a leaf out of one of the old English fairy tales that Andrew Lang or Joseph Jacobs has rescued for us. A difference there is, however, and Baum has done with mere words what Denslow has done with his delightful draughtsmanship. The story has humor and here and there stray bits of philosophy that will be a moving power on the child mind and will furnish fields of study and investigation for the future students and professors of psychology. Several new features and ideals of fairy life have been introduced into the "Wonderful Wizard," who turns out in the end to be only a wonderful humbug after all. A scarecrow stuffed with straw, a tin woodman, and a cowardly lion do not, at first blush, promise well as moving heroes in a tale when merely mentioned, but in actual practice they take on something of the living and breathing quality that is so gloriously exemplified in the "Story of the Three Bears," that has become a classic.

The book has a bright and joyous atmosphere, and does not dwell upon killing and deeds of violence. Enough stirring adventure enters into it, however, to flavor it with zest, and it will indeed be strange if there be a normal child who will not enjoy the story.

Unsigned, "A New Book for Children," *New York Times Saturday Review of Books and Art*, 8 September 1900, p. 605

EDWARD WAGENKNECHT   Perhaps the best key to the Oz books is found in a passage in *The Royal Book of Oz*, written from Mr. Baum's notes, after his death, by Miss Thompson. In this book, the Scarecrow, having gone out to look for his family tree, has inadvertently slid down the bean pole and landed in a mysterious kingdom where, very uncomfortably for himself, he has come to be regarded as the incarnation of a long lost Emperor. Making the best of a bad situation, the Scarecrow gathers the fifteen little princes together and tries to amuse them. They are very literal-minded children, however, and he does not succeed very well. For example, when he tries to tell them of the wonders of the Land of Oz, the oldest prince immediately flips out a map, and not being able to find the Land of Oz located therein, at once announces serenely that he does not believe there is such a place. Well, I once knew a boy who started to read Howard Pyle's *Men of Iron* and threw it aside in disgust when he found it was a romantic story of knights and knighthood. He had expected a story of the Gary, Indiana, steel mills. Now that is the kind of child Mr. Baum did not believe in and the kind of child he did not write for. ⟨. . .⟩

The use of machinery in the Oz books is also characteristically American. In general, magic may be said to inhere not in persons but in things. Whoever has the magical instrument can perform magic deeds. Continually, the forces of Nature, as we know them in America, are used for purposes of conveyance. In *The Wizard of Oz*, it is a Kansan cyclone which carries Dorothy and her house over the desert and deposits them in the Land of Oz. In *Ozma of Oz*, Dorothy is shipwrecked. In *Dorothy and the Wizard of Oz*, Dorothy, in California, is swallowed by an earthquake and carried down into the center of the Earth, from whence she makes her way to Oz. In *The Scarecrow of Oz*, Trot and Cap'n Bill are sucked down by a whirlpool. And in *The Road to Oz*, the Wizard sends people home from Ozma's birthday celebration in soap bubbles.

Indeed the United States is well represented in Oz. Dorothy is from Kansas; the Shaggy Man comes from Colorado; and Betsy Bobbin's home is Oklahoma. The Wizard of Oz himself is a native of Omaha. There he was connected with Bailum and Barney's Consolidated Shows, and his magic was, all of it, pure fake. He used to go up in a balloon on exhibition days to draw the crowds, and it was thus, on one occasion, when he lost control of his balloon, that he was carried to the Land of Oz. Though he was a good ruler, his pretended magic was all imposture, as Dorothy learns when she wants him to send her home to Kansas. It is not until later in his career when the Wizard becomes a pupil of the great sorceress, Glinda the Good, that he learns something about real magic.

Now what is the significance of all this? Not surely that American magic is any better than French magic or German magic. No. Simply that Mr. Baum has enlarged the resources of fairyland. He has not destroyed European magic: he has simply added to it. And he has done one thing more. He has taught American children to look for the element of wonder in the life around them, to realize that even smoke and machinery may be transformed into fairy lore if only we have sufficient energy and vision to penetrate to their significance and transform them to our use.

Edward Wagenknecht, *Utopia Americana* (Seattle: University of Washington Book Store, 1929), pp. 22–23, 27–29

MARIUS BEWLEY   Perhaps it was the nature of the land whose history he was writing that drew Baum's style away from literary realism. At any rate, after several more books, one becomes aware of allegorical themes and attitudes that put one in mind of Hawthorne's short stories. In *The Scarecrow of Oz* Baum tells the story of a Princess whose heart was frozen by witchcraft so that she could no longer love:

> Trot saw the body of the Princess become transparent, so that
> her beating heart showed plainly. But now the heart turned from a
> vivid red to gray, and then to white. A layer of frost formed
> about it and tiny icicles clung to its surface. Then slowly
> the body of the girl became visible again and the heart was
> hidden from view.

It is possible that Jack Pumpkinhead was suggested to Baum by Hawthorne's "Feathertop: A Moralized Legend," but he draws nearest to Hawthorne in his treatment of certain themes that, without breaking the frame of a children's story, explore the heart and personality with a good deal of subtlety. In *The Tin Woodman of Oz* (1918) Baum searches into the ambiguities of identity and one's relation to one's own past in a remarkable episode. The Tin Woodman, whose man's body was gradually replaced by tin parts as his limbs, torso, and head were successively severed by an enchanted ax, sets out in this book to recover his past and to rectify certain sins of omission of which he had been guilty in his youth. In a remote part of the Munchkin country he comes face to face with his severed but still living head:

> The Tin Woodman had just noticed the cupboards and was curious to know what they contained, so he went to one of them and opened the door. There were shelves inside, and upon one of the shelves which was about on a level with his tin chin the Emperor discovered a Head—it looked like a doll's head, only it was larger, and he soon saw it was the Head of some person. It was facing the Tin Woodman and as the cupboard door swung back, the eyes of the Head slowly opened and looked at him. . . .
>
> "Dear me!" said the Tin Woodman, staring hard. "It seems as if I had met you somewhere, before. Good morning, sir!"
>
> "You have the advantage of me," replied the Head. "I never saw you before in my life."

A pilgrim in search of his own past, its recovery proved impossible for the Tin Woodman, and he and his former head remain strangers without a common ground of meeting. The pilgrimage back through time to one's origins and source was a favorite theme of many American writers—for example, of Hawthorne in his last fragmentary novels, or of James in *The Sense of the Past* or "A Passionate Pilgrim." Baum, who handles the theme expertly enough on his own level, also finds that the past cannot be repeated, or even rediscovered in any satisfying way.

Marius Bewley, "The Land of Oz: America's Great Good Place" (1964), *Masks and Mirrors: Essays in Criticism* (New York: Atheneum, 1970), pp. 259–60

FRED ERISMAN   It is perhaps asking too much of Baum to call his works a parable of Progressive reform idealism, but the notion is a tempting one. In the two series ⟨the Oz books and the Aunt Jane's Nieces books⟩, he establishes the dichotomy that appears throughout the entire Progressive movement—on the one hand, the vision of an ideal state in which the law is supreme and the people are the law, and on the other, the bleak realization that this ideal state must be built with the clay and straw of 20th century America. His statement of this comes in an Oz book written in 1910, shortly after ⟨the character⟩ Quintus Fogerty's second appearance. In a comment that can only be called wistful, he observes: "You will know, by what I have here told you, that the Land of Oz was a remarkable country. I do not suppose such an arrangement would be practical with us, but Dorothy assures me that it works finely with the Oz people."

This statement marks Baum's surrender to the demands of reality, and the beginning of his escape to Oz. In the process, it points up the reason that Baum (like the nieces) failed in his quest for an ideal America. Both Baum and the Progressives were faced with the inadequacy of traditional values in the modern world. The Progressives, like Fogerty, by flexibility, by adaptation and in a great part by luck saw many of their goals become reality. Baum, on the other hand, clung rigidly to his convictions. If, as the creation of Fogerty implies, he realized that they were unsuitable, he still held them, refusing to modify them in any way. For his application of them, he had to turn to the ephemeral yet enduring realm of imagination.

And yet, Baum may well have achieved a success not immediately apparent from a consideration of his works. Both series, Oz and Aunt Jane's Nieces, depend upon the question of "what if." The adventures of Merrick and the nieces are, in their own way, fantastic: they record what might happen should a few people try to practice traditional ideals in a modern context. But the fantastic world of Oz builds upon a slightly different question—"What if everyone practiced these ideals?" Baum's success does not lie in his own answer to the question, for his answer is impossible. Instead, his success and his vindication lie in the audience of whom he asks the question.

Baum wrote for children—children who would become the adults of the next generation. He presents to them a twofold picture of the world: in one form it is flawed, but still possesses, in the traditional values, the seeds of perfection; in the other, it is perfect. His generation, he seems to say, has failed to achieve this perfection, blocked by unexpected and unprecedented changes. Despite this, the traditional values, that strengthened the Founding Fathers and carried America through many trials, remain valid. If Baum's generation failed in applying these values to the modern world, perhaps the next generation would succeed.

Fred Erisman, "L. Frank Baum and the Progressive Dilemma," *American Quarterly* 20, No. 3 (Fall 1968): 622–23

ROGER SALE As one might expect, it is in the early Oz books, when there are still fresh journeys to Oz to be taken, that Baum is at his very best. After Dorothy moves to Oz permanently as part of Baum's strategy for writing no more Oz books, she loses a good deal of her sparkle and becomes like most of the other residents of the Emerald City. Baum tried with Betsy Bobbin and Trot to find substitutes for Dorothy, but his heart wasn't in such journeys any more; he knew too completely how they went and where they would end up before he started. For this reason some of his admirers wish he had been able to stop after *The Emerald City*, when he first said he wanted to be done with Oz. The later books often do, indeed, show a marked falling off in quality. ⟨. . .⟩

This way of arguing the case, however, distorts Baum's talents and achievements even if it does isolate his very best things. Baum wrote quickly and never seems to have worried if he could sustain his interest for the length of a whole book. He seems to have known when he began a book how he wanted it to start, and perhaps where he wanted it to end, but he left the middle to be contrived as he went along. Rereading *The Wizard*, for instance, is always a strange experience for anyone who has come to know Victor Fleming's movie. Book and movie each begin wonderfully and in different ways; the movie has its spectacular cyclone and shift from brown-and-white to color, and Baum's matter-of-factness about Kansas, cyclones, and the Munchkins is winning. From then on, though, the advantages seem to belong to the movie. Baum's admirers may complain about having the whole thing be a dream, but the movie makes the dream create its own kind of sense, by emphasizing two characters, the Wizard and the Wicked Witch of the West, whom Baum uses only as part of his zoo. The second Oz book, *The Land*, and the fifth, *The Road*, are wonderful for a hundred or more pages, but then fade, while the fourth, *Dorothy and the Wizard*, and the sixth, *The Emerald City*, are among the weakest in the series. We can't, thus, imagine Baum doing wonderfully well with Oz until he lost interest because he was always capable of losing interest, of falling into slapdash writing, easy satire, or trivial zoo-keeping inventiveness. Furthermore, two of the later books, *Rinkitink* and *The Lost Princess*, though they take no journey to magic lands and therefore lack some of the moment-to-moment sparkle of some of the early books, are very good at sustaining their narrative propositions through to the end; and the last book, *Glinda*, has a fine central situation and ⟨. . .⟩ one spectacular stretch.

The essence of Baum is his restless, careless ease, his indifference to the complexities of life, his eagerness to describe what enchanted him without ever exploring or understanding it. Such people often become entertainers of one sort or another, but they seldom become writers. It might be said he had a knack for writing the way some people have a knack for singing or dancing or hitting a baseball. He obviously enjoyed writing, but his view of himself as a pleaser of audiences and his indifference to any disciplining of his genius meant he often wrote a good deal he didn't want to write.

Roger Sale, "L. Frank Baum and Oz," *Fairy Tales and After: From Snow White to E. B. White* (Cambridge, MA: Harvard University Press, 1978), pp. 236–38

BEN P. INDICK   What was it that gave ⟨Baum⟩ such popularity, even while his work, from the first, was ignored by critics and librarians? The children never had doubts. If his style seemed wooden or lame to some critics, much given to a *deus ex machina* which guaranteed happy endings, the children knew that Oz was the very essence of imagination. It was neither the exoticism of dark medieval countries and folk peoples, nor the terror that underlay classic fairy tales. Oz was the literal transplanting into magical settings of their own lives. Baum never forgot what was important to his young readers, their sense of wonder combined with their need for security. The problems of food and shelter are never ignored in Oz; Dorothy's weird friends, made of metal, glass, wood or even stranger materials, often remind her that not being meat-people, they do not have need for such, while she does. Obligingly, Oz is plentiful with food, and even packed lunch-boxes grow on trees. If the young heroines are in danger, at heart they know their every action is being observed by the calm mother-figure of Glinda, who will rescue them if necessary. The most dangerous of animals must succumb to love: the Hungry Tiger, who allows Princess Ozma to weave ribbons in his hair, admits to a secret desire to eat fat babies; however, he says ruefully, his soft heart will never allow it. The bugaboo of schooling, which annoyed Baum in his youth, is handily solved by Prof. Woggle-Bug, who has invented pills which provide learning painlessly. The most outlandish and even potentially frightening creatures are rendered harmless by the inclusion of very human individuals who resourcefully confront their situation. ⟨. . .⟩

In spite of the ultimately enormous cast of characters, many of whom appear frequently, as the author capitalizes on their individual popularity, he never loses sight of the human aspects of the story. The marvels of the fantasy world enhance but do not replace human verities, so that the stories remain true. Other writers have been less successful with similar material;

indeed, on the heels of the success of his first novel, it was natural that imitations would appear. One such which appeared a year after *Wizard*, *Zauberlinda the Wise Witch* by Eva Katherine Gibson, apes the very shape of *The Wizard of Oz* as well as the typography and illustration layout. Baum commences: *"Dorothy lived in the midst of the great Kansas prairies . . ."* and Gibson begins *"It stood in the midst of wheat fields, the little brown house where Annie lived."* Where this book failed while Baum's succeeded was in the position of the story-teller: the former *told* its story, as to an obedient auditor, whereas Baum allowed his reader to *live* the story, in full empathy, as though the child was the actual hero. Baum also was endowed with a gentle and satiric humor, as is evident from the names and natures of some of the ⟨. . .⟩ characters. Furthermore, it is a satire which operates on several levels, to the child and to the adult (who will read the book to the very young child) as well. The Women's Liberation movement of General Jinjur amuses the male adult (and revenges Baum on his wife and mother-in-law) by its foolish excesses, but also amuses the child who is accustomed to seeing the women, or at least until our own time, in quite different roles. Scraps, the Patchwork Girl, is literally an adult-sized living doll, gloriously unbeautiful, made of patches, scraps and buttons, slapstick, brash and clownish for the young readers, and a reflection of an independent, lively, unintimidatable young woman to the adult. Her courtship by the Scarecrow is hilarious on either level.

Ben P. Indick, "L. Frank Baum: The Wonderful Wizard of Oz," *Anduril: Magazine of Fantasy* No. 7 (February 1972): 10–12

BRIAN ATTEBERY   It is too much to say, as Henry Littlefield does, that *The Wizard* is a "Parable on Populism," but it does share many of the Populist concerns and biases. Taken loosely, with a grain of salt, Littlefield's readings help indicate much about the relationship between Kansas and Oz: the silver shoes are a little like William Jennings Bryan's silver ticket to prosperity, the Scarecrow is, in a sense, the troubled farmer, the Tin Woodman can stand for the industrial laborer, the Cowardly Lion is a witty analog of Bryan himself, the Wizard could be any ineffectual President from Grant to McKinley, and the band of petitioners are another Coxey's Army descending on Washington (Littlefield, throughout). I might even propose one more analogy. Dorothy, bold, resourceful, leading the men around her toward success, is a juvenile Mary Lease, the Kansas firebrand who told her neighbors to raise less corn and more hell, or an Annie Diggs, the Populist temperance reformer. Baum and the Populists promoted an active role for women in the rural utopia. Incidentally, the real surname of the Wizard of Oz is Diggs.

Baum created Oz, then, with the aid of a paradox. It is Kansas—or rather, let us say, since most of the elements we are dealing with are applicable to a broader area than Dorothy's Kansas, it is the United States—and it is also everything that conditions in the United States make us wish for. ⟨. . .⟩ What Dorothy finds beyond the Deadly Desert is another America with its potential fulfilled: its beasts speaking, its deserts blooming, and its people living in harmony.

If Oz is America, then Dorothy is its Christopher Columbus. *The Wizard of Oz* is primarily a story of exploration, and one of its principal strengths is the feeling of "wild surmise" that Keats ascribed to Cortez and his men. Dorothy is the discoverer who opens up the newest new world; later she and other children—the Cabots, Drakes, and Hudsons of this fairyland— chart the unknown regions remaining in Oz and the lands around it. ⟨. . .⟩ The journey motif owes something to traditional fairy tale structure, ⟨. . .⟩ but it owes as much or more to an American tradition of restlessness and curiosity. Happily, the discovery of Oz undoes some of the evils that accompanied the discovery of America. The natives accept the invaders, who, in turn, leave them in possession of their lands. Profit and progress are firmly excluded, and Oz remains the sleepy paradise it began.

> Brian Attebery, *The Fantasy Tradition in American Literature from Irving to Le Guin* (Bloomington: Indiana University Press, 1980), pp. 86–87

WILLIAM R. LEACH   Many analysts have argued that Baum presents a veiled critique of American industrial society in *The Wizard of Oz*. Some have called the book a "parable of Populism," and others have claimed that by emphasizing the supposedly agrarian virtues of simplicity and goodheartedness it brings into question the ethical character of the industrial order. But there is no trace of such a critique in the book. Rather, Baum, who had been a resourceful and enterprising merchant nearly all his life, fully accepted the new economic and social norms. As he had always done, he blocked out whatever grimness or suffering there was in the world, concentrating instead on the rewards of America's new culture and economy of consumption.

This ideological vision was shaped by new forces and institutions in American society: by the new stores and theaters; by the proliferation of more and more manufactured goods; by inventions and technologies; and by major changes in religious life, exemplified most clearly by the abandonment of older religious beliefs and practices and by the rise of new spiritual therapies such as theosophy. Broadly speaking the new ideology was shaped by late nineteenth-century capitalist society itself, which seemed to many people to promise prosperity and opportunity to all Americans. (The reality, of course, was another matter.) Just as Baum had been affected by these forces and institutions, so had most urban middle-class Americans been affected as well. But many of these people felt guilt and anxiety over the changes. Herein lay perhaps the lasting cultural importance of *The Wizard of Oz*: It helped relieve some of the guilt people may have felt in living in the new America.

> William R. Leach, "A Trickster's Tale: L. Frank Baum's *The Wonderful Wizard of Oz*," *The Wonderful Wizard of Oz by L. Frank Baum* (Belmont, CA: Wadsworth, 1991), pp. 160–62

▨ *Bibliography*

Baum's Complete Stamp Dealers Directory. 1873.

The Book of the Hamburgs. 1886.

Mother Goose in Prose. 1897.

By the Candelabra's Glare. 1898.

Father Goose, His Book. 1899.

A New Wonderland ⟨*The Surprising Adventures of the Magical Monarch of Mo and His People*⟩. 1900.

The Army Alphabet. 1900.

The Art of Decorating Dry Goods Windows and Interiors. 1900.

The Navy Alphabet. 1900.

The Songs of Father Goose. 1900.

The Wonderful Wizard of Oz. 1900.

Dot and Tot of Merryland. 1901.

American Fairy Tales. 1901.

The Master Key: An Electrical Fairy Tale. 1901.

The Life and Adventures of Santa Claus. 1902.

The Enchanted Island of Yew. 1903.

The Marvelous Land of Oz. 1904.

The Fate of a Crown. 1905.

Queen Zixi of Ix: A Story of the Magic Cloak. 1905.

The Woggle-Bug Book. 1905.

Daughters of Destiny. 1906.

John Dough and the Cherub. 1906.

Annabel. 1906.

Sam Steele's Adventures on Land and Sea ⟨*The Boy Fortune Hunters in Alaska*⟩.
    1906.

Aunt Jane's Nieces. 1906.

Twinkle Tales. 1906. 6 vols.

Aunt Jane's Nieces Abroad. 1907.

Father Goose's Year Book. 1907.

In Other Lands Than Ours by Maud Gage Baum (editor). 1907.

Tamawaca Folks. 1907.

Ozma of Oz. 1907.

Sam Steele's Adventures in Panama ⟨*The Boy Fortune Hunters in Panama*⟩. 1907.

Policeman Bluejay. 1907.

The Last Egyptian: A Romance of the Nile. 1908.

Dorothy and the Wizard of Oz. 1908.

The Boy Fortune Hunters in Egypt. 1908.

Anut Jane's Nieces at Millville. 1908.

The Road to Oz. 1909.

The Boy Fortune Hunters in China. 1909.

Aunt Jane's Nieces at Work. 1909.

The Emerald City of Oz. 1910.

The Boy Fortune Hunters in the Yucatan. 1920.

Aunt Jane's Nieces in Society. 1910.

L. Frank Baum's Juvenile Speaker. 1910.

The Sea Fairies. 1911.

The Daring Twins: A Story for Young Folk. 1911.

The Boy Fortune Hunters in the South Seas. 1911.

Aunt Jane's Nieces and Uncle John. 1911.

The Flying Girl. 1911.

Sky Island. 1912.

Phoebe Daring: A Story for Young Folk. 1912.

Aunt Jane's Nieces on Vacation. 1912.

The Flying Girl and Her Chum. 1912.

The Patchwork Girl of Oz. 1913.

The Little Wizard Series. 1913. 6 vols.

Aunt Jane's Nieces on the Ranch. 1913.

Tik-Tok of Oz. 1914.

Aunt Jane's Nieces Out West. 1914.

The Scarecrow of Oz. 1915.

Aunt Jane's Nieces in the Red Cross. 1915.

Rinkitink in Oz. 1916.

The Snuggle Tales. 1916–17. 6 vols.

Mary Louise. 1916.

Mary Louise in the Country. 1916.

The Lost Princess of Oz. 1917.

Mary Louise Solves a Mystery. 1917.

The Tin Woodman of Oz. 1918.

Mary Louise and the Liberty Girls. 1918.

Mary Louise Adopts a Soldier. 1919.

The Magic of Oz. 1919.

Glinda of Oz. 1920.

The Royal Book of Oz. Ed. Ruth Plumly Thompson. 1921.

L. Frank Baum's "Our Landlady." 1941.

Jaglon and the Tiger Fairies. 1953.

The High-Jinks of L. Frank Baum. 1959.

A Kidnapped Santa. 1961.

Animal Fairy Tales. 1969.

The Purple Dragon and Other Fantasies. Ed. David L. Greene. 1976.

William Beckford
1759–1844

WILLIAM BECKFORD was born on October 1, 1759, at Fonthill Gifford, Wilt-shire. His father, who received a large income from a Jamaica sugar planta-tion, was twice lord mayor of London, and upon his death in 1770 Beckford inherited a large fortune. After having been privately tutored, Beckford set out in 1777 on a tour of the Continent, which he described in *Dreams, Waking Thoughts, and Incidents*; this book was published in 1783 but was rapidly withdrawn, perhaps because Beckford feared that its wildness would hurt his aristocratic standing. Portions of the book were incorporated in *Italy; with Sketches of Spain and Portugal* (1834).

In 1783 Beckford married Lady Margaret Gordon; she died, however, in 1786, after the birth of their second daughter. Beckford spent many years abroad and published several accounts of his travels, including his 1834 book on Italy, Spain, and Portugal as well as *Recollections of an Excursion to the Monasteries of Alcobaça and Batalha* (1835). Most of the material for these books was drawn from his travel diaries, which were published in their original form in 1928 by Guy Chapman. His *Journal in Spain and Portugal 1787–1788* was edited by Boyd Alexander in 1954.

From 1796 onward Beckford lived a retired existence at Fonthill Abbey, Wiltshire, which he helped design and for which he amassed an enormous collection of paintings and books. In 1822 his extravagance obliged him to sell the house, which shortly afterward collapsed into ruins. Beckford himself died at Bath on May 2, 1844.

Vathek, the "Arabic tale" for which Beckford is today chiefly remembered, was first written in French in 1782. Beckford commissioned Samuel Henley to make an English translation, intending to publish the two versions simul-taneously. In 1786, however, while Beckford was distracted by his wife's death, Henley anonymously published the English version, claiming in the preface that it was based on an Arabic original; when Beckford published his own French version in the following year it was largely ignored. Nonethe-less, this story of a caliph who sells himself to the Devil was greatly admired and widely imitated. Among Beckford's other books are *Modern Novel Writing; or, The Elegant Enthusiast* (1796) and *Azemia* (1797), burlesques of the novel of sensibility. *The Episodes of Vathek*, narratives intended to be inserted into *Vathek*, were lost until 1910, when Lewis Melville discovered them in the course of compiling *The Life and Letters of William Beckford* (1910). They were published in 1912 in a translation from the original French by Sir Frank T. Marzials. The fragmentary third episode was later completed by American fantasist Clark Ashton Smith. *Life at Fonthill 1807–1822*, a selection of Beckford's letters, edited by Boyd Alexander, appeared in 1957.

▦ *Critical Extracts*

GEORGE GORDON, LORD BYRON

> On sloping mounds, or in the vale beneath,
> Are domes where whilome kings did make repair;
> Yet ruin'd splendour still is lingering there.
> And yonder towers the Prince's palace fair:
> There thou, too, Vathek! England's wealthiest son,
> Once form'd thy Paradise, as not aware
> When wanton Wealth her mightiest deeds hath done,
> Meek Peace voluptuous lures was ever wont to shun.
>
> Here didst thou dwell, here schemes of pleasure plan,
> Beneath yon mountain's ever beauteous brow:
> But now, as if a thing unblest by Man,
> Thy Fairy dwelling is as lone as thou!
> Here giant weeds a passage scarce allow
> To halls deserted, portals gaping wide:
> Fresh lessons to the thinking bosom, how
> Vain are the plesaunces on earth supplied;
> Swept into wrecks anon by Time's ungentle tide!

George Gordon, Lord Byron, *Childe Harold's Pilgrimage*, 1812, Canto 1, Stanzas 22–23

CYRUS REDDING   In person ⟨Beckford⟩ was scarcely above the middle height, slender, but well formed, with features indicating great intellectual power. His eyes were wonderfully acute, his apprehension exceedingly quick, his enunciation rather more rapid than that of the average of speakers in general. His constitution had not, according to his own account, been strong. In early life he had been unable in consequence to remain in parliament, though he had sat both for Wells and Hindon. By activity, temperance, and care, more than all by spending as much time as possible in the open air with plenty of exercise, he had rendered himself comparatively hale. He was dressed in a green coat with cloth buttons, a buff striped waistcoat, breeches of the same kind of cloth as the coat, and brown topboots, the fine cotton stockings appearing over them, in the fashion of a gentleman thirty or forty years ago. I never saw him in any other costume when indoors. To return to my interview. ⟨. . .⟩

"I am fond of the East," said Mr. Beckford.

I replied I should have thought as much from his tale of *Vathek*. It was one of the works which had delighted me from my youth—the most striking and imaginative I ever read. Mr. Beckford seemed to forget he had volunteered to be Cicerone. Neither of us rose from our chairs to the book-cases. His conversation was exceedingly interesting. I lamented I knew nothing of Eastern literature, endeavouring to return to the subject of *Vathek*.

"I thought of the Tower of the Caliph just now," I remarked, "while I was upon Lansdown, fancying the youthful idea carried on through later life—the towers in *Vathek*, at Fonthill, and here, lead to such a conclusion."

"No," he replied, "I have extraordinary sight; God rarely gives men such eyes. I am partial to glancing over a wide horizon—it delights me to sweep far along an extended landscape. I must elevate myself to do this, even on Lansdown. The tower at Fonthill was as necessary an appendage to such a structure as it would have been to a real abbey. I love building, planting, gardening—whatever will keep me employed in the open air. I like to be among workmen. I never kept less at one time than a hundred when at Fonthill. Wishing to have something besides a study on the summit of the hill where the view is so extensive, I determined upon erecting the tower."

"It was a conclusion from the advantageous site then?" I observed.

"It was—every body is deceived in judging of the motives of others, though your conclusion was natural."

"The Tower of the Caliph is so prominent in *Vathek* that I am not the only person who labours under the mistake. *Vathek* made a great sensation when it appeared?" I continued, wishing to obtain all the information possible about a favourite book.

"You will hardly believe how closely I was able to apply myself to study when young. I wrote *Vathek* when I was barely twenty-two years of age. I wrote it at one sitting, in French. I cost me three days and two nights of hard labour. I never took off my clothes the whole time. This severe application made me very ill."

"Your mind must have been ardent, and deeply imbued with the literature of the East?"

"I revelled day and night in that sort of reading for a good while—I preferred it to the classics, and began it as a relief from their dryness. I was a much better Latin than Greek scholar—the Greek and Latin were set tasks. I began Persian of my own accord."

"The 'Hall of Eblis,' Byron praises highly for its sublimity."

"Byron several times complimented me upon that story."

"I never read a description in the Eastern writings, through translation of course, that contains any thing like the 'Hall of Eblis,' " I observed.

"You could hardly find any thing like it there, for that was my own. Old Fonthill had a very ample, lofty, loud echoing hall, one of the largest in the kingdom. Numerous doors led from it into different parts of the house, through dim, winding passages. It was from that I introduced the hall—the idea of the 'Hall of Eblis' being generated by my own. My imagination magnified and coloured it with the Eastern character. All the females in *Vathek* were portraits of those in the domestic establishment of old Fonthill, their fancied good or ill qualities exaggerated to suit my purpose."

"I have heard that Sir Walter Scott copied most of his characters and landscape descriptions from such as really existed," I remarked.

"I did something of the sort by accident in *Vathek*—it was the impulse of my own mind—but I had to elevate, exaggerate, and orientalize every thing. I was soaring on the Arabian bird roc, among genii and enchantments, not moving among men. I have the French edition of *Vathek* recently printed—pray accept a copy." ⟨. . .⟩

I inquired whether the three episodes of *Vathek* were still in existence, remarking how strongly Byron had expressed his desire to see them—the histories of Alasi and Firouz, of Prince Barkiarokh, of Kalilah and Zulkais, who were shut up in the palace of subterranean fire.

He replied that he had destroyed one of these histories, because he thought it would be deemed too wild, but that the other two might some day see the light. ⟨. . .⟩

No sketch or plan of *Vathek* appears to have been made; it was struck off from the author's mind *currente calamo*.

Cyrus Redding, "Recollections of the Author of *Vathek*," *New Monthly Magazine* No. 282 (1844): 148–51

LAFCADIO HEARN   And now we come to the subject of Beck-ford's connection with the 18th century literature. One might suppose that a man so wonderfully gifted, and so great a lover of books would give the world something very remarkable, either for scholarship or for literary beauty. But he gave it only one small story,—the story of *Vathek* and a few notes of travel in Southern Europe. All this writing is excellent of its kind; it has the finest possible hard polish; but it is quite insignificant as to bulk. No doubt Beckford would have thought it beneath him to work very hard at literature. His studies and his tastes were prosecuted or indulged for his own private gratification, not for the sake of the public. But it must be confessed that *Vathek* is the most perfect bit of prose romance in the purely classic style which the 18th century has given to us. It was first written in French, 1783; and as a French effort it is simply perfect—a flawless imitation of the style of the great masters of French literature. Even in English it preserves admirably the correct elegance and flexibility of French forms; and I am inclined to call it a unique classic in this respect. Certainly it is a much finer piece of work than Johnson's *Rasselas* or than any brief romance which preceded it. Sterne, of course, reproduced in English the brilliancy and wit of French forms of the lighter sort; but I do not know any English writer of romance who has given us a perfect imitation of the old French classical style such as Beckford did. Work like this reminds us especially of the short stories of Voltaire and his school. As for the conception, it is even more unique than the form. It is not really an imitation of Arabian literature;— it is something suggested by Oriental romance, but not imitated from it. The imagination of Beckford is entirely his own; and the closing chapter of his romance is universally acknowledged to be a very grand painting of fancy. Beckford's idea of Hell will always live in literature: it is an idea so powerful and original that we can compare it only to the grand conceptions of the greatest poets. But this is all that one of the most fortunate, cultivated, and studious Englishmen really bequeathed to English literature. But for this single book, his name and eccentricities would probably have been forgotten. By reason of it, they will be remembered through other centuries.

Lafcadio Hearn, "William Beckford" (1899), *Some Strange Literary Figures of the Eighteenth and Nineteenth Centuries*, ed. R. Tanabé (Tokyo: Hokuseido Press, 1927), pp. 47–49

H. P. LOVECRAFT   Classic in merit, and markedly different from its fellows because of its foundation in the Oriental tale rather than the Walpolesque Gothic novel, is the celebrated *History of the Caliph Vathek* by the wealthy dilettante William Beckford ⟨. . .⟩ Beckford, well read in Eastern romance, caught the atmosphere with unusual receptivity; and in his fantastic volume reflected very potently the haughty luxury, sly disillusion, bland cruelty, urbane treachery, and shadowy spectral horror of the Saracen spirit. His seasoning of the ridiculous seldom mars the force of his sinister theme, and the tale marches onward with a phantasmagoric pomp in which the laughter is that of skeletons feasting under Arabesque domes. *Vathek* is a tale of the grandson of the Caliph Haroun, who, tormented by that ambition for super-terrestrial power, pleasure, and learning which animates the average Gothic villain or Byronic hero (essentially cognate types), is lured by an evil genius to seek the subterranean throne of the mighty and fabulous pre-Adamite sultans in the fiery halls of Eblis, the Mahometan Devil. The descriptions of Vathek's palaces and diversions, of his scheming sorceress-mother Carathis and her witch-tower with the fifty one-eyed negresses, of his pilgrimage to the haunted ruins of Istakhar (Persepolis) and of the impish bride Nouronihar whom he treacherously acquired along the way, of Istakhar's primordial towers and terraces in the burning moonlight of the waste, and of the terrible Cyclopean halls of Eblis, where, lured by glittering promises, each victim is compelled to wander in anguish forever, his right hand upon his blazingly ignited and eternally burning heart, are triumphs of weird colouring which raise the book to a permanent place in English letters. 〈. . .〉 Beckford, however, lacks the essential mysticism which marks the acutest form of the weird; so that his tales have a certain knowing Latin hardness and clearness preclusive of sheer panic fright.

H. P. Lovecraft, "Supernatural Horror in Literature" (1927), *Dagon and Other Macabre Tales*, ed. S. T. Joshi (Sauk City, WI: Arkham House, 1987), pp. 383–84

JORGE LUIS BORGES   William Beckford of Fonthill was a rather ordinary sort of millionaire—a distinguished gentleman, a traveler, a bibliophile, a builder of palaces, and a libertine. 〈Guy〉 Chapman, his biographer, fathoms (or tries to fathom) his labyrinthine life, but omits an analysis of the novel *Vathek*, on the final ten pages of which Beckford's fame rests. 〈. . .〉

Saintsbury and Andrew Lang declare or suggest that the invention of the Palace of Subterranean Fire is Beckford's greatest achievement. I maintain that it is the first truly atrocious Hell in literature. And I shall hazard this paradox: the most famous literary Avernus, the *dolente regno* of the *Divine Comedy*, is not an atrocious place; it is a place where atrocious things happen. The distinction is valid. 〈. . .〉

I have given several examples; perhaps the observation that Dante's Hell magnifies the notion of a jail, and Beckford's, the tunnels of a nightmare, would have sufficed. The *Divine Comedy* is the most justifiable and the most solid of all literature, *Vathek* is a mere curiosity, "the perfume and suppliance of a minute"; and yet I believe that *Vathek* prognosticates, at least in a rudimentary way, the satanic splendors of Thomas de Quincey and Poe, of Charles Baudelaire and Huysmans. There is an untranslatable English epithet, the epithet "uncanny," to denote supernatural horror; that epithet (*unheimlich* in German) is applicable to certain pages of *Vathek*, but not, as far as I recall, to any other book before it.

> Jorge Luis Borges, "About William Beckford's *Vathek*" (1943), *Other Inquisitions 1937–1952*, tr. Ruth L. C. Simms (Austin: University of Texas Press, 1964), pp. 138–40

BOYD ALEXANDER   *Life at Fonthill* shows that he lived in complete social isolation there for nearly thirty years after his disgrace in October 1784. The scandal was engineered and spread by a political enemy, who 'framed' him during a house-party at Powderham Castle and accused him of illicit relations with the sixteen-year-old William Courtenay, later Earl of Devon. Beckford, still only twenty-four, was robbed of his promised peerage; no book could ever appear under his own name; and he laboured under a sense of grievance as a man unjustly accused and condemned without a hearing (particulary after he was publicly blamed for his beloved wife's death in 1786).

Beckford's struggle with his homosexual tendencies, and the consequent ostracism contributed, then, more than anything else to his literary sterility. ⟨. . .⟩

Had Beckford's literary impulse not been crushed at Fonthill by his incessant internal conflict and the weight of boredom, bitterness and remorse, this Gloomy Egoist might have given us a savage novel to equal *Wuthering Heights*.

This, of course, presupposes that Beckford had a certain genius, and that he was capable of sustaining it from within, despite external disappointments. Was this so? Swinburne, in the fairest verdict on Beckford which I know, wrote to Mallarmé:

> I have always pictured Beckford as a most unhappy man, more
> deeply consumed by malaise, ennui and melancholy than
> ever his admirer Byron was. This is sometimes bottled up and

> simmering, and sometimes breaks out and explodes
> everywhere in *Vathek* and in all that is told of him, both true
> and false. To be a millionaire and to want to be a poet—
> and only to be half a one! To be conscious of something like
> genius, but to turn out not to be one after all and nothing
> more than an *à peu près!* Almost to succeed in finding the path
> to artistic creation, and then to fall back on one's riches!
> All this must make the life of the poet *manqué* something much
> more gloomy than the Hall of Eblis.

Already, before his coming-of-age in 1781, when his prospects seemed most splendid and his position unassailable, Beckford voiced his self-doubt, his gnawing anxiety: "I fear I shall never be . . . good for anything in this world, but composing airs, building towers, forming gardens, collecting old Japan, and writing a journey to China or the moon."

Boyd Alexander, "The Decay of Beckford's Genius" (1960), *William Beckford of Fonthill 1760–1844: Bicentenary Essays*, ed. Fatma Mousa Mahmoud (Port Washington, NY: Kennikat Press, 1972), pp. 20, 27–28

KENNETH W. GRAHAM   If Beckford owes anything to Walpole, it is to the inspiration derived from Walpole's theory rather than his practice. *Vathek* is unembarrassedly improbable, an embodiment of the bizarre and fantastic. Yet it leaves the impression that the tale is true to life, that it states profound truths about the nature of humanity. How Beckford was able to achieve a successful blending of the improbable and the true is owing to a further successful yoking, perhaps suggested by Walpole's *Castle of Otranto*. Among other remarkable characteristics of Beckford's Oriental romance is its unified sensibility, its presentation of emotional opposites, sometimes yoked by violence to provide an ironic contrast, and sometimes homogeneously blended to provide a clear vision of life's complexity. Of all the fabulists of the late eighteenth century, Beckford is the most successfully metaphysical.

An appreciation of Beckford's achievement begins with an examination of the period of composition of *Vathek*. *Vathek* was published in 1786, during a period that has been denominated, with some justification, pre-romantic. The term has been criticized for suggesting a state of anticipation in the writers of the time of the coming romantic revolution, and, hence, for arising from an after-the-fact critical bias. Walpole's second preface makes it apparent, however, that writers *were* conscious of the movement of literature away from the literature of an age of reason. The forces of unreason, held artificially in check by the influence of Pope and the genius of Dr. Johnson, were gaining in momentum. ⟨. . .⟩

Beckford's *Vathek* arose from this period of aesthetic unease. It reflects its period not, as did many works of fiction, by replacing in the picaresque framework a robust sense of the comic with a pallid, sentimental refinement, but rather by combining an optimistic view of man's capabilities with a pessimistic sense of man's anti-heroic ludicrousness. The obvious manifestation of Beckford's merging of an earlier and later concept of man is in his transformation of his central character from a romantic Faust-figure into a kind of Don Quixote. More broadly, Beckford's unified sensibility operates by the reversal of expectations, whether these expectations be romantic or neoclassical, optimistic or pessimistic. In *Vathek* he expresses a classical distaste for religious enthusiasm but combines it with a romantic awareness of the struggle of good and evil at the cosmic level, an awareness we find in Blake, Shelley and Byron. Lurking beneath the device of reversal of expectations is an awareness of the limitations of neoclassical trends, going out of popularity, and romantic trends, coming into popularity: the limitations of both aristocratic rationalism and democratic emotionalism. In sum, Beckford's *Vathek* is characterized by a vision of the inadequacy of most current political, social and philosophical tendencies.

> Kenneth W. Graham, "Beckford's *Vathek*: A Study in Ironic Dissonance," *Criticism* 14 (Summer 1972): 244–45

ROBERT J. GEMMETT   It is difficult not to believe that Beckford is very close to his subject in "The Story of Prince Alasi and the Princess Firouzkah." In the Vathekian mode, Alasi, the narrator of the tale, displays the same restless craving for the forbidden. He is betrothed to Rondabah, princess of Ghilan, for reasons of State, but with an "almost misanthropic repulsion from the ordinary ways of men" finds the idea of marriage distasteful. Alasi is in many ways a portrait of Beckford. He is a perpetual dreamer and a man of taste and refinement, more impressed, it seems, by a "superb collation" than by public duties, which he regards as "a burden very heavy to be borne." Instead of to the woman he is about to marry, his interests are directed toward winning the affections of a young boy named Firouz, the son of the King of Shirvan. Initially, Alasi appears blind to the true nature of his feelings for his new friend, but before long he finds them perplexing. "The fascination he exercised upon me," Alasi confesses, "was extraordinary, to myself, quite inexplicable." In effect, Firouz becomes a fictional counterpart for William Courtenay and the story itself becomes an opportunity for Beckford to explore his own ambivalent relationship with the young heir of Powderham Castle. "What is there in common between the affection I shall owe to my wife," he asks of Firouz, "and the affection I shall ever entertain for yourself?"

The subject of the tale and the guiding principle of composition is homosexual love. "Love, which in its own shape would have been repelled," says Alasi at the opening of the narrative, "took Friendship's shape, and in that shape effected my ruin." As the relationship develops, however, innocent friendship gives way to sexual feelings so strong that Alasi is even willing to become a partner in Firouz's crimes: "The sound of Firouz's voice, his words, his looks, seemed to confuse my reason, and made my speech come low and haltingly. He perceived the tumult raging in my breast, and, to appease it, abandoned a certain languour and tenderness of demeanor that he had so far affected, and assumed the childish gaiety and vivacity natural to his years; for he did not appear to be much more than thirteen." The sudden reversal half way through the story which changes Firouz's sex is unconvincing and does no violence to the theme, particularly in view of the fact that "she" dons male clothing at the end. This deliberate blurring of sexual identity simply suggests Beckford's own uneasiness in dealing with such a delicate subject. That Firouz becomes an expression of evil, one of the more arrogant and perverse characters of the *Vathek* cycle, likewise does not diminish the possibility that this tale, in its treatment of aberrant love, represents a vehicle for the projection of Beckford's own private predicament. From one point of view, Firouz's evil can be considered an expression of Beckford's own guilt. But there is also evidence in his biography to show that in time he actually viewed Courtenay as "the meanest traytor and the blackest enemy." Admittedly, it is slippery activity to become too literal in establishing a relationship between the fictional and the actual world, but, in this case, the correspondences are too significant to overlook.

Robert J. Gemmett, "Introduction," *The Episodes of Vathek* (Rutherford, NJ: Fairleigh Dickinson University Press, 1975), pp. xxxviii–xl

---

R. D. STOCK   The story ⟨of *Vathek*⟩ itself is simple enough. The opulent Caliph Vathek is motivated by hedonism, the *libido dominandi*, and some slight degree, it can hardly be underestimated, of intellectual curiosity. Encouraged in his desires by his mother Carathis, a redoubtable astrologer and witch, he abjures Mahomet, devotes himself to a malignant giaour, and promises to "adore the terrestrial influences." As recompense, he will be brought to the fabled Palace of Subterranean Fire, where he will receive talismans to render him omnipotent and the treasures of the pre-Adamite sultans. A stretch of episodes follows showing Vathek's decadence, egoism, and fatuous cruelty. 〈. . .〉 The last two paragraphs point the moral: this shall be the punishment "of unrestrained passions and atrocious deeds . . . of that blind curiosity, which would transgress those bounds the wisdom of the Creator has prescribed to human knowledge."

But if the story is uncomplicated, the style and tone are troublesome. The tale begins with a description of Vathek:

> His figure was pleasing and majestic: but when he was angry,
> one of his eyes became so terrible, that no person could bear
> to behold it; and the wretch upon whom it was fixed instantly
> fell backward, and sometimes expired. For fear, however, of
> depopulating his dominions and making his palace desolate, he
> but rarely gave way to anger.

Here is the penetrating, terrifying glance of the alchemists in *St. Leon*, Schedoni, and legions of daemonic hero-villains—but ludicruously hyperbolized. If it be thought that such hyperbole is only a trait of the oriental style, the last sentence communicates an ironic detachment reminiscent of Pope, Swift, or Voltaire. Note, too, the grotesqueness: it is just *one* of Vathek's eyes that is thus demolitionary. This sort of thing runs practically throughout the tale, and to ironic hyperbole we may add outright comedy— for example, when Nouronihar tricks Vathek's chief eunuch into falling into her bath; and burlesque, as when the Satanic giaour transforms himself into a ball and is propelled about the court by Vathek's increasingly frenzied subjects. Voltairean irony, gross exaggeration, grotesquerie, comedy, burlesque: few of these have been thought to comport with spiritual horror, and they explain H. P. Lovecraft's rather understated remark that "Beckford . . . lacks the essential mysticism which marks the acutest form of the weird."

R. D. Stock, *The Holy and the Daemonic from Sir Thomas Browne to William Blake* (Princeton: Princeton University Press, 1981), pp. 292–93

R. B. GILL   *Vathek* repays frequent reading with an increased sense of its complexity and tight structure. Throughout the novel Beckford has carefully prepared for many aspects of his striking conclusion: the curiosity theme, for example, the loss of hope, even little details like the whirling of Carathis. And that worrisome moral at the end, "that the condition of man upon earth is to be—humble and ignorant," is foreshadowed in a multitude of ways. This moral, which we might call the public voice of *Vathek* and Beckford, is the key to continuing interest in the novel, for many readers sense that it does not coincide with Beckford's emotional concerns, however much its surface details may have been foreshadowed. The result is a tension that leaves the end somewhat unfocused. As Roger Lonsdale notes, "the official moral framework is in practice constantly subverted by the conduct of the tale." We suspect Beckford of hidden motives and begin looking for psychological explanations, for a private Beckford lurking beneath the public persona.

But the biographical Beckford is not hidden within *Vathek*. Rather, Beckford has included himself as a public and prominent part of the novel. Robert Kiely writes that Beckford "created an image of himself which became almost inseparable from his literary achievement." I would drop the word "almost" from Kiely's statement and claim that this image is an integral and indispensable part of Beckford's literary achievement, for it is a created, public image that appears in the novel. Our modern impulse to psychoanalyze causes us to look for an inner man, but the eighteenth-century Beckford was entirely ready to accept his created, public image as his real self.

An important consideration as we look for Beckford in his novel is the fact that the fundamental style or approach of *Vathek* is an exterior one. It is a public work whose surface meanings are the intended meanings. In some respects *Vathek* is a philosophical tale like *Candide* and *Rasselas*, but it rejects their moderate and personal conclusions; Beckford has used the external forms of Enlightenment moderation without belief in their internal justification. Although each of these works is a series of variations on the vanity of human wishes, a consideration of the self being accommodated to its world, Beckford relies on the literal meaning of his story, avoiding its potential as an exploration of inner psychology or a statement of universal significance, in spite of its closing moral.

> R. B. Gill, "The Enlightened Occultist: Beckford's Presence in *Vathek*," *Vathek and the Escape from Time*, ed. Kenneth W. Graham (New York: AMS Press, 1990), pp. 131–32.

◈ Bibliography

Biographical Memoirs of Extraordinary Painters. 1780.

Dreams, Waking Thoughts, and Incidents: In a Series of Letters, from Various Parts of Europe. 1783.

Vathek. 1786 (as An Arabian Tale; tr. Samuel Henley), 1787 (French original),
　　1929 (2 vols.; with The Episodes of Vathek; ed. Guy Chapman).
Modern Novel Writing; or, The Elegant Enthusiast; and Interesting Emotions of
　　Arabella Bloomville: A Rhapsodical Romance. 1796. 2 vols.
Azemia: A Descriptive and Sentimental Novel. 1797. 2 vols.
The Story of Al Raoui: A Tale from the Arabic. 1799.
[A Dialogue in the Shades. 1819.]
Epitaphs: Some of Which Have Appeared in the Literary Gazette of March &
　　April 1823. 1825.
Italy; with Sketches of Spain and Portugal. 1834. 2 vols.
Recollections of an Excursion to the Monasteries of Alcobaça and Batalha. 1835.
The Episodes of Vathek (tr. Frank T. Marzials). Ed. Lewis Melville. 1912.
Travel-Diaries. Ed. Guy Chapman. 1928. 2 vols.
The Vision; Liber Veritatis. Ed. Guy Chapman. 1930.
Journal in Spain and Portugal 1787–1788. Ed. Boyd Alexander. 1954.
Life at Fonthill 1807–1822, with Interludes in Paris and London: From the Corre-
　　spondence of William Beckford. Ed. Boyd Alexander. 1957.

James Branch Cabell
1879–1958

JAMES BRANCH CABELL was born in Richmond, Virginia, on April 14, 1879, to an old and distinguished Virginia family. As a boy Cabell was fascinated with a children's book about King Arthur, and he also heard stories of the Civil War from his elders; these two influences may have helped to foster his creation of imaginary realms of fantasy where flamboyant aristocrats behave like Southern gentlemen.

Cabell attended the College of William and Mary from 1894 to 1898, teaching Greek and French there while still an undergraduate. One of his college acquaintances was Ellen Glasgow, who would remain a lifelong friend. After graduating Cabell spent several years as a newspaper reporter in New York and Richmond, then a decade as a genealogical researcher, traveling to England, Ireland, and France. This genealogical work clearly influenced his later fantasy writing, which involves the tracing back of a Virginia family to its remote ancestors in the imaginary medieval realm of Poictesme. Cabell also traced his own genealogy in two early volumes, *Branchiana* (1907) and *Branch of Abingdon* (1911).

Cabell had already begun writing during his college years, and some of his poems appeared in the *William and Mary College Monthly*. Beginning in 1902 he contributed stories to *Argosy*, *Smart Set*, *Red Book*, *Harper's Monthly*, and other periodicals. These tales, archly depicting the lives and loves of pseudo-medieval knights and ladies and written in a gorgeous but richly ironic prose style, became popular with the intelligentsia but not with the general public; his first book, *The Eagle's Shadow* (1904), was a critical but not a financial success.

Cabell returned to the United States in 1911, and dismayed his family by working in a West Virginia coal mine for two years. In 1913 he married Rebecca Priscilla Bradley Shepherd, a widow with five children; they remained happily married for thirty-five years, and she bore Cabell a son, Ballard Hartwell. With *The Soul of Melicent* (1913; later retitled *Domnei*) and *The Rivet in Grandfather's Neck* (1915), Cabell began shaping his eighteen-novel "Biography of the Life of Manuel," a racy phantasmagoria set largely in Poictesme. *The Cream of the Jest* (1917) and *Beyond Life* (1919) continued to establish Cabell's critical reputation, but he achieved both fame and notoriety when *Jurgen* (1919) was seized by John S. Sumner of the New York Society for the Suppression of Vice. The ensuing obscenity trial did not take place until 1922, but ended as expected in an acquittal. Cabell defended the aesthetic sincerity of his novel in a pamphlet, *The Judging of* Jurgen (1920), wrote a popular sequel to it entitled *Figures of Earth* (1921), and viciously satirized Sumner in *Taboo* (1921).

During the 1920s Cabell, now one of the most popular authors of the day, ran something of a literary salon in his Richmond home, playing host to H. L. Mencken and other figures. He wrote several volumes of poetry, as well as a play, *The Jewel Merchants* (1921), while continuing to produce novels at a prolific rate, among them *The High Place* (1923), *The Silver Stallion* (1926), and *Something about Eve* (1927). Cabell's publishers, Robert M. McBride & Company, issued a lavish collected edition of the "Biography" in eighteen volumes (1927–30). In his spare time Cabell researched genealogies for the Virginia aristocracy, and served as editor of the Virginia War History Commission.

The 1930s saw a change of mood in the national temper, and Cabell's irony and sophistication came to seem remote from harsh economic realities. Cabell's reputation suffered a backlash, and he was no longer the darling of the intelligentsia. He continued to write through the 1940s, producing three trilogies of novels and two trilogies of essays and autobiographical writings. From 1932 to 1935 he was coeditor of the *American Spectator*. Cabell's wife died in 1949; he married Margaret Freeman the following year. His autobiography, *As I Remember It,* was published in 1955. James Branch Cabell died in Richmond on May 5, 1958. His *Letters* appeared in 1975.

◈ *Critical Extracts*

JAMES BRANCH CABELL   ⟨. . .⟩ my thoughts have turned again to you and Jurgen. Indeed, bereft of a manuscript to play with, I have already begun to feel lonely. So do you begin returning it, with all imaginable suggestions, as soon as you can. Some of your ideas, of course, I already have in mind. To the idea of a privately printed edition, which will preserve the tale's immoral integrity, I cling in particular. All that is a part of the book's fundamental idea—"the journeying, resplendent and procreative sun." Much can be done by starting off the reader with the honest belief that a sword or a staff is actually being discussed, and then permitting the evil-minded, such as you, to become suspicious. But, but, but, the more I meditate upon your suggestion that the Cocaigne chapters be rewritten so as to keep Jurgen in a state of vague horror, the more inclined I am to rank it with Allen's suggestion that I re-model *The Rivet* by omitting the last book and marrying Colonel Musgrave to Anne Charteris. The whole point of the Cocaigne experience is that after a week it was very much like being at home with Lisa. So I charitably attribute this whim of yours to the table d'hôte wine: and for the rest, entreat you to draw up in full all objections to the book as it stands. But let's be as roguish as the law permits. You know I really thought I had removed everything really "improper." Even now, I stick to it there is not an indecent sentence or any shocking word like "whore" or (that last favorite) "urinal" anywhere in the book. However, you may now at your convenience unloose your evil-mindedness.

James Branch Cabell, Letter to Guy Holt (11 December 1918), *The Letters of James Branch Cabell*, ed. Edward Wagenknecht (Norman: University of Oklahoma Press, 1975), p. 26

EDMUND WILSON   To begin with the contemporary American novel—which is commonly assumed to be our principal glory—I must confess that I have difficulty in reading our novelists. ⟨. . .⟩ Joseph Hergesheimer, though he knows how to tell a story, writes nearly as badly in a fancy way as Dreiser does in a crude one: the judgment of him that I most agree with is the remark attributed to Max Beerbohm: "Poor Mr. Hergesheimer, he wants so much to be an artist." Cabell, though a man of real parts, is, at his worst, a case of the same kind: *Beyond Life* I regard as one of the most obnoxiously written books I have ever read. *Jurgen* certainly had its merits: it was well-planned and curiously successful in the artificial evocation of the atmosphere of primitive folklore. But, except at Cabell's moments of highest imaginative intensity, which are neither very frequent nor very intense, he is likely to be simply insipid. His genealogies and maps of Poictesme bore me beyond description, and the whole Poictesme business strikes me as the sort of thing with which ingenious literary schoolboys sometimes amuse themselves. I dislike also Cabell's Southern sentimentality, which leaves him soft when he thinks he is most cynical. One cannot help feeling that, in the impression he gives of living and working in a vacuum, he furnishes a depressing illustration of the decay of the South since the Civil War.

Edmund Wilson, "The All-Star Literary Vaudeville" (1926), *The Shores of Light* (New York: Farrar, Straus & Giroux, 1952), pp. 230–32

EDD WINFIELD PARKS   Like Boccaccio, Cabell is frequently lewd, and sometimes blasphemous. The Italian writer devoted many pages to demonstrating, in a period of rigid Christian orthodoxy, that the mythological gods of Greece and Rome were entitled to a place in the minds of men; and considerable scholastic arguments to prove that "not only is poetry theology, but also that theology is poetry." Symbolism, allegory, and fiction are their common properties, and their common device for showing without direct statement the existence of mystic correspondences. For a poet, religious or pagan, intuitively understood that which could not be comprehended through logic or reason; but neither could it be expressed directly, for it "proceeds from the bosom of God."

Mr. Cabell has avoided this old-fashioned phraseology, but the difference is mainly in the wording. He is enough of today to believe that man is an animal; he talks in terms of aspiration rather than inspiration; not only is he aware of the imperfections of this world but he is frankly sceptical about the perfection of any possible world to come. What he has is an abiding faith in man's spirit, however much he may doubt the existence of any God. He puts his faith in the artist, especially the literary artist, rather than in the priest ⟨. . .⟩

This is the humanist Cabell, concerned with the ethical conflict in the individual; concerned with doubt and belief; concerned always with what man is and what he may—or might—be; concerned, in short, with philosophical and religious problems that have troubled man from the beginning, and one hopes will trouble him to his eventual end. Cabell is writing of man's impossible yet somehow not improbable journey toward perfection, toward self-realization, toward a possible afterpiece in the form of salvation. Yet a phrase ⟨. . .⟩ hints at the fundamental weakness in Cabell's philosophy: men dwindle and subside into being "responsible citizens."

This to Cabell is the supreme and yet inevitable crime of the artist. It reveals the essential dichotomy of his mind. If the first refrain running through his non-fictional books is that man alone of animals plays the ape to his dreams, the second and almost equally important one is that the artist should create force-producing illusions by writing perfectly of beautiful happenings. The artist is always in conflict with every-day life. When he accepts and conforms, as so many of Cabell's protagonists eventually do, he may become reasonably contented but he ceases to be an artist. In *Quiet Please* (1952), Cabell has rephrased but not changed the attitude voiced in earlier books:

> In brief, I esteem it the hall mark of a literary genius not ever
> to sympathize with our human living here, and not ever to arrange
> with it a satisfying compromise, whether in his personal over-
> transitory flesh or in print. Rather it is his vocation, his
> exalted calling—or it may be, his mania—to invent an
> expurgated and a re-colored and a generally improved version
> of life's botcheries . . .

This is the purpose of art and the justification of romance, that it gives us a glimpse of the supremely beautiful and that it whispers to us of the unattainable. The ordinary doings of mankind are not the concern of the artist: "veracity is the one unpardonable sin, not merely against art, but against human welfare." This is a denial of the importance of facts, not a denial of truth in the ultimate sense, "for in life no fact is received as truth until the percipient has conformed and colored it to suit his preferences: and in this also literature should be true to life." All enduring art must be an allegory; it must deal with contemporary life by means of symbols; it must be faithful to what man has dreamed of becoming rather than a portrait of what he is.

Edd Winfield Parks, "James Branch Cabell," *Southern Renascence: The Literature of the Modern South* (Baltimore: Johns Hopkins Press, 1953), pp. 251–54

ARVIN R. WELLS   It is not ⟨. . .⟩ merely detachment or aloofness which accounts for Cabell's transcendence of the naturalistic dilemma, but wholeness of vision as well. For Theodore Dreiser man is "a mechanism, undevised and uncreated, and a badly and carelessly driven one at that." For Cabell also this may be true, but it is equally and more certainly true that man is a gullible, dreaming consciousness and that the physical processes in which he participates and of which he is an expression are for him perpetually fruitful in moral principles. "So has man's vanity made a harem of his instincts and walled off a seraglio wherein to beget the virtues and refinements and all ennobling factors in man's long progress from gorillaship." Man is cajoled, hoodwinked, and betrayed; yet—behold the miracle!—he is in some sense the better for it. Man wanders blindly through a universe which is largely hostile to him and in which he is subject to the treachery of his own instincts and to the merciless attrition of time; yet— behold the miracle!—the human spirit endures, and endures precisely because of these apparently unamiable conditions.

However, to get at what is really integral to human existence, to get at the essential pattern of human living, obviously involves a high degree of abstraction. For the philosopher it is permissible and necessary to end in abstraction, but for the literary artist it is not permissible. The literary artist must find some means of giving dramatic expression to his vision; he must embody it in specific objects and actions so as to make it available to his reader on something like the level of experience. Cabell solved this problem by turning his back upon verisimilitude, by turning to those vaguely yet complexly symbolic figures out of legend and folklore and myth which have always attracted the romantic, and by adopting a technique of allegorical and symbolic fantasy. The fantasy assures detachment and provides for that frustration of the reader's normal orientation which is necessary if the reader is to transcend both the particularity of human experience and his own prepared responses. The symbolic and allegorical figures with which Cabell worked or from which he modeled his characters bring with them an immedi- ate depth of meaning. They express or suggest segments of the essential pattern without eliciting an immediately personal and possibly irrelevant response. Moreover, because their symbolic value is inexhaustible, they are susceptible to endless rehandling. And, by constantly exploiting the incongruity between their assumed symbolic value and a deliberately inade- quate representation of them, Cabell sustains the comic mood; by playing them off one against the other—Odysseus against Faust—he manages to suggest the way in which, in the general flux of character and experience, the tragic implications of existence are cancelled out. ⟨. . .⟩

In essence, the achievement was the creation of a kind of comedy which threads the line between comedy and tragedy without being tragicomedy. Whereas tragicomedy is a hybrid, depending for its effect upon a last minute reversal by means of which the action is deflected from impending disaster toward an at least unexpectedly happy ending, Cabellian comedy is in its overall effect comic, despite frequent modulations in tone and mood. Like all seriously intended comedy, Cabellian comedy may be said to rejoice over the endless fertility of life, but unlike most comedy, it expresses a comic vision which has been arrived at not by exclusion but by inclusion. It approaches tragedy in its attempt to transcend the whole of the finite predicament (for Cabell, the naturalistic dilemma) and thereby to reconcile man to his role in the scheme of things.

Arvin R. Wells, *Jesting Moses: A Study in Cabellian Comedy* (Gainesville: University of Florida Press, 1962), pp. 134–36

DESMOND TARRANT   Looking back over the full vista of Cabell's works, we see a remarkably ordered, intricate, and beautiful landscape. To begin with, the first writings—the short stories and early novels including those on contemporary life and *The Soul of Melicent*—treat life largely as a challenge to youth, although, from the beginning, Cabell has been unusually fair in seeing both sides of every question including that of youth and age. With the major works of the Biography the challenge is directed at mature man over the full range of his dilemma throughout his lifetime; the response to this challenge of life is presented, in depth and breadth, in all its spiritual and—symbolically—physical ramifications. The later writings place the emphasis more on age as Hamlet's Uncle rather than Hamlet receives the bulk of the treatment, or the King of Melphé rather than Cesario, although both sides of the questions are still acknowledged. Toward the end, treatment becomes satiric rather than ironic, the stature of the achievement tends to return to that of the early contemporary novels although in each case, even in *The St. Johns*, the artistic aim is fulfilled even as it becomes less ambitious, as seen even in the last two of Cabell's novels. The prose writings begin, continue and end on the very highest level of human intellectual endeavor and constitute the objective analytical soil from which the art was to flower into magnificent synthesis.

So everything seems most symmetrical. Symmetry is perfection. The pursuit of perfection is a universal impulse retained according to individual strength or weakness—which would appear to be a matter not so much of chance but of constitution. Cabell pursues it both in the form and in the content of his writings; the difficulties of the pursuit, difficulties which, from another point of view, are temptations to abandon it, add doubts to desires, doubts which capture the double nature of good and evil and, in so doing, guarantee the status of classical literature.

Thus we come to the summing up:

> But I at least, who have found human living and this world
> not wholly admirable, and who have here and there made
> formal admission of the fact, feel that in honor one ought to
> acknowledge all courtesies too. With life, then, I, upon the

> whole, have no personal quarrel; she has mauled, scratched and
> banged, she has in all ways damaged me; but she has
> permitted me to do that which I most wanted.

This is the conclusion of all Cabell's books, including *As I Remember It*.
He sees life as a pursuit of beauty. Beauty embodies order, harmony, symmetry, and unity not only in the external and tangible but in the ultimately
more solid reality of the intangible spirit. The pursuit of integration demands
integrity, which needs courage, mostly the courage to face facts, mostly facts
concerning self-knowledge. In the end, age must win and man must fail.
But this fact does not release him from his obligation. His obligation is
never stated, never defined, and it is not known to whom or what it is
owed. Yet it fulfills a purpose not entirely contained in individual satisfaction.
That which he most wanted was to write perfectly of beautiful happenings,
not to throw light upon the universe, not to persuade others to a faith or
creed, but to divert himself. In doing so, he has thrown considerable light
upon the universe and stated a creed. His faith, vision, or creed consists of
a hope in evolutionary progress at the command of an artist-God, a hope
augmented by the keenest of intellectual observations in his art. The philosophical light upon the universe expresses not only that the ways of the
artist-God are wonderful but that, ultimately, they are incomprehensible
and, either way, are illusions.

Desmond Tarrant, *James Branch Cabell: The Dream and the Reality* (Norman: University
of Oklahoma Press, 1967), pp. 278–80

LESLIE A. FIEDLER   ⟨. . .⟩ Cabell appeals to a new generation of
what he considered the mindless young (the grandchildren of his original
audience) not as a pornographer or an old-fashioned spinner of romantic
yarns, but as a writer of up-to-date fantasy. Cabell is "probably the only
American fantasy writer of genius," Lin Carter writes of him, apparently
forgetting that other Richmond author, Edgar Allan Poe. But we are dealing
with "hype" rather than criticism: an introduction to a series of Cabell
reprints which Ballantine Books obviously hoped would reach in the late
seventies the ready-made audience for what Edmund Wilson was already
describing in 1956 as "juvenile trash," meaning specifically *The Lord of the
Rings*. At that point, Wilson still thought it possible to distinguish between
the fairy tales of Tolkien, which he was proud to despise, and the fantasy
of Cabell, which he was not ashamed to admire. The former, he believed,
demanded of adult readers, eager to share the enthusiasms of the young,

the abrogation of all "standards," ethical as well as aesthetic, normally associated with maturity and sophistication.

It seems to me, however, that though there is a real difference between the two, it is one of degree rather than kind, Cabell substituting for the naïveté of extended childhood the callowness of prolonged adolescence. The pleasure, therefore, which despite myself I continue to find in his fiction, seems to me an understandable but rather ignoble response to what are essentially the wet dreams of an eternal fraternity boy, wish-fulfillment fantasies set in a realm between dawn and sunrise, in which time is unreal and crime without consequence. In this crepuscular Neverland, all males are incredibly urbane and phallic, all women fair and delightfully stupid up to the point of marriage. After that dread event, the former become genitally inadequate, and the latter shrewish and nagging, though dedicated, for reasons never made quite clear, to nurturing and protecting their doddering mates so that they can produce romances celebrating not those wives, of course, but certain phantom girls whom they have not married and who consequently remain forever desirable and eighteen.

How is it possible today to respond without guilt to Cabell's travesties of male/female relations, when women everywhere around us are protesting such stereotypes of them and us? ⟨. . .⟩ Guilty or not, we who do regard our sisters as human, read him still in large part, I suspect, not in spite of his "sexism" but because of it; since in the unreconstructed dark underside of our minds the notion of the eternally unattainable lady which we do not dare to confess in full daylight continues to lead a crepuscular life.

Indeed, it would seem as if popular "fantasy" exists precisely in order to indulge "immortal longings" in us which our conscious pities and allegiances have taught us to continue. Cabell, to be sure, had completely different notions about the function of nonmimetic art. To him the enemy was "realism," which he identified not just with the bourgeois world of compromise and accommodation, but with the best sellers that celebrated its values. His elite "romances" he thought of as subverting and transcending that world in the imagination, thus preparing a chosen few for achieving in fact an evolutionary leap to a new level of humanity. But the survival of his books as merely another kind of best seller (preferred above all others at the moment by the youth audience) suggests that their function may all along have been "regressive" rather than "progressive," though therapeutically so—encouraging, as the psychiatrists would put it, "regression in service of the ego."

Leslie A. Fiedler, "The Return of James Branch Cabell; or, The Cream of the Jest," *James Branch Cabell: Centennial Essays*, ed. M. Thomas Inge and Edgar E. MacDonald (Baton Rouge: Louisiana State Unversity Press, 1983), pp. 139–40

JAMES D. RIEMER   In addition to depicting the impossibility of
arriving at definitive meaning or absolute reality, *Jurgen* shares with modern
subversive fantasies a concern with the dissolution of boundaries between
the conceptual categories we use to order and understand experience, thus
exposing the relativity or limitations of such categories and "discrete units
of meaning." Through his ironic depiction of supernatural and mythical
beings, showing them as subject to the same irritations as humans, Cabell
moves towards the dismantling of our distinctions between the supernatural
and the natural, the mythic and the mundane. Even more central to *Jurgen*,
and to many of the later fantasies, is Cabell's exposure of the relativity and
limits of our conceptual differentiation between belief and objective reality.
As Cabell suggests through Jurgen's adventures, there is negligible difference
between what is believed to be truth and reality and what is shown to
have objective, actual existence. In fact, Cabell clearly illustrates Jackson's
observation that conceptual categories define what is real while relegating
those things which it cannot contain to the category of the unreal or
imaginary. ⟨. . .⟩

Throughout the book, Cabell satirizes the power of the human will to
attribute objective reality to what is in fact unreal or imaginary. With
each successive adventure, Jurgen claims for himself titles of increasing
importance, progressing from duke to prince, king, emperor, and pope.
Through the willingness of others to believe, Jurgen's claims gain the aura
of authenticity. In other instances, the assurance with which Jurgen glibly
cites the names of authorities he has improvised on the spot, combined
with the willingness of others to accept his references to avoid appearing
ignorant, gives Jurgen's fabrications the effect and substance of reality. The
Philistine judges take this a step further by using feigned knowledge of
Jurgen's created sources to refute his argument. Thus Cabell challenges not
only our ability to distinguish between the real and the unreal, but also
blurs the distinctions between the two categories.

Cabell takes the dissolution of our conceptual distinctions between the
unreal and the real, between belief and objective reality, even further,
moving his treatment of it from an essentially metaphorical level to a
metonymical one. He integrates primarily figurative statements that belief
creates reality with instances in which belief literally creates objective,
physical reality. During his visit to the Master Philologist in Cocaigne,
Jurgen learns that through the power of mortal philologists he has been
declared a solar legend. He therefore is forced to travel with the Equinox,
which itself has attained actual physical form because of people's treatment
of it as a reality.

The power of belief to create physical, objective reality is also evident when the judges of Philistia sentence Chloris and Jurgen, relegating them to the limbos envisioned by their respective forefathers. While Chloris is sent to the forgetfulness of the river Lethe, Jurgen descends to the Christian conception of Hell, which he learns was created out of men's proud belief that their worldly wickedness was of such importance that it was worthy of infernal punishment. Furthering the idea that belief literally created reality, Jurgen discovers that the devils in Hell did not "differ from the worst that anybody had been able to imagine." Later, when Jurgen ascends to Heaven, he finds that it has been conjured up out of the religious beliefs of an old woman, Jurgen's own grandmother Steinvor. By integrating situations in which belief literally affects or creates objective reality, with circumstances in which belief gives the potency of reality to that which, in effect, has no objective reality, Cabell further subverts the validity of our distinctions between objective and subjective reality.

James D. Riemer, *From Satire to Subversion: The Fantasties of James Branch Cabell* (Westport, CT: Greenwood Press, 1989), pp. 20–22

▣ *Bibliography*

The Eagle's Shadow. 1904.

The Line of Love. 1905.

Branchiana: Being a Partial Account of the Branch Family in Virginia. 1907.

Gallantry: An Eighteenth Century Dizain in Ten Comedies. 1907.

The Cords of Vanity. 1909.

Chivalry. 1909.

Branch of Abingdon. 1911.

The Soul of Melicent. 1913, 1920 (as *Domnei: A Comedy of Woman-Worship*).

The Rivet in Grandfather's Neck: A Comedy of Limitations. 1915.

The Majors and Their Marriages. 1915.

The Certain Hour (Dizain des Poëtes). 1916.

From the Hidden Way: Being Seventy-five Adaptions in Verse. 1916.

The Cream of the Jest: A Comedy of Evasions. 1917.

Beyond Life: Dizain des Demiurges. 1919.

Jurgen: A Comedy of Justice. 1919.

The Judging of Jurgen. 1920.

Figures of Earth: A Comedy of Appearances. 1921.

Taboo: A Legend Retold from the Dirghic of Saevius Nicanor. 1921.

Joseph Hergesheimer: An Essay in Interpretation. 1921.

The Jewel Merchants. 1921.

The Lineage of Lichfield: An Essay in Eugenics. 1922.

The High Place: A Comedy of Disenchantment. 1923.

Straws and Prayer-Books: Dizain des Diversions. 1924.

The Silver Stallion: A Comedy of Redemption. 1926.

The Music from Behind the Moon: An Epitome. 1926.

Something about Eve: A Comedy of Fig-Leaves. 1927.

Works (Storisende Edition). 1927–30. 18 vols.

The White Robe: A Saint's Summary. 1928.

Ballades from The Hidden Way. 1928.

Sonnets from Antan. 1929.

The Way of Ecben: A Comedietta Involving a Gentleman. 1929.

Between Dawn and Sunrise: Selections from the Writings of James Branch Cabell.
          Ed. John Macy. 1930.

Some of Us: An Essay in Epitaphs. 1930.

The Romaunt of Manuel Pig-Tender. 1931.

These Restless Heads: A Trilogy of Romantics. 1932.

Special Delivery: A Packet of Replies. 1933.

Smirt: An Urbane Nightmare. 1934.

Ladies and Gentlemen: A Parcel of Reconsiderations. 1934.

Smith: A Sylvan Interlude. 1935.

Preface to the Past. 1936.

Smire: An Acceptance in the Third Person. 1937.

The Nightmare Has Triplets: An Author's Note on Smire. 1937.

Acrostic. 1938.

The King Was in His Counting House: A Comedy of Commonsense. 1938.

Of Ellen Glasgow. 1938.

Hamlet Had an Uncle: A Comedy of Honor. 1938.

The First Gentleman of America: A Comedy of Conquest. 1942.

The St. Johns: A Parade of Diversities (with A. J. Hanna). 1943.

There Were Two Pirates: A Comedy of Division. 1946.

Let Me Lie: Being in the Main an Ethnological Account of the Remarkable Common-
          wealth of Virginia and the Making of Its History. 1947.

The Witch-Woman: A Trilogy about Her ⟨*The Music from Behind the Moon;*
          The White Robe; The Way of Ecben⟩. 1948.

The Devil's Own Dear Son: A Story of the Fatted Calf. 1949.

Quiet, Please. 1952.

As I Remember It: Some Epilogues in Recollection. 1955.

Between Friends: Letters of James Branch Cabell and Others. Ed. Padraic Colum
        and Margaret Freeman Cabell. 1962.
The Nightmare Has Triplets: Smirt, Smith, and Smire. 1972.
Letters. Ed. Edward Wagenknecht. 1975.

Lewis Carroll
1832–1898

LEWIS CARROLL was born Charles Lutwidge Dodgson in Darebury, Cheshire, on January 27, 1832, the son of the Reverend Charles Dodgson. He was educated at the Richmond Grammar School in Yorkshire (1844–46) and at Rugby (1848–50). From an early age he wrote and published prose, verse, and drawings in a series of family magazines such as *Useful and Instructive Poetry*, *The Rectory Umbrella*, and *Mischmasch*. Between 1850 and 1854 he studied at Christ Church College, Oxford, where he became a lecturer in mathematics in 1855. He remained at Oxford for the rest of his life, teaching and writing. He never married. He was ordained a deacon in 1861 but never assumed clerical duties.

While still an undergraduate Carroll began to establish himself as a humorist, contributing stories and poems to the *Oxonian Advertiser* and the *Whitby Gazette*. The first works to appear under the pseudonym "Lewis Carroll" were a number of parodies published in the *Train* in 1856. That year he also bought his first camera (he is regarded as one of the greatest Victorian photographers), and first made the acquaintance of Alice Pleasance Liddell, who was then nearly four years old. Alice was the daughter of Henry George Liddell, a Greek scholar and the Dean of Christ Church College. Over the next several years Dodgson frequently photographed her and devised stories for her; they became great friends.

On July 4, 1862, Dodgson went boating with the three Liddell sisters— Lorina, Alice, and Edith—and to amuse them invented a story that Alice requested he write down. This was *Alice's Adventures Under Ground* (1863), which he then revised and expanded, retitling it *Alice's Adventures in Wonderland*. In this form it was published in 1865, with illustrations by John Tenniel. *Phantasmagoria and Other Poems* appeared in 1869, followed by *Through the Looking-Glass, and What Alice Found There* in 1871 and *The Hunting of the Snark: An Agony in Eight Fits*, a long, mock-heroic, possibly nonsensical poem, illustrated by Henry Holiday, in 1876. *Sylvie and Bruno* (1889) and *Sylvie and Bruno Concluded* (1893), a novel in two volumes, is partially based on some earlier short stories, including "Bruno's Revenge," which originally appeared in *Aunt Judy's Magazine* in 1867. In addition, Carroll wrote a number of lighthearted treatises on mathematics and logic, including *Euclid and His Modern Rivals* (1879), *A Tangled Tale* (1885), *The Game of Logic* (1887), and *Symbolic Logic* (1896), the last three of which were written for children. Lewis Carroll died at his sister's home in Guildford on January 14, 1898.

Critical Extracts

ARTHUR MACHEN   The artist must not suffer for the sins of the copyist, and *Alice* remains and will long remain classic, the masterpiece of a curious *genre* in literature. Its author reigns "over the realms of nonsense absolute," and though he established a school he has left no successor. And yet, though we are all delighted with *Alice*, it would be perhaps a little difficult to analyze the sources of our pleasure. For on the surface both the *Wonderland* and the *Looking Glass* appear to be nonsense, *simpliciter*, and critics of the Johnsonian school, who regard literature as the expression of the intelligence, could hardly admit that nonsense, in itself, can amuse anybody. There are, of course, the verbal contortions we have alluded to— the fishes who indulged in "reeling, and writhing, and fainting in coils"— but it will be acknowledged that fun of this description is not, in any sense of the word, inimitable. And the Mock Turtle who wept because he was not a real turtle, he, too, is a purely verbal creature, not, surely, a humorous reality, an *ens entium* of wit. Where, then, as Dr. Johnson remarked on a memorable occasion, is the merriment? The inquiry would be a singular one, and certainly nobody would have been more delighted than Mr. Dodgson if a chain commencing with *Alice* had been shown to extend, not merely into logic and mathematics, but into the farther Wonderland of metaphysics and psychology. And yet it seems probable that we relish "Lewis Carroll's" nonsense because in it we see mirrored certain dark and mysterious portions of our nature. In the 18th century philosophy had come to the conclusion that man was a purely rational animal, and from this standpoint Johnson judged "Lycidas" to be rubbish, or something very near it. But it seems probable that man is not only born rational but also irrational, that deep in the heart there is a dungeon, where two-sided triangles abound, where Achilles chases the tortoise in vain, eternally, where parallel straight lines are continually meeting. It is the world of contradictions, of the impossible realized, the world of which we dream at nights, and, above all, it is the world which is the home of children, far more true and real to them than all the assemblage of rational sublunary things.

Arthur Machen, "Obituary: Lewis Carroll," *Literature*, 22 January 1898, p. 88

MAX BEERBOHM   Behind Lewis Carroll, the weaver of fantastic dreams, the delighter in little children, there was always Mr. Dodgson, the ascetic clergyman, the devoted scholar in mathematics. And the former had to pay constant toll to the latter—to report himself, as it were, at very brief intervals. It was as though the writer never could quite approve of his deviations into the sunny path that he loved best. When he was not infusing mathematics into his humor, he was stiffening out his fantasy with edification. In his latter books, mathematics and morals triumphed. Humour lay crushed in "The Tangled Skein," fantasy in *Sylvie and Bruno*. Readers of Walter Pater will remember the story of Prior Saint-Jean; will remember how the last volume of that treatise on mathematics which had occupied his life was never completed. "Whereas in the earlier volumes you found by way of illustration no more than the simplest indispensible diagrams, the scribe's hand had strayed here into mazy borders, long spaces of hieroglyph, and as it were veritable pictures of the theoretic elements of his subject. Soft wintry auroras seemed to play behind whole pages of crabbed textural writing, line and figure bending, breathing, flaming into lovely 'arrangements' that were like music made visible. . . ." Well! (as Pater himself would have said) Lewis Carroll's history was the history of Prior Saint-Jean reversed. In him the fair luxuriance of a Pagan fancy was gradually overcome by the sense of duty to his cloth, and by the tyranny of an exact science. In the two books about Alice, however, you have a perfect fusion of the two opposing elements in his nature. In them the morality is no more than implicit, and the mathematics are not thrust on you. Though modern adults are apt to resent even implicit morality in a book for children, children delight in it. They delight in feeling that, in some way or other, Alice is being "improved" by her adventures. Orally, she seems to be an awful prig, but various internal evidence makes them suspect her of having "a past"— of having been naughty; and they feel that, somehow or other, the Caterpillar and the Red Queen and all the rest of them are working out her redemption.

Max Beerbohm, " 'Alice' Again Awakened" (1900), *Around Theatres* (New York: Alfred A. Knopf, 1930), Vol. 1, pp. 140–41

WILLIAM EMPSON   To make the dream-story from which *Wonderland* was elaborated seem Freudian one has only to tell it. A fall into a deep hole into the secrets of Mother Earth produces a new enclosed soul wondering who it is, what will be its position in the world, and how it can get out. It is in a long low hall, part of the palace of the Queen of Hearts (a neat touch), from which it can only get out to the fresh air and the fountains through a hole frighteningly too small. Strange changes, caused by the way it is nourished there, happen to it in this place, but always when it is big it can not get out and when it is small it is not allowed to; for one thing, being a little girl, it has no key. The nightmare theme of the birth-trauma, that she grows too big for the room and is almost crushed by it, is not only used here but repeated more painfully after she seems to have got out; the rabbit sends her sternly into its house and some food there makes her grow again. In Dodgson's own drawing of Alice when cramped into the room with one foot up the chimney, kicking out the hateful thing that tries to come down (she takes away his pencil when it is a juror), she is much more obviously in the foetus position than in Tenniel's. The White Rabbit is Mr. Spooner to whom the Spoonerisms happened, an undergraduate in 1862, but its business here is as a pet for children which they may be allowed to breed. Not that the clearness of the framework makes the interpretation simple; Alice peering through the hole into the garden may be wanting a return to the womb as well as an escape from it; she is fond, we are told, of taking both sides of an argument when talking to herself, and the whole book balances between the luscious nonsense-world of fantasy and the ironic nonsense-world of fact.

William Empson, *"Alice in Wonderland," Some Versions of Pastoral* (London: Chatto & Windus, 1935), pp. 270–71

MARTIN GARDNER   It is this agony, the agony of anticipating one's loss of being, that pecks at the heart of Carroll's poem ⟨*The Hunting of the Snark*⟩. Did he realize that B, the dominant letter of his Ballad, is a symbol of "be"? I sometimes think he did. At any rate, the letter sounds through the poem like a continuous drum beat, starting softly with the introduction of the Bellman, the Boots, and the others, then growing more and more insistent until, in a final thunderclap, it becomes the Boojum.

The *Snark* is a poem about being and nonbeing, an existential poem, a poem of existential agony. The Bellman's map is the map that charts the course of humanity; blank because we possess no information about where we are or whither we drift. The ship's bowsprit gets mixed up with its rudder and when we think we sail west we sail east. The Snark is, in Paul Tillich's fashionable phrase, every man's ultimate concern. That is the great search motif of the poem, the quest for an ultimate good. But this motif is submerged in a stronger motif, the dread, the agonizing dread, of ultimate failure. The Boojum is more than death. It is the end of all searching. It is final, absolute extinction. In a literal sense, Carroll's Boojum means nothing at all. It is the void, the great blank emptiness out of which we miraculously emerged; by which we will ultimately be devoured; through which the absurd galaxies spiral and drift endlessly on their nonsense voyages from nowhere to nowhere.

Perhaps you are a naturalist and humanist, or a Sartrean existentialist. You believe passionately in working for a better world, and although you know that you will not be around to enjoy it, you take a kind of comfort— poor substitute that it is!—from the fact that future generations, perhaps even your own children, may reap the rewards of your labors. But what if they won't? Atomic energy is a Snark that comes in various shapes and sizes. A certain number of intercontinental guided missiles—the U.S. Air Force has one it calls the Snark—with thermonuclear warheads can glide gently down on the just and the unjust, and the whole of humanity may never be met with again.

Martin Gardner, "Introduction," *The Annotated Snark* (New York: Simon & Schuster, 1962), pp. 23–24

HARRY LEVIN   The stuff of dreams is as illusory as those scented rushes which lose their fragrance and beauty when Alice picks them. Yet Dodgson catches the cinematographic movement of dreams when the grocery shop, after changing into the boat from which she gathers the dream-rushes, changes back into the shop which is identifiable as an Oxford landmark. The next phase is the egg on the shelf, which becomes Humpty Dumpty on his wall. The narration, with its corkscrew twists, carefully observes the postulate that Dodgson formulated in his seriocomic treatise, "Dynamics of a Particle": "Let it be granted that a speaker may digress from any one point to any other point." Alice proceeds by digression through Wonderland, since it does not really matter which way she goes. In the Looking-Glass Land, which is regulated by a stricter set of ground rules, she is forced to move backward from time to time. Dodgson had given himself his *donnée* by sending her down the rabbit-hole "without the least idea what was to happen afterwards." What extemporaneously followed seemed to consist, as he subsequently recounted it, "almost wholly of fits and scraps, single ideas which came of themselves." Though it may have been obsession which gave them a thematic unity, it was artistry which devised their literary form.

Symmetrically, each of the two books comprises twelve chapters. Both of them conflate the dream vision with the genre known as the *voyage imaginaire;* in effect, they merge the fairy tale with science fiction. The journey, in either case, is not a quest like *The Hunting of the Snark*—or that logbook it almost seems to parody, *Moby-Dick*. Rather, it is an exploration—underground, in the first instance, and so originally entitled *Alice's Adventures Under Ground*. This relates it to a wealth of symbols for the claustral limits of the human condition, from Plato to Dostoevsky. Falling can betoken many things: above all, the precondition of knowledge. Subterranean descent can land in an underworld, be it Hell or Elysium or the other side of the earth, the Antipodes, which Alice malapropistically calls "the Antipathies"—not so exact an opposite to our side as the Looking-Glass Country, but a topsy-turvydom of sorts like Butler's *Erewhon*. As we approach it, it seems to be a juvenile utopia, what with its solemn games and half-remembered lessons and ritualized performances of nursery rhymes. Before we leave it, it becomes an unconscious *Bildungsroman*, projecting and resisting the girlish drama of physical and psychological development. "What do you suppose is the use of a child without any meaning? [fumes the Red Queen.] Even a joke should have some meaning—and a child's more important than a joke, I hope."

Harry Levin, "Wonderland Revisited," *Kenyon Review* 27, No. 4 (Autumn 1965): 604–5

JOHN FISHER   Dodgson had ⟨. . .⟩ found the basic key that would release him from the disappointments of conformity long before he revealed himself as Lewis Carroll. As a boy, amid the sheltered innocence and prim propriety of a childhood which presents its own parallels to the academic and emotional seclusion of the Oxford of his later years, he had stumbled, surprisingly for the son of an archdeacon with principled objections to the stage, across the secrets of the conjuror's craft, a fascination that persisted throughout his life. His nephew and authorised biographer, Stuart Dodgson Collingwood, describes how his favorite fantasy as a child entailed dressing up for exotic effect in astrological nightshirt and flowing brown wig in order to entertain his brothers and sisters at special performances of sleight of hand, displays sometimes supplemented by his equally deft manipulation of the toy theatre and 'penny plain, tuppence coloured' marionettes of cardboard on wood built by his agile fingers with the help of the village carpenter. A born entertainer, he wrote his own plays for the latter, the most popular of which were *The Tragedy of King John* and *La Guida di Bragia*, an operatic burlesque of *Bradshaw's Railway Guide*. He was in his element conjuring up voices and effects out of nowhere from behind a discreet screen, 'just like a conjuring-trick', and always requiring, at a White Knight's insistence, 'plenty of practice!' At the age of twenty-three he was still organizing these performances and finding cause to complain in his diary on April 11, 1855 of the lack of suitable plays for puppet theatres: 'All existing plays for such objects seem to me to have one of two faults—either (1) they are meant for real theatres, and are therefore not fitted for children, or (2) they are overpoweringly dull—no idea of fun in them.'

The itch to baffle and mystify, and to entertain into the bargain, remained with him until his death. And yet the reciprocal rewards for Carroll himself were far greater than for his average wand-wielding contemporary. With a magician's instinct for tracking down the impossible, he was able to apply something more than the straightforward academic approach to his studies in mathematics and logic, sources of mystification no conventional magician had ever tapped. He did not need long to realise that not only did mathematics present an infinite means of bewilderment in stark contrast to the stereotyped repertoire of the drawing-room entertainer, but even more remarkably often displayed a baffling aspect which he, the magician himself, could not account for. Logic professed fallacies which when decked out with entertaining characters were far more spellbinding than the contrived red-herring patter used to misdirect an audience's awareness away from a more tangible secret. Here was as near as he would ever come to discovering real magic.

> John Fisher, "Introduction," *The Magic of Lewis Carroll* (London: Thomas Nelson & Sons, 1973), pp. 8–9

EDMUND MILLER   In the *Alice* books dream may be seen as an escape from our normal reality. Dream has a more psychologically sophisticated (or adult) function in *Sylvie and Bruno*. The Red God dreams a new game of creation, but the reader is quite awake through it all—or at least confident that he *can* awake to reality. But *Sylvie and Bruno* is contrived to make it much more difficult for the reader to maintain this sort of psychical distance from the material. He drifts in and out of Fairyland with the Narrator. Thus he is gradually taught to understand that the limits of reality are blurred, that it is not so easy to say that this is the world of reality while that is the world of nonsense and fantasy. Ruth Berman has plausibly suggested that what she calls the dullness of the English scenes ("earnestness" would perhaps be more relevant and charitable) has a structural significance at least for the modern reader of the novel in making the Fairyland and particularly the Outland scenes seem more lively, more free, and finally more "real" in contrast.

Dreaming functions in *Sylvie and Bruno* as problem solving—as it often does in life. Dreams can restructure reality by omitting, changing, and adding details so that we can work out at least partial solutions to the continual problems we have in the real world. This can sometimes be materially helpful, and it can often be psychologically helpful. In *Sylvie and Bruno*, the characters of dream are vitally necessary to the solving of problems in the real world. Because they are, the work becomes a flux of reality and dream. It is no accident that here we find Carroll inventing the Time Machine (he is several years before Wells). An Outlandish Watch would be pointless in Wonderland because there we have lost all sense of what time it "really" is; the Mad Hatter's watch "doesn't tell what o'clock it is." But real time and eerie time exist simultaneously in the world of *Sylvie and Bruno*, and Carroll means for us to discover that neither is all there is. Reality is not enough; we need nonsense too. Drifting into a world of fantasy is not an escape from reality but a significant education about the nature of life. And reality is not an escape from nonsense. Our education goes on everywhere. Arthur teaches us most directly, but there are professors everywhere in this work (and college officers, the Warden and the Sub-Warden). And it is only natural that the Narrator's dreams discover Bruno at his lessons, twiddling his eyes to see what letters do not spell, for example, and then seeing in EVIL only LIVE backwards. Eric Lindon learns the greatest lesson, that God answers prayer. This too is a lesson of love. And if we do not learn the lesson of love . . . why, we turn into porcupines.

Edmund Miller, "The *Sylvie and Bruno* Books as Victorian Novel," *Lewis Carroll Observed*, ed. Edward Guiliano (New York: Clarkson N. Potter, 1976), pp. 135–36

PETER HYLAND   Now although *Alice's Adventures* is very clearly about the opposed states of childhood and adulthood, I do not believe that it is a book about growing up if by that it is meant that Alice's adventures lead to her maturity in any sense. I do not believe that Alice grows up at the end of the book, or that the book deals with a process of development. Rather the book throughout juxtaposes, for comic effect, the child's and the adult's responses to the world. Since these different responses are frequently combined in the figure of Alice herself, it is hardly surprising that we are sometimes left with ambivalent feelings.

We should not see Alice as a character of the kind we normally expect to encounter in Victorian novels; rather, she represents two different viewpoints which separate or combine throughout the book, and these two viewpoints are presented quite explicably in the first chapter. Here, the fallen and tiny Alice, unable to reach the golden key to the lovely garden, begins to cry:

> 'Come, there's no use in crying like that!' said Alice to herself, rather sharply. 'I advise you to leave off this minute!' She generally gave herself very good advice, (though she very seldom followed it), and sometimes she scolded herself so severely as to bring tears into her eyes; and once she remembered trying to box her own ears for having cheated herself in a game of croquet she was playing against herself, for this curious child was very fond of pretending to be two people.

What we have here, very clearly, is an adult talking to a child. The 'adult' Alice gives advice, imposes rules, the 'child' Alice ignores or rejects rules. Alice's attempt to chastise herself is equivalent to an attempt to impose order upon anarchy, but the anarchy remains intractable. The pattern works throughout the book: Alice embodies the perspectives of adult and child, alternately or simultaneously, and we can no more expect consistency from her viewpoint than we can expect it from her size. Thus the book is not simply showing, as Elise Leach thinks, 'the illogical ways of adults' seen through the eyes of a child, because sometimes the eyes are an adult's eyes, and sometimes the point of view is closer to a complication of both. This is where the ambiguity arises, and this is why it is not really helpful to talk of Alice's 'favoured' position, since her position is not fixed, but fluctuates between the adult's and the child's—neither of which, of course, is 'right' in any absolute sense.

Peter Hyland, "The Ambiguous Alice: An Approach to *Alice in Wonderland*," *Jabberwocky* 11, No. 4 (Autumn 1982): 105–6

ANNE CLARK AMOR   Dodgson's first recorded river expedition with Alice, Lorina and Edith in the summer of 1862 was on 26 May, when Southey helped him row to Iffley and back. Although the distance covered was not great, it was hard work rowing because the current was so strong. The second occasion was on 14 June, when Robinson Duckworth, of Trinity College, helped with the rowing. Dodgson's aunt, Lucy Lutwidge, and his sisters Fanny and Elizabeth, for whom Dodgson had secured rooms at Mrs Golding's lodgings, were also in the boat with them, and the little girls found their presence somewhat inhibiting. On the return journey they were caught in a heavy shower, and abandoning the boat, Dodgson deposited the female members of the party at a house in Sandford where they could dry their clothes, and went on with Duckworth to Iffley to send them a fly.

The third river expedition that year, planned to compensate the children for the soaking they had received on the second expedition, was planned for 3 July, but was rained off. Instead it took place on 4 July 1862.

'Duckworth and I made the expedition *up* the river to Godstow with the three Liddells: we had tea on the bank there, and did not reach Christ Church again until quarter past eight, when we took them to my rooms to see my collections of microphotography, and restored them to the Deanery just before nine', he wrote. The fact that on this occasion for the first time Dodgson told them the story of *Alice's Adventures* did not even rate a mention at the time, but on 10 February 1863 Dodgson seemed suddenly to have a vague inkling of the importance of the occasion, for he added on the facing page. 'On which occasion I told them the fairy-tale of *Alice's Adventures Underground,* which I undertook to write out for Alice, and which is now finished (as to the text) though the pictures are not yet nearly done.'

There is not a single word in the extant diaries and letters to suggest that Alice was his favourite before that golden afternoon. Probably he chose her for his heroine for no better reason that she was the middle Liddell. But it seems that with that single act of choosing her as the heroine of his fairytale, and writing it down for her, he unleashed in the little girl more love and gratitude than he had ever believed possible in a child. For his part, Dodgson responded by polishing and refining his story until he had made that child immortal. By simply begging him to write out the story, Alice Liddell had shown him the way to achieve that literary masterpiece that he had been waiting all his life to create. She was now unique in his life, his muse and his heroine combined. As the realisation slowly dawned on him of her unique double role in his life, his fondness for her grew beyond all measure. He now loved Alice Liddell more than he had loved anyone in his entire life. Her place in his heart was unparalleled, and could never be threatened.

Anne Clark Amor, "Lewis Carroll and His Alice," *Jabberwocky* 20, No. 1 & 2 (Winter/ Spring 1991): 14–15

▣ *Bibliography*

Rules for Court Circular: (A New Game of Cards for Two or More Players). 1860.

Photographs. 1860.

Notes on the First Two Books of Euclid. 1860.

A Syllabus of Plane Algebraical Geometry: Part I. 1860.

The Formulae of Plane Trigonometry. 1861.

Notes on the First Part of Algebra. 1861.

Endowment of the Greek Professorship. 1861.

An Index to In Memoriam. 1862.

The Enunciations of the Propositions and Corollaries, Together with Questions on the Definitions, Postulates, Axioms, &c. in Euclid, Books I. and II. 1863.

General List of (Mathematical) Subjects, and Cycle for Working Examples. 1863.

Croquêt Castles: For Five Players. 1863, 1866 (as *Castle-Croquêt for Four Players*).

Examination Statute. 1864.

The New Examination Statute. 1864.

A Guide to the Mathematical Student in Reading, Reviewing, and Working Examples: Part I. 1864.

American Telegrams: Summary. 1865.

The New Method of Evaluation, as Applied to π. 1865.

The Dynamics of a Particle. 1865.

Alice's Adventures in Wonderland. 1865.

Symbols and Abbreviations for Euclid. 1866.

The Elections to the Hebdomadal Council. 1866.

Condensation of Determinants. 1866.

Enigma. 1866.

Explication of the Enigma. 1866.

The Deserted Parks. 1867.

Elementary Treatise on Determinants. 1867.

The Offer of the Clarendon Trustees. 1868.

The Telegraph-Cipher. 1868.

The Alphabet-Cipher. 1868.

The Fifth Book of Euclid, Treated Algebraically. 1868.

Algebraical Formulae for Responsions. 1868.

Phantasmagoria and Other Poems. 1869.

The Guildford Gazette Extraordinary. 1869.

Algebraical Formulae and Rules. 1869.

Arithmetical Formulae and Rules. 1870.

The Songs from Alice's Adventures in Wonderland (with William Boyd). 1870.

Suggestions for Committee to Consider the Expediency of Reconstituting Senior Studentships at Christ Church. 1871.

To All Child-Readers of Alice's Adventures in Wonderland. 1871.

Through the Looking-Glass, and What Alice Found There. 1871.

Circular to Hospitals Offering Copies of the Two "Alice" Books. 1872.

The New Belfry of Christ Church, Oxford. 1872.

Number of Propositions in Euclid. 1872. Lost.

The Enunciations of Euclid I–VI. 1873.

The Vision of the Three T's: A Threnody. 1873.

Objections, Submitted to the Governing Body of Christ Church, Oxford, against Certain Proposed Alterations in the Great Quadrangle. 1873.

A Discussion of the Various Modes of Procedure in Conducting Elections. 1873.

The Blank Cheque: A Fable. 1874.

Notes by an Oxford Chiel. 1874.

Suggestions as to the Best Method of Taking Votes, Where More Than Two Issues Are to Be Voted On. 1874.

Examples in Arithmetic. 1874.

Euclid, Book V: Proved Algebraically So Far As It Relates to Commensurable Magnitudes. 1874.

Some Popular Fallacies about Vivisection. 1875.

Euclid: Books I, II (editor). 1875, 1882.

Song for Puss in Boots. 1876.

Professorship of Comparative Philology. 1876.

A Method of Taking Votes on More Than Two Issues. 1876.

The Hunting of the Snark: An Agony, in Eight Fits. 1876.

An Easter Greeting to Every Child Who Loves "Alice." 1876.

Letter and Questions to Hospitals. 1876. Lost.

Fame's Penny-Trumpet. 1876.

Responsions, Hilary Term, 1877. 1877.

A Charade. 1878.

Word-Links: A Game for Two Players, or a Round Game. 1878.

Euclid and His Modern Rivals. 1879.

Doublets: A Word-Puzzle. 1879.

Doublets Already Set. 1879.

A Game for Two Players. 1879.

A New Method of Scoring. 1880.

⟨Letter from Mabel to Emily.⟩ 1880.

Lanrick: A Game for Two Players. 1881.

On Catching Cold. 1881.

Notice re Concordance to In Memoriam. 1881.

Dreamland (with C. E. Hutchinson). 1882.

A Letter to Friends and to Members of the Dramatic Profession. 1882.

An Analysis of the Responsions-Lists from Michaelmas 1873 to Michaelmas 1881. 1882.

Mischmasch. 1882.

Lawn Tennis Tournaments: The True Method of Assigning Prizes. 1883.

A Circular to Friends about Appointments, &c. 1883.

Rules for Reckoning Postage. 1883. Lost.

Rhyme? and Reason? 1883.

Christmas Greetings from a Fairy to a Child. 1884.

Twelve Months in a Curatorship. 1884.

Supplement to Twelve Months in a Curatorship. 1884.

Postscript ⟨to Twelve Months in a Curatorship⟩. 1884.

The Principles of Parliamentary Representation. 1884.

The Profits of Authorship. 1884.

The Principles of Parliamentary Representation: Supplement. 1885.

The Principles of Parliamentary Representation: Postscript to Supplement. 1885.

Supplement to Euclid and His Modern Rivals. 1885.

The Proposed Procuratorial Cycle. 1885.

Postscript: Addressed to Mathematicians Only. 1885.

The Proctorial Cycle to Be Voted On in Congregation on Tuesday, Nov. 10, 1885. 1885.

Suggestions as to the Election of Proctors. 1885.

A Tangled Tale. 1885.

Three Years in a Curatorship. 1886.

Remarks on the Report of the Finance Committee. 1886. Lost.

Remarks on Mr. Sampson's New Proposal. 1886.

Observations on Mr. Sampson's New Proposal. 1886.

Suggestions as to the Election of Proctors. 1886.

First Paper on Logic. 1886.

Second Paper on Logic. 1886.

Third Paper on Logic. 1886.

Fourth Paper on Logic. 1886.

The Game of Logic. 1886, 1887.

Alice's Adventures Under Ground. 1886.

Questions in Logic. 1887.

Fifth Paper on Logic. 1887.

Sixth Paper on Logic. 1887.

Seventh Paper on Logic. 1887.

To My Child-Friend. 1888.

Memoria Technica. 1888.

Curiosa Mathematica, Part I: A New Theory of Parallels. 1888.

The Nursery Alice. 1889.

Sylvie and Bruno. 1889.

Circular Billiards, for Two Players. 1889.

The Wonderful Postage-Stamp Case. 1890.

The Strange Circular. 1890.

Eight or Nine Wise Words about Letter-Writing. 1890.

A Postal Problem. 1891.

A Postal Problem: Supplement. 1891.

⟨A Circular Addressed to the Governing Body of Christ Church, Oxford.⟩ 1891.

⟨A Circular about Resignation of Curatorship.⟩ 1892.

⟨A Circular about "Unparliamentary" Words.⟩ 1892.

Curiosissima Curatoria. 1892.

Eighth Paper on Logic. 1892.

Ninth Paper on Logic. 1892.

Notes to Logic Papers Eight and Nine. 1892.

A Challenge to Logicians. 1892.

Syzygies and Lanrick: A Word-Puzzle and a Game for Two Players. 1893.

Curiosa Mathematica, Part II: Pillow-Problems Thought Out during Wakeful Hours. 1893.

Second-Hand Books. 1893.

Sylvie and Bruno Concluded. 1893.

A Disputed Point in Logic. 1894.

A Theorem in Logic. 1894.

A Logical Puzzle. 1894.

Symbolic Logic: Specimen-Syllogisms, Premisses. 1894.

Symbolic Logic: Specimen-Syllogisms, Conclusions. 1894.

Symbolic Logic: Questions. 1894. 2 parts.

⟨A Circular for Mechanics' Institutes.⟩ 1894.

What the Tortoise Said to Achilles. 1894.

Three Problems. 1895.

Logical Nomenclature, Desiderata. 1895.

A Fascinating Mental Recreation for the Young. 1895.

Symbolic Logic, Part I: Elementary. 1896.

Resident Women-Students. 1896.

Quadrilateral Diagrams. c. 1896.

Quinquilateral Diagrams. c. 1896.

Three Sunsets and Other Poems. 1898.

The Lewis Carroll Picture Book. Ed. Stuart Dodgson Collingwood. 1899.

Freeing the Mind. Ed. William H. Draper. 1907.

Six Letters. Ed. Wilfred Partington. 1924.

Some Rare Carrolliana. Ed. Sidney Herbert Williams. 1924.

Bruno's Revenge. Ed. John Drinkwater. 1924.

Novelty and Romancement. 1925.

Further Nonsense Verse and Prose. Ed. Langford Reed. 1926.

Tour in 1867 ⟨The Russian Journal⟩. 1928.

Collected Verse. Ed. John Francis McDermott. 1929.

A Christmas Carroll. 1930.

To M. A. B. 1931.

Collected Verse. 1932.

For the Train: Five Poems and a Letter. Ed. Hugh J. Schoenfield. 1932.

The Rectory Umbrella and Mischmasch. 1932.

A Selection of the Letters of Lewis Carroll to His Child-Friends, Together with Eight or Nine Wise Words about Letter-Writing. Ed. Evelyn M. Hatch. 1933.

Logical Nonsense. Ed. Philip C. Blackburn and Lionel White. 1934.

The Russian Journal and Other Selections. Ed. John Francis McDermott. 1935.

Complete Works. 1936.

How the Boots Got Left Behind. 1943.

Diaries. Ed. Roger Lancelyn Green. 1953. 2 vols.

Useful and Instructive Poetry. Ed. Derek Hudson. 1954.

Mathematical Recreations of Lewis Carroll. 1958. 2 vols.

The Annotated Alice. Ed. Martin Gardner. 1960.

The Annotated Snark. Ed. Martin Gardner. 1962.

Works. Ed. Roger Lancelyn Green. 1965.

Lewis Carroll on Education. Ed. John Fleming and Joan Fleming. 1972.

The Magic of Lewis Carroll. Ed. John Fisher. 1973.

Photos and Letters to His Child Friends. Ed. Guido Almansi. 1975.

The Rectory Magazine (editor). 1975.

Symbolic Logic, Parts I & II. Ed. William Warren Bartley III. 1977.

The Wasp in a Wig: A "Suppressed" Episode of Through the Looking-Glass and What Alice Found There. Ed. Edward Guiliano. 1977.

Lewis Carroll's Photographs of Nude Children. Ed. Morton N. Cohen. 1978.

Letters. Ed. Martin N. Cohen and Roger Lancelyn Green. 1979. 2 vols.

Lewis Carroll: Victorian Photographer. Ed. Helmut Gernsheim. 1980.

Complete Illustrated Works. Ed. Edward Guiliano. 1982.

Lewis Carroll. Ed. Cornel Capa et al. 1984.

Logic and Tea: The Letters of Charles L. Dodgson to Mrs. Emily Rowell and Her Daughters Ethel and Hattie. Ed. Jan Susine and F. Brewer. 1984.

Looking-Glass Letters. Ed. Thomas Hinde. 1991.

Oxford Pamphlets, Leaflets, and Circulars. Ed. Edward Wakeling. 1993.

Lord Dunsany
1878–1957

EDWARD JOHN MORETON DRAX PLUNKETT was born on July 24, 1878, at 15 Park Square near Regent's Park, London. He was descended from an aristocratic Anglo-Irish line that could trace its origins to the twelfth century, and Plunkett spent his early years alternately at homes in England and at his ancestral castle in County Meath, Ireland. He attended Eton and Sandhurst and served in the Boer War. In 1899, upon the death of his father, he became the eighteenth Lord Dunsany. In 1904 he married Beatrice Villiers, daughter of the Earl of Jersey; they had one son, Randal.

Although Dunsany had published a poem, "Rhymes from a Suburb," in 1897, he otherwise showed little inclination for writing; but in 1904 he began the composition of a book of stories and fables, *The Gods of Pegāna*, which introduced an entire imaginary cosmogony complete with gods, demigods, priests, and worshippers. Having no literary reputation, he paid for the publication of the volume, which appeared in 1905; its surprising *succès d'estime*, as well as the warm reception of his other early collections of tales—*Time and the Gods* (1906), *The Sword of Welleran* (1908), *A Dreamer's Tales* (1910), *The Book of Wonder* (1912)—made Dunsany one of the most popular and fashionable authors in the English-speaking world.

In 1909 W. B. Yeats asked Dunsany to write plays for the Abbey Theatre, and Dunsany obliged with *The Glittering Gate*. This and later plays—*The Gods of the Mountain* (1911), *King Argimēnēs and the Unknown Warrior* (1911), *A Night at an Inn* (1916)—became spectacularly popular, and in 1916 Dunsany became the only playwright to have five plays running simultaneously on Broadway. His early plays were collected in *Five Plays* (1914), *Plays of Gods and Men* (1917), and *Plays of Near and Far* (1922). Both his plays and his stories were extensively published in the United States, where Dunsany gained a particularly avid following.

Dunsany, who remained for his entire life a Unionist who wished Ireland to retain its ties to England, was about to be sent overseas to serve in World War I in 1916, but instead assisted in subduing the Dublin riots during the

Eastern Rebellion; he was seriously injured by gunfire, but recovered and went to Flanders later that year. At about this time appeared *The Last Book of Wonder* (1916), which marked an end to the imaginary-world fantasy that marked his early period.

After the war Dunsany and his wife lived alternately in Dunsany Castle and in a home, Dunstall Priory, in Sevenoaks, Kent, although they traveled widely. Dunsany made extensive lecture tours in the United States in 1919–20 and 1928, and also traveled to Africa, India, and elsewhere to pursue his ardent hobby of big-game hunting. He also became one of the world's greatest amateur chess players. Between the wars Dunsany was a much sought-after writer and contributed stories, essays, and poetry extensively to the *Atlantic Monthly*, *Saturday Evening Post*, *Collier's*, and other periodicals. He began writing novels, among them *The Chronicles of Rodriguez* (1922), *The King of Elfland's Daughter* (1924), *The Charwoman's Shadow* (1926), and *The Blessing of Pan* (1927).

In 1932 Dunsany took offense at being rejected as a full member of the Irish Academy of Letters then being formed by W. B. Yeats; the reason given was that he had not written specifically of Ireland, so Dunsany turned his attention to Irish themes in the novels *The Curse of the Wise Woman* (1933), *Rory and Bran* (1936), and *The Story of Mona Sheehy* (1939), in the ruminative volume *My Ireland* (1937), and in many short stories. Dunsany also achieved great popularity with his five collections of tales about the clubman Joseph Jorkens, beginning in 1931 with *The Travel Tales of Mr. Joseph Jorkens*. His three autobiographies—*Patches of Sunlight* (1938), *While the Sirens Slept* (1944), and *The Sirens Wake* (1945)—are full of accounts of his writings, travels, and encounters with fellow writers.

In 1940 Dunsany accepted the Byron Professorship of English Literature at Athens University but had to be evacuated the next year when the Germans invaded, returning home via a very circuitous route through the Middle East and Africa. He wrote about this adventure in the novel *Guerrilla* (1944) and in the long poem *A Journey* (1944). In 1943 he delivered the Donnellan lectures at Trinity College, Dublin, and in 1945 he wrote a series of essays on the future of civilization, *A Glimpse from a Watch Tower*, in which he wrote of his reaction to the dropping of the atomic bomb: "I think that a new era started yesterday . . . henceforth we are all people with a mission, a strange mission, not to destroy the world." In the 1950s he made several trips to California to visit Hazel Littlefield, and was still received with enthusiasm by readers and reporters. He continued writing prolifically to the end of his life, with such late story collections as *The*

Man Who Ate the Phoenix (1949) and *The Little Tales of Smethers* (1952) and such novels as *The Strange Journeys of Colonel Polders* (1950) and *The Last Revolution* (1952). Lord Dunsany died on October 25, 1957. A biography by Mark Amory was published in 1972, and a comprehensive bibliography, compiled by S. T. Joshi and Darrell Schweitzer, appeared in 1993.

✛ *Critical Extracts*

W. B. YEATS   Some of the writers of our school have intended, so far as any creative art can have deliberate intention, to make this change ⟨the revival of Irish literature⟩, a change having more meaning and implications than a few sentences can define. When I was first moved by Lord Dunsany's work I thought that he would more help this change if he could bring his imagination into the old Irish legendary world instead of those magic lands of his with their vague Eastern air; but even as I urged him I knew that he could not, without losing his rich beauty of careless suggestion, and the persons and images that for ancestry have all those romantic ideas that are somewhere in the background of all our minds. He could not have made Slieve-na-Mon or Slieve Fua incredible and phantastic enough, because that prolonged study of a past age, necessary before he could separate them from modern association, would have changed the spontaneity of his mood to something learned, premeditated, and scientific. ⟨. . .⟩

⟨. . .⟩ Had I read 'The Fall of Babbulkund' or 'Idle Days on the Yann' when a boy I had perhaps been changed for better or worse, and looked to that first reading as the creation of my world; for when we are young the less circumstantial, the further from common life a book is, the more does it touch our hearts and make us dream. We are idle, unhappy and exorbitant, and like the young Blake admit no city beautiful that is not paved with gold and silver. ⟨. . .⟩

These plays and stories have for their continual theme the passing away of gods and men and cities before the mysterious power which is sometimes called by some great god's name but more often 'Time'. His travellers, who travel by so many rivers and deserts and listen to sounding names none heard before, come back with no tale that does not tell of vague rebellion against that power, and all the beautiful things they have seen get something of their charm from the pathos of fragility. This poet who has imagined colours, ceremonies and incredible processions that never passed before the eyes of Edgar Allan Poe or of De Quincey, and remembered as much fabulous beauty as Sir John Mandeville, has yet never wearied of the most universal of emotions and the one most constantly associated with the sense of beauty; and when we come to examine those astonishments that seemed so alien we find that he has but transfigured with beauty the common sights of the world. He describes the dance in the air of large butterflies as we have seen it in the sun-steeped air of noon. 'And they danced but danced idly, on the wings of the air, as some haughty queen of distant conquered lands might in her poverty and exile dance in some encampment of the gipsies for the mere bread to live by, but beyond this would never abate her pride to dance for one fragment more.' He can show us the movement of sand, as we have seen it where the sea shore meets the grass, but so changed that it becomes the deserts of the world: 'and all that night the desert said many things softly and in a whisper but I knew not what he said. Only the sand knew and arose and was troubled and lay down and the wind knew. Then, as the hours of the night went by, these two discovered the foot-tracks wherewith we had disturbed the holy desert and they troubled over them and covered them up; and then the wind lay down and the sand rested.' Or he will invent some incredible sound that will yet call before us the strange sounds of the night, as when he says, 'sometimes some monster of the river coughed'. And how he can play upon our fears with that great gate of his carved from a single ivory tusk dropped by some terrible beast; or with his tribe of wanderers that pass about the city telling one another tales that we know to be terrible from the blanched faces of the listeners though they tell them in an unknown tongue; or with his stone gods of the mountain, for 'when we see rock walking it is terrible' 'rock should not walk in the evening'.

Yet say what I will, so strange is the pleasure that they give, so hard to analyse and describe, I do not know why these stories and plays delight me. Now they set me thinking of some old Irish jewel work, now of a sword covered with Indian Arabesques that hangs in a friend's hall, now of St Mark's at Venice, now of cloud palaces at the sundown; but more often still of a strange country or state of the soul that once for a few weeks I entered in deep sleep and after lost and have ever mourned and desired.

W. B. Yeats, "Introduction to *Selections from the Writings of Lord Dunsany*" (1912), *Prefaces and Introductions* (The Collected Works of W. B. Yeats, Volume VI), ed. William H. O'Donnell (New York: Macmillan, 1989), pp. 140–42

PADRAIC COLUM   We are all fictionists nowadays: Lord Dunsany, however, is that rare creature in literature, the fabulist. He does not aim at imposing forms on what we call reality—graceful, impressive or significant forms: he aims at transporting us from this reality altogether. He is like the man who comes to the hunters' lodges and says "You wonder at the moon. I will tell you how the moon was made and why." And having told them about the moon he goes on to tell them about marvellous cities that are beyond the forest and about the jewel that is in the unicorn's horn. If such a one were rebuked for filling the folk with dreams and idle tales, he might (had he the philosophy) make reply: "I have kept alive their spirit of wonder, and wonder in man is holy." Lord Dunsany speaking for himself would say with Blake "Imagination is the man." He would, I think, go on to declare that the one thing worth doing for mankind is to make their imaginations more and more exalted. One can hardly detect a social idea in his work. There is one there, however. It is one of unrelenting hostility to everything that impoverishes man's imagination—to mean cities, to commercial interests, to a culture that arises out of material organization. He dwells forever upon things that arouse the imagination—upon swords and cities, upon temples and palaces, upon slaves in their revolt and kings in their unhappiness. He has the mind of a myth-maker, and he can give ships and cities and whirlpools vast and proper shapes.

> Padraic Colum, "Introduction," *A Dreamer's Tales and Other Stories* (New York: Boni & Liveright [Modern Library], 1917), p. xiii

---

AE (GEORGE WILLIAM RUSSELL)   ⟨. . .⟩ *The King of Elfland's Daughter* ⟨. . .⟩ is a highly sustained piece of fantasy, written in a prose whose melody never fails and never tires. It compares well, I think, with any of William Morris's prose romances, for their defect is that they are almost altogether literature in one dimension. They are on the flat, like wall paper or tapestry, even though the figures worked upon it have unending comeliness. The invention of an Elfland that can, by the magic of its king, come close to our world or be inconceivably remote, gives a richness to Dunsany's romance, so that it may be said to be two-dimensional, though not in his tale any more than in Morris's romances do recognizable human entities move about. His people loom before us like a dance of animated and lovely shadows and grotesques, but we follow their adventures with excitement, and that means that in some way they are symbolic of our own spiritual adventures. We have all known that fading of Elfland from just beyond the familiar woods and lakes and hills which comes after childhood, and how inconceivably remote Elfland seems once it has gone from us, and what purifications and sacrifices and labors of the soul we must endure if we are to regain the child vision we have lost. The fading away of Elfland from the vision of Alveric in the tale, and his years of search for it, do not appear to us unreal as we read, for have we not, most of us, lost vision of the enchanted land? And though some have sought to regain it, how few they are who have won it back so that it glows again beyond the familiar fence! *The King of Elfland's Daughter* is the most purely beautiful thing Lord Dunsany has written. There may be better or more exciting things in some of the short tales, but nowhere else has he had such a long run on that Pegasus of his that carries him east of the East and west of the West—not curving round the world, as he once said to me, but going on straight into regions that the makers of the Arabian tales of enchantment knew, or which lay in neighboring kingdoms of romance.

> AE (George William Russell), "A Maker of Mythologies," *Living Age*, 29 May 1926, pp. 464–65

H. P. LOVECRAFT   Dunsany has a peculiar appeal for me. Casual and tenuous though any one of his fantastic flights may seem, the massed effect of his whole cycle of theogony, myth, legend, fable, hero-epic and dream-chronicle on my consciousness is that of a most potent and particular sort of cosmic liberation. When I first encountered him (through *A Dreamer's Tales*) in 1919 he seemed like a sort of gate to enchanted worlds of childhood dream, and his temporary influence on my own literary attempts ⟨. . .⟩ was enormous. Indeed, my own mode of expression almost lost itself for a time amidst a wave of imitated Dunsanianism. There seemed to me to be in Dunsany certain poetic adumbrations of the cosmic lacking elsewhere. I may have read some of them in myself, but am sure that a goodly number must have been there to start with. Dunsany knows a certain type of dream and longing and vague out-reaching natural to the Nordic mind and shaped in childhood by the early folklore and literary impressions afforded by our culture—the Germanic fairy-tale, the Celtic legend, the Biblical myth, the Arabian-Nightish Orientale, the Graeco-Roman epic, and so on. This vision or longing or out-reaching he is able to crystallise in terms of certain elements drawn from all these simple and familiar sources, and the result has an odd universal magic which few can deny. The philosophy behind his work is essentially that of the finer minds of our age—a cosmic disillusion plus a desperate effort to retain those fragments of wonder and myth of significance, direction, and purpose which intellectual progress and absorption in material

things alike tend to strip away. Of course Dunsany is uneven, and his later work (despite the different sort of charm in *The Curse of the Wise Woman*) cannot be compared with his early productions. As he gained in age and sophistication, he lost in freshness and simplicity. He was ashamed to be uncritically naive, and began to step aside from his tales and visibly smile at them even as they unfolded. Instead of remaining what the true fantaisiste must be—a child in a child's world of dream—he became anxious to shew that he was really an adult good-naturedly pretending to be a child in a child's world. This hardening-up began to show, I think, in *The Book of Wonder*—though it did not creep into the plays so soon. A decade later it relaxed slightly in the novels *Chronicles of Rodriguez* and *The King of Elfland's Daughter*, but it shews at its worst in the "Jorkens" tripe. Alas that no writer can ever keep up to the level of his best! When I think of Dunsany, it is in terms of *The Gods of the Mountain*, "Bethmoora", "Poltarnees, Beholder of Ocean", "The City of Never", "The Fall of Babbulkund", "In the Land of Time", and "Idle Days on the Yann".

> H. P. Lovecraft, Letter to Fritz Leiber (15 November 1936), *Selected Letters: 1934–1937*, ed. August Derleth and James Turner (Sauk City, WI: Arkham House, 1976), pp. 353–54

LORD DUNSANY   On the back of the hill that faced Dunstall, the slope of which I could now see facing West from the end of Sir Joseph ⟨Prestwich⟩'s garden, I first saw a hare one summer's evening: my father pointed him out to me and clapped his hands for me to see it run; and it ran along the slope under the woods. If ever I have written of Pan, out in the evening, as though I had really seen him, it is mostly a memory of that hare. If I thought that I was a gifted individual whose inspirations came sheer from outside earth and transcended common things, I should not write this book; but I believe that the wildest flights of the fancies of any of us have their homes with Mother Earth, and I only retail my early memories because amongst them must be the origins of any fancies of mine that may have been so happy as to entertain any reader. Of course it is by no means always that one can trace any earthly origin to one's own fancies or to those of other people, which helps us to suppose that all inspirations are from beyond the paths of the planets; and yet every now and then I hit on the mundane origin of some fancy that almost seemed as though it scorned earth; and these discoveries I make, when I make them at all, with a certain impartiality, among the inspirations of others and of myself. ⟨. . .⟩

The source of all imagination is here in our fields, and Creation is beautiful enough for the furthest flights of the poets. What is called realism only falls far behind these flights because it is too meticulously concerned with the detail of material; mere inventories of rocks are not poetry; but all the memories of crags and hills and meadows and woods and sky that lie in a sensitive spirit are materials for poetry, only waiting to be taken out, and to be laid before the eyes of such as care to perceive them. For this reason I have dwelt awhile on the trivial scenes of childhood, because a child's eyes are brighter than they will ever be again, and a child's spirit is sensitive, and the few memories still mirrored there are likely to be clearer reflections of the beauty of England than any that will come to me any more.

Lord Dunsany, *Patches of Sunlight* (London: William Heinemann, 1938), pp. 9, 20–21

OLIVER ST. JOHN GOGARTY   Many of his plays were written before the First World War, between 1909 and April, 1913. They reveal a high distinction and one quite unusual in modern drama. There is an unearthly liturgic quality about them, a language measured appropriately to the inexorable utterance of outlandish gods in far inaccessible fastnesses, strong places high above the lowly world of men.

His first play was *The Glittering Gate*. It was produced in the Abbey Theatre, Dublin, April 29, 1909. It was such a success that Lady Gregory, who controlled the Abbey Theatre, took it off the program with the excuse that it was not sufficiently long. In spite of this rebuff (perhaps it was so disguised that it did not seem a rebuff) he offered his next play to the same management two years later. Its title was *King Argimēnēs and the Unknown Warrior*. This time the characters were dressed in the dregs of the Abbey greenroom, so no longer was the discouragement disguised. For a while I thought Dunsany's resentment was not altogether justified, until I saw to what extent the management of the Abbey would go to make one of Yeats's plays or the plays of Lady Gregory a success. Dunsany's dislike of Yeats grew from this. The Abbey Theatre saw Dunsany no more.

Since he tried his prentice hand in the Abbey, he has since written some of the greatest plays in the English language: *Alexander*, *The Queen's Enemies*, and *A Night at an Inn*, to name but three.

It is not quite fair to attribute a trend to a dramatist; but sometimes unfair things are quite allowable; so I can see that Dunsany judges men by the gods they worship. It may not be so; that is why I have taken the unfairness to myself. To prosecute the thought further, there is in the Irish defiance in the midst of destruction and desolation, in Irish bravery in the face of ruin, that which is akin to the dramatic attitude toward life: regarding it from a detached point of view. The judgment on men by the gods they choose!

The Abbey Theatre, being a one man and woman show, could not hold such an independent and self-contained spirit as Dunsany long. So the world became his stage, and on it he was a success second to none—certainly not to those who deal with passing and ephemeral things.

Oliver St. John Gogarty, "Lord Dunsany," *Atlantic Monthly* 195, No. 3 (March 1955): 67

HAZEL LITTLEFIELD   Every morning the *Los Angeles Times* was left in plain sight near the breakfast table. Without a glance he pushed it aside. He would not clutter his mind with reports of crime and political crises that were the usual grist of news. He knew that preoccupation with human relationships of the workaday world is apt to dull one's sense of the spiritual yearnings and imaginative flights of which the human soul is capable. But he had a shrewd idea of what was happening in the arena of world politics and sometimes, in conversation, he dropped a caustic comment that blasted the folly of dull diplomats and power-seeking radicals.

Among older people it began to be remembered that his plays had once been the rage in New York and his *Wonder Tales* the delight of those who love fantasy. The voices of strangers spoke to me over the telephone asking if they might come to meet him: authors, actors, poets, a dancer, a diplomat. One awestruck woman's voice asked if it were really true that he was in Palos Verdes. "Oh," she sighed, "to think I am breathing the same air with him." I invited her to come nearer and take a deep breath.

Invited and uninvited they came to morning coffee and afternoon tea. They sat and adored him. His impeccable dignity and natural charm were all that they could have desired. He enchanted them. ⟨. . .⟩

Describing his flight over Arizona, he said, "The sun shone on the ramparts of uninhabited cities and there was a parliament of mountains sitting around their council tables." And of the period between the two great wars, "The dance of death paused only long enough to change partners." He described a river in Africa which he had seen from the air as, "A dark sluggish river, like an old cart horse, when suddenly stung by a whip, plunging forward, the river plunges over a precipice." To a man who was discussing the tremendous increase given our defensive power by the hydrogen bomb,

Dunsany threw off this comparison: "It is as if, walking in a garden, two men watched snails crawling, and one man said, 'My snail will win,' and the other replied, 'My horse will win the Derby.' We've increased our power to destroy a million times, but how much have we increased our wisdom?"

Hazel Littlefield, *Lord Dunsany: King of Dreams: A Personal Portrait* (New York: Exposition Press, 1959), pp. 47–48

SEAMUS HEANEY   ⟨The⟩ hero ⟨of *The Curse of the Wise Woman*⟩ is abroad, engaged on some diplomatic business for the new Irish Free State, and the book is a nostalgic evocation of an adolescence during the Troubles. The emotional division in the heart of a Unionist landlord, living in a newly independent Ireland, is emblematically realised in the setting. The boy hovers between the privileged structures of Eton and his walled estate, and the mysterious lure of the bog and its denizens. The hero's world is masculine and feudal, its spirit in the gun and dog; the primeval landscape beyond the walls is feminine, its spirit is the wise woman. Both are threatened by the impersonal enterprise of the Peat Development (Ireland) Syndicate. While the characters are two-dimensional and some of the dialogue a parody of stage Irish, these are the constituents of what might be a myth of the shaping of modern Ireland, and while the author balks it with a happy ending that is imaginatively unsatisfactory and geologically improbable (a tidal wave of bog engulfs the machines), the book contains many exhilarating sportsman's sketches, and there is a seam of memorable beauty running through the whole story, in the evocations of the mythopoeic bog. It is a pity he didn't spend more time and intellect exploring these peaty obsessions.

Seamus Heaney, "The Labourer and the Lord," *Listener*, 28 September 1972, p. 409

ARTHUR C. CLARKE   ⟨. . .⟩ Lord Dunsany's delightful and deservedly popular fantasies had a great influence on me, and I was privileged to meet their author in the late 1940s; we also had an extensive correspondence, which may one day be published. He wrote several tongue-in-cheek stories about space travel: one of my favorites ⟨"Our Distant Cousins," in *The Travel Tales of Mr. Joseph Jorkens*⟩ is about a man who flies to Mars and discovers, among other wonders, a herd of *very* small elephants. He brings one back to Earth with him, but unfortunately it escapes. The only

evidence he has to prove his story is the broken matchbox out of which it
battered its way. . . . Yes, Martian elephants are *very* small indeed.

Arthur C. Clarke, "The Poetry of Space" (1981), *1984: Spring: A Choice of Futures*
(New York: Ballantine Books, 1984), pp. 165–66

JOHN WILSON FOSTER   There is in the fiction of Lord Dunsany
an absence of that self-consciousness we discovered in fiction of the ⟨Irish
literary⟩ revival. The selflessness of his work is of no urgently personal or
patriotic kind; indeed, there is very little presentation of the self at all, few
heroes with whom he or we can identify save on a purely narrative level
and through the technical device of point of view. We might account for
the composure of Dunsany's fiction in terms of his imagination which,
Colum's opinion to the contrary that Dunsany has "the *mind* of a myth-
maker," seems to me to lack the *Einfühlung* which ⟨James⟩ Stephens' imagination had in abundance and which is the basis of mythopoeia. Stephens,
Blake, and Lawrence seem to me essentially mythopoeic writers, creators
of myth; Tolkien, Dunsany, Morris, even Joyce, seem to me formally mythopoeic writers, users of myth. Yeats stands between, a maker of legends. Of
course, the conventions of fantasy (like those of the folktale) are impersonal
ones, highly suitable for authors who wish to create selfless worlds without
the pain of transcending the self through various forms of self-expression.

But we might also take into account, and possibly could do so in the
cases of ⟨C. S.⟩ Lewis and Tolkien as well as Dunsany, a social self-confidence.
Lord Dunsany, whose social station and sense of self seem to have been so
closely entwined, apparently considered no reason for self-questioning to
exist. Perhaps we could see in his double life, fantasy and literature on the
one hand, snipe-shooting and safaris on the other, the Irish law of the
excluded middle, or in his fashioning of otherworlds an Ascendancy longing
for social security (dreaming his fracturing world intact), yet his English
literary affinities suggest otherwise. If he and his literature are Irish, they
are so in a peculiar and negative way, which might, after all, be said equally
of the orthodox Ascendancy during the Irish struggle for independence.
Colum chose to see Dunsany's imaginings as socially innocent. But surely
there is a connection between, firstly, Dunsany's ignoring of Irish folk and
bardic material and the purity of his fantasy, and, secondly, the conservatism
of mind (he detested modern poetry, for example) as well as of his politics. His
freedom from self-questioning and political anxiety released his imagination

from the demands of social reality. The social ideas are there in his work, but like nineteenth century landlords, are detectable by their absenteeism.

John Wilson Foster, *Fictions of the Irish Literary Revival: A Changeling Art* (Syracuse: Syracuse University Press, 1987), pp. 297–98

S. T. JOSHI   An honest reader of Dunsany must get beyond the early work, siren song as it is; one must explore what he chose to do in the nearly four decades of writing after *Tales of Three Hemispheres* (1919) and read this material with the expectation that it will be significantly different from— but not necessarily inferior to—the earlier work. I resolutely refuse to pass judgment on whether his earlier or his later writing is superior: there are times when I, like most readers, want to genuflect before *The Gods of Pegāna* or *A Dreamer's Tales*, but I would never wish to part with *The Blessing of Pan, The Curse of the Wise Woman, The Story of Mona Sheehy,* or *The Strange Journeys of Colonel Polders*. But it is not a matter of likes or dislikes: Dunsany, quite simply, was always evolving as a writer. ⟨. . .⟩

In the end the career of Lord Dunsany is both unique and edifying. Let us by all means reverence the early work, the work we unconsciously designate when we use the adjective "Dunsanian"; but let us learn that the later work is just as Dunsanian, just as representative of his temperament at a later stage. Let us marvel at his seemingly effortless mastery of so many different forms (short story, novel, play, even essay and lecture), his unfailingly sound narrative sense, and the amazing consistency he maintained over a breathtakingly prolific output. Like Lovecraft, like Machen, Dunsany claimed aesthetic independence from his time and culture, became a sharp and unrelenting critic of the industrialism and plebeianism that were shattering the beauty both of literature and of the world, wrote works almost obtrusively and aggressively unpopular in tone and import yet retained a surprising popularity—at least in terms of the sale of his work—through the whole of his career. The criticism of Dunsany is at an even more primitive level than that of Machen, Lovecraft, or M. R. James, and certainly more than that of Poe and Bierce. In part I think this is because many critics—and I will include myself in this number—find his early work so flawless of its kind as to be virtually uncriticizable, and most have not considered the later work at all. But it is also because Dunsany is seen by many simply as a *predecessor*: a dominant influence on Lovecraft, Tolkien, and others, to whom an obligatory tip of the hat and no more is necessary. Lovecraft died in 1937, the year *The Hobbit* was published; Dunsany continued to write for nearly two decades after this. I have done all I can to indicate the compelling interest in the whole of his work; later critics must continue the task of explication so that Lord Dunsany becomes more than just a hallowed name.

S. T. Joshi, "Lord Dunsany: The Career of a *Fantaisiste*," *The Weird Tale* (Austin: University of Texas Press, 1990), pp. 84–86

◈ Bibliography

The Gods of Pegāna. 1905.

Time and the Gods. 1906.

The Sword of Welleran and Other Stories. 1908.

The Fortress Unvanquishable, Save for Sacnoth. 1910.

A Dreamer's Tales. 1910.

Selections from the Writings of Lord Dunsany. [Ed. W. B. Yeats.] 1912.

The Book of Wonder. 1912.

Five Plays. 1914.

Fifty-one Tales. 1915.

The Last Book of Wonder 〈*Tales of Wonder*〉. 1916.

A Night at an Inn. 1916.

Plays of Gods and Men. 1917.

A Dreamer's Tales and Other Stories. 1917.

The Book of Wonder 〈and *Time and the Gods*〉. 1918.

Tales of War. 1918.

Nowadays. 1918.

Unhappy Far-Off Things. 1919.

Tales of Three Hemispheres. 1919.

If. 1921.

The Chronicles of Rodriguez 〈*Don Rodriguez: Chronicles of Shadow Valley*〉. 1922.

The Laughter of the Gods. 1922.

The Tents of the Arabs. 1922.

The Queen's Enemies. 1922.

Plays of Near and Far. 1922.

Plays of Near and Far (Including If). 1923.

The Compromise of the Queen of the Golden Isles. 1923.

The Flight of the Queen. 1923.

Cheezo. 1923.

A Good Bargain. 1923.

If Shakespeare Lived To-day. 1923.

Fame and the Poet. 1923.

The Gods of the Mountain. 1923.

The Golden Doom. 1923.

King Argimēnēs and the Unknown Warrior. 1923.

The Glittering Gate. 1923.

The Lost Silk Hat. 1923.

The King of Elfland's Daughter. 1924.

Alexander and Three Small Plays. 1925.

Alexander. 1925.

The Old King's Tale. 1925.

The Evil Kettle. 1925.

The Amusements of Khan Kharuda. 1925.

Why the Milkman Shudders When He Perceives the Dawn. 1925.

The Charwoman's Shadow. 1926.

The Blessing of Pan. 1927.

Seven Modern Comedies. 1928.

Atalanta in Wimbledon. 1928.

The Raffle. 1928.

The Journey of the Soul. 1928.

In Holy Russia. 1928.

His Sainted Grandmother. 1928.

The Hopeless Passion of Mr. Bunyon. 1928.

The Jest of Hahalaba. 1928.

Fifty Poems. 1929.

The Old Folk of the Centuries. 1930.

The Travel Tales of Mr. Joseph Jorkens. 1931.

A City of Wonder. 1932.

Lord Adrian. 1933.

The Curse of the Wise Woman. 1933.

If I Were Dictator. 1934.

Building a Sentence. c. 1934.

Jorkens Remembers Africa. 1934.

Mr. Faithful. 1935.

Up in the Hills. 1935.

Rory and Bran. 1936.

My Talks with Dean Spanley. 1936.

My Ireland. 1937.

Plays for Earth and Air. 1937.

Patches of Sunlight. 1938.

Mirage Water. 1938.

The Story of Mona Sheehy. 1939.

Jorkens Has a Large Whiskey. 1940.

War Poems. 1941.

Wandering Songs. 1943.

A Journey. 1944.

Guerrilla. 1944.

While the Sirens Slept. 1944.

The Donnellan Lectures 1943. 1945.

The Sirens Wake. 1945.

The Year. 1946.

A Glimpse from a Watch Tower. 1946.

The Odes of Horace (translator). 1947.

The Fourth Book of Jorkens. 1947.

To Awaken Pegasus. 1949.

The Man Who Ate the Phoenix. 1949.

The Strange Journeys of Colonel Polders. 1950.

Carcassonne. c. 1950.

The Last Revolution. 1951.

His Fellow Men. 1952.

The Little Tales of Smethers and Other Stories. 1952.

Jorkens Borrows Another Whiskey. 1954.

The Sword of Welleran and Other Tales of Enchantment. 1954.

The Collected Works of Horace (translator; with Michael Oakley). 1961.

At the Edge of the World. Ed. Lin Carter. 1970.

Beyond the Fields We Know. Ed. Lin Carter. 1972.

Gods, Men and Ghosts: The Best Supernatural Fiction of Lord Dunsany. Ed.
    E. F. Bleiler. 1972.

Over the Hills and Far Away. Ed. Lin Carter. 1974.

The Ghosts of the Heaviside Layer and Other Fantasms. Ed. Darrell Schweitzer.
    1980.

*An Enemy of Scotland Yard and Other Whodunits / Ein Feind vom Scotland Yard
    und andere Kurzkrimis.* 1985.

Verses Dedicatory: 18 Previously Unpublished Poems. Ed. Lin Carter. 1985.

The Ghosts. 1992.

Kenneth Grahame
1859–1932

KENNETH GRAHAME was born in Edinburgh on March 8, 1859, to James Cunningham Grahame and Bessie Ingles Grahame. His family moved first to Loch Fyne, then to Inveraray, in Argyllshire, where Grahame's mother died in 1864 shortly after the birth of her fourth child. Shattered by the loss, James Grahame distanced himself from his family and allowed his wife's mother to raise his children and to move them to Cookham Dene in Berkshire, England. Although James Grahame did reclaim his children for a year in 1866–67, he thereafter left for Europe and would never see his children again. Kenneth and his siblings returned to live with their grandmother in Cranbourne, Berkshire.

Grahame attended St. Edward's School in Oxford from 1868 to 1876. He wished to attend Oxford University, but his family decided that he should secure a position at the Bank of England. While waiting for a position there, he went to work for his uncle, John Grahame, a parliamentary agent. At this time Grahame settled in London, living in various quarters for the next thirty years. From 1879 to 1908 he worked for the Bank of England, first as a clerk, later as a secretary.

Grahame's banking career allowed much time for leisure activities, including boating, sightseeing, and athletics. Through contact with the scholar F. J. Furnivall, Grahame met Tennyson, Browning, and other literary figures. He had begun writing in the 1880s, and his prose sketches appeared in the *St. James's Gazette*, the *Scots Observer*, and the *National Observer*, the latter two edited by W. E. Henley, whose conservative political and social philosophy influenced Grahame significantly. Grahame's first book, a collection of essays and sketches entitled *Pagan Papers*, was dated 1894 but appeared in October 1893, with a frontispiece by Aubrey Beardsley.

In 1894 Grahame began writing stories for the *Yellow Book*, an avant-garde journal that promoted the "art for art's sake" credo. One long story published there in October 1894, "The Headswoman," appeared as a chapbook in 1898. It is the only one of Grahame's major works of fiction to deal with adults, and in its depiction of a woman who takes over the job of executioner in a medieval French town can be read as a satire against "strong" women.

Grahame initiated the phase of his writing for which he is now best known with *The Golden Age* (1895) and *Dream Days* (1898), which both seek to depict the idyllic life of a family of five children. These books, although not actually written for children, became very popular and Grahame came to be regarded as an authority on children's literature.

In 1899 Grahame, who had hitherto led the life of a carefree bachelor, fell seriously ill and was nursed back to health by Elspeth Thomson; he married her later that year, and with her had one son, Alastair, who was born blind in one eye and had other physical ailments. Grahame's literary work lapsed after his marriage, and his work at the Bank of England also suffered. In 1906 he moved his family back to his childhood home of Cookham Dene, and two years later he gave up work at the bank.

The bedtime stories Grahame told Alastair beginning in 1904 became *The Wind in the Willows* (1908), a milestone in the history of children's literature. Written in a rich, ornate prose, it was not didactic or moralistic in its portrayal of the characters Rat, Mole, Badger, and Toad. The book—as with Grahame's work as a whole—can also be read as a plea for the maintenance of rural life as opposed to industrialism and urbanization. Its popularity has continued to grow since its publication; A. A. Milne wrote a successful stage adaptation, *Toad of Toad Hall* (1929).

For the last twenty-five years of his life Grahame wrote little; but he had never been a full-time writer, preferring instead to roam the countryside and live the life of a country squire. He was able to retire on the proceeds of *The Wind in the Willows*, and in 1910 he purchased a farmhouse in Blewbury, Berkshire. Alastair Grahame was run over by a train in 1920. The Grahames, devastated by the loss, went to Europe, staying there (mostly in Rome) for four years. Upon their return, they moved to Church Cottage, Pangbourne, on the Thames, where Grahame died on July 6, 1932.

▨ *Critical Extracts*

WALTER CLAYTON   *The Wind in the Willows* is a poem in praise of the glory that can never really pass away from the earth, unless we allow ourselves to grow up and forget—which, you may be sure, we shall never do, until what time the birds shall cease to sing about the tomb of Tusitala. It reveals anew the miracle of out-of-doors. The romance of the river, the allurement of the open road, the tremendous ecstatic terrors of the wild wood, the sad sweet tug of heart-strings by the sense of home, the poignant wander-longing, the amusement of adventure,—all these moods of simple wonderment are told and sung in its enchanting pages. ⟨. . .⟩ *The Wind in the Willows* is fun to read because the author wrote it for fun. It ranges through all the moods of natural enjoyment: it is humorous and beautiful, it combines satire with sentiment, it is serious and jocund. An uproarious chapter, which satirizes the modern subservience to the latest fad, is followed by a chapter in which, mystically, we are brought face to face with the very God of out-of-doors. Mr. Grahame talks in whatever mood most enchants him at the time: his range is as various and as free as the æolian breathing of the wind in the willows.

The actors in the present rambling narrative bear the names of animals; and a certain inconsistency may be noted in the handling of them. At times they are endowed with human traits and used to satirize the foibles of mankind; and at other times they are exhibited as animals indeed, and are used to reveal an infra-human view of life. This inconsistency is sometimes jarring; and as a consequence, the critic is moved to set the book on a plane a little lower than that of the perfect expositions of the mood of wonder,— like *Alice in Wonderland*, for example.

Ten years ago, before his disquieting silence, Mr. Grahame demonstrated that he held command of the most finished and perfected English prose style that had been listened to since Stevenson's. *The Wind in the Willows* is written in the same style, ripened and matured. To be a great artist is, of course, a lesser thing than to be an undiscouragable child; but it is reassuring to record that Mr. Grahame is the one as well as the other. We need him, both to play with and to listen to. Those of us who refuse to grow up and forget are banking on the future. May he fulfil his future, even if he has to neglect his Bank!

Walter Clayton, "An Interrupted Pan Resumes His Piping," *Forum* 41, No. 1 (January 1909): 84–85

A. A. MILNE   One can argue over the merits of most books, and in argument understand the point of view of one's opponent. One may even come to the conclusion that possibly he is right after all. One does not argue about *The Wind in the Willows*. The young man gives it to the girl with whom he is in love, and if she does not like it, asks her to return his letters. The older man tries it on his nephew, and alters his will accordingly. The book is a test of character. We can't criticize it, because it is criticizing us. As I once wrote: It is a Household Book; a book which everybody in the household loves, and quotes continually; a book which is read aloud to every new guest and is regarded as the touchstone of his worth. But I must give you one word of warning. When you sit down to it, don't be so ridiculous as to suppose that you are sitting in judgment on my taste, or on the art of Kenneth Grahame. You are merely sitting in judgment on yourself. You may be worthy: I don't know. But it is you who are on trial.

> A. A. Milne, "Introduction," *The Wind in the Willows* (London: Methuen, 1951), pp. vii–viii

---

PETER GREEN   Grahame's attitude to Socialism was very much that of ⟨W. E.⟩ Henley—who must have influenced him considerably—or of ⟨William⟩ Cobbett before him. He was all for individual freedom to the point of eccentricity as long as it was contained 'within the fabric of a firm but self-reformative social structure'—as long, that is, as the rural *status quo* was preserved, complete with its attendant class-structure. Anything that threatened this he regarded as destructive Philistinism. His attitude, like Cobbett's, was semi-patriarchal; he had the same characteristic distaste for the education of the lower orders, which he 'regarded much as a modern man would receive a suggestion that his old nurse was useless without a course of Pelmanism'.

This static rural traditionalism which Grahame idealized was, of course, in many ways a product of ardent wish-fulfilment. We have already seen how actual village life was visibly breaking up, and no one was more acutely aware of the changes going on—especially in his early essays—than Grahame himself. Nor, indeed, did he have any illusions about the crimes, brutality, violence, and poverty, which characterized the earlier England of Fielding. The social picture which *The Wind in the Willows* presents is not life as Grahame thought it was, or once had been: it is his ideal vision of what it *should* be, his dream of the true Golden Age. It is precisely because he knew at heart that the dream was lost beyond any hope of realization that his imaginary world acquired such compulsive fascination for him. The contrast is brought out sharply when Grahame's attitude is compared with that of the actual villagers of Cookham Dene, who 'were ever child-like admirers of Progressive Stunts—and not given to nostalgia'. Again, of course, something of this local addiction to the new-fangled has been gently satirized in the character of Toad.

Throughout the whole book there runs the *leitmotif* which may be roughly described as the conflict between Us and Them—or more specifically, the attempts made by Grahame's ideal rural society to defend itself against encroachment. (The curious thing is that though Grahame set out to create a trouble-free Arcadia he could not stifle his private anxieties: the Wild Wood loomed menacingly across the River, stoats and weasels lurked ready to invade Toad's ancestral home.) This society is specifically identified with the River-Bankers: Rat, Mole, Badger, Otter, and their friends form a close-knit community of leisured landowners who observe an extremely strict code of responsible behaviour.

Peter Green, *Kenneth Grahame 1859–1932: A Study of His Life, Work and Times* (London: John Murray, 1959), pp. 243–45

CLIFTON FADIMAN   Out of the conflict between the imposed life and the buried life came four slim books. One, *Pagan Papers*, is Stevenson-and-water: arty, wistful essays, perfectly in the *fin de siècle* mood of the nineties. *The Golden Age* and *Dream Days* are re-creations of the life of childhood, oddly mingling an affectionate sympathy for the young and a restrained bitterness toward grownups—the 'Olympians', as he ironically termed them.

The only one of Grahame's books that will last is *The Wind in the Willows*. This story of the riverside adventures of the Mole, the Water Rat, the Badger, and the Toad is generally received as a delightful animal fantasy. Indeed it can be so read, particularly by children. But many readers have often vaguely felt it to be more than that, just as they know *Gulliver* to be more than a story about little people and big people. Some of us perhaps find ourselves wondering about the conceited Mr Toad, in many ways an odd character for a child's book. By making Mr Toad a rich man was not Grahame quietly expressing his opinion on his money-making era, as Dickens did more explicitly? By making Mr Toad motor-mad was he not suggesting that the nineteenth century was to its own cost abandoning a life lived simply and naturally?

And then the book is not of one piece. Part of it seems simple and pleasant enough: the conversion of Mole to the delights of river life; the dangers Mole and Rat run in the Wild Wood and their rescue by Badger; Toad's transgressions and his final rehabilitation by the sorely tried but loyal friends. But other parts of the book are allegorical, even philosophical, and young readers will almost surely pass over them lightly. With the chapter called 'The Piper at the Gates of Dawn' and at several other points the tone alters. What was a humorous fancy about talking animals turns into a pagan hymn or a sly but not trivial commentary on the inferiority of humans to beasts.

> Clifton Fadiman, "Professionals and Confessionals: Dr Seuss and Kenneth Grahame"
> (1962), *Only Connect: Readings on Children's Literature*, ed. Sheila Egoff, G. T. Stubbs,
> and L. F. Ashley (New York: Oxford University Press, 1969), pp. 318–19

WILLIAM W. ROBSON   The handling of the animal/as/human, human/as/animal convention in *The Wind in the Willows* has come in for some comment. If it is to be categorized as a beast-fable, it sits a good deal more loosely to the beast-fable mode than some other famous examples. It obviously breaks many of the rules enforced so sternly to-day by the young ladies in the editorial departments of publishers of children's books, who condemn such transgressions with the severity of the *Académie française* coming down on Corneille. It is full of inconsistencies, which children notice. What size are the characters? How are we to imagine them? When Toad is disguised as a washerwoman he seems to be washerwoman size, but when the bargewoman detects him he is toad-size (she picks him up by the leg and throws him into the river). Any reader of the book will be able to think of dozens of other examples. Children notice these things.

Children notice; but do they mind? In the view of one critic of authority, they do not.

Kenneth Grahame says:

> It is the special charm of the child's point of view that the dual
> nature of these characters does not present the slightest
> difficulty to them. It is only the old fogies, who are apt to begin
> 'Well, but . . .' and so on. To the child it is all entirely
> natural and as it should be.

But whether children mind or not, the question why the characters have this 'dual nature' remains. ⟨. . .⟩

Perhaps the best explanation for the animal-device is this. The contradiction which the child notices may be the cover for a deeper contradiction which he does not notice. The characters belong to the timeless ideal world of children, freed from adult cares and responsibilities. Yet they have the

independence of adults. The indispensable ingredient of 'messing about in
boats', and the whole River Bank way of life, is freedom. *The Wind in the
Willows* is an artistic expression of the human longing to 'have it both ways',
to break down the antithesis of the Grecian Urn, to take the coldness out
of the 'cold pastoral'. Its success can be measured by the corresponding
failure in *Peter Pan* to achieve a similar resolution in human terms.

> William W. Robson, "On *The Wind in the Willows*," *Hebrew University Studies in
> Literature* 9, No. 1 (Spring 1981): 80–81, 83–84

MICHAEL STEIG   The reviewer for *Victorian Studies* of Peter
Green's centenary biography of Kenneth Grahame remarked only that it
was "comprehensive" and "disturbing." I cannot speculate on this particular
reviewer's personal reasons for feeling disturbed, but potential sources of
disturbance in the biography are clear enough. Green puts forth the thesis,
amply supported by the details of Grahame's life, that *The Wind in the
Willows* is a transformation into symbolic form of rebellious and hedonistic
impulses mildly evident in his earlier works, a process taking place under
the extreme pressures of a late, unhappy, and unfulfilling marriage, being
the father of a handicapped (half-blind) child, and tedious work in the
Bank of England. Such an analysis might indeed be disturbing to anyone
for whom reading *The Wind in the Willows* has formed a special, private set
of experiences, and who does not wish those experiences to be sullied by
the misery and frustration of Grahame's life.

Yet I found my adult rereading of Grahame's book more perplexing than
my subsequent reading of his biography, and it is from this perplexity that
the present attempt at interpretation issues. On the one hand, *The Wind
in the Willows* continues to be important to many who read it, and my own
childhood reading of it was an important event for me. On the other hand,
there seem to be several reasons why I, and at least some of its other adult
devotees, should really dislike it. One may note that this novel's fantasy
seems to be a very narrow one as an analogue of the real world. Its principal
animal characters are all male, all bachelors, and all independently wealthy,
conditions that obtain for few people and fewer wild animals. It is, seemingly,
"clean of the clash of sex," as Grahame wrote for the publisher's blurb, as
well as being a demonstrably conservative satire of aspects of upper-middle-
class life, a satire whose point is now largely lost in North America and
increasingly irrelevant in Britain. Furthermore, it contains a good deal of
what is, on the face of it, terribly sentimental writing. We can perhaps

imagine why an Edwardian reader of a certain social class might find the book delightful because of these very attributes; it is difficult to understand why it should have any appeal for modern readers who have some awareness of the exclusion of females and the class presumption of the four major characters.

Michael Steig, "At the Back of *The Wind in the Willows*: An Experiment in Biographical and Autobiographical Interpretation," *Victorian Studies* 24, No. 3 (Spring 1981): 307–9

HUMPHREY CARPENTER   All Grahame's writing was produced by tension between these two poles, the Wanderer and the Home-lover. *The Wind in the Willows* was the outstanding result of it, but one may also observe it in *The Golden Age* and *Dream Days*, which are explorations of the security and home-lovingness of childhood, and also a search for some more distant goal, which can only be achieved by the child wandering away from home, either in imagination or in actual fact.

Neither book conveys any sense of deep unhappiness, of regret for parents dead and lost, of a lack of love. The two books describe a family of parentless children living in the house of some maiden aunts, under the supervision of these ladies, a governess, and the occasional visiting uncle; and after the narrator's initial observation that he and his brothers and sisters lacked 'a proper equipment of parents' there is not even a hint of regret for what might have been. Certainly Aunt Eliza (who is the nearest we get to a portrait of Grahame's grandmother) is a rather unlikeable, unsympathetic Victorian who lacks even the slightest understanding or tolerance of what children like doing and thinking; and she and the others of her kind are characterised by the narrator as 'the Olympians', both stupid and indifferent to children's needs. But the Olympians play only a small part in the story. Sometimes, quite unpredictably, they intervene in the doings of Edward, Harold, Selina, Charlotte, and the nameless boy-narrator, as when a circus visit is promised by them, and is then suddenly withdrawn to be replaced by a threatened garden party. They may be relied upon, too, to punish apparent wrongdoing without any questioning of its real nature or cause. But for most of the time the Olympians are simply not in evidence; the children are left free to do what they want, to an extent that would astonish their modern successors, and such rules as do exist—for instance, attendance at schoolroom lessons—are broken again and again without dire consequences:

> Harold would slip off directly after dinner, going alone, so as
> not to arouse suspicion, as we were not allowed to go into the town
> by ourselves. It was nearly two miles to our small metropolis,
> but there would be plenty of time for him to go and return
> . . . Besides, he might meet the butcher, who was his friend and
> would give him a lift . . .

⟨. . .⟩ And though the circus visit has been called off, the children neverthe-less manage to get there, accepting a random offer of a lift from a neighbour, the Funny Man. The Olympians have about as little actual influence on their lives as did the original Olympians on the daily lives of the Greeks; Grahame, who knew his classical literature pretty well, chose their name carefully.

These books, then, are not the product of an unhappy childhood. On the contrary, they are a record of a time so free from worry, so peculiarly happy, that later life could never quite measure up to it.

Humphrey Carpenter, "Kenneth Grahame and the Search for Arcadia," *Secret Gardens: A Study in the Golden Age of Children's Literature* (Boston: Houghton Mifflin, 1985), pp. 117–18

SARAH GILEAD   A striking example of the fully elaborated plot and counterplot is Kenneth Grahame's *Wind in the Willows,* which is con-structed on two interlocked narratives, the stories of Mole and Toad. At first glance, these hardly seem to oppose each other or to generate significant internal tensions. Both narratives feature comic adventures and accidents in which real danger or unhappiness is either averted or short-lived; good fellowship rules over personal interaction, so that loyalty, tolerance, mutual aid, and sympathy predominate; necessity, work, mortality, family life, and illness hardly exist; there is abundance of food and leisure; and evil can be conquered by luck, by the protection of stronger and wiser fellows, or by a good fight whose happy outcome is providentially ordained. Though Toad repeatedly threatens to violate the pastoral order, each time he is brought back to it.

And yet, the pattern of alternation between the two plots does imply a certain rivalry. The first, the Mole/Rat narrative (chapters 1, 3–5, 7, 9), is a version of pastoral idyll. The second, Toad's adventures (chapters 2, 6, 8, 10–12), takes place in a more socialized narrative landscape where class differences, money, modern technology, social criticism through satire, polit-ical allegory, overt moral dramas and didacticism, all come into play. Such elements are virtually excluded from the Mole/Rat narrative. If the stress through chapter 5 is on Mole, the middle section alternates the two plots, and after chapter 9 the balance shifts in favor of Toad. Gradually, one plot displaces the other.

The comic spirit rules both the opening and the conclusion of Grahame's novel. Chapter 1, which initiates the Mole/Rat plot, celebrates individual freedom, conviviality, leisure, and innocence; the final chapter, which concludes the Toad plot, as its title indicates, is a comic parody of "The Return of Ulysses." While the opening invitation to release and hedonism establishes a light-hearted, brilliantly escapist comic mode, the more conservative final chapter develops into conservative social comedy. There fellowship based on play, echoed in the reunion of Toad with Badger, Mole, and Rat, is transmuted into communal solidarity against a common class enemy, the lower-class weasels and stoats. The "squire" is restored to his hereditary rights and learns to restrict his egotistic boasting to the secrecy of his chambers; in short, the social (class) as well as the psychological bases of civilization have been preserved. As an uninhibited comic impulse yields to a much soberer one, the protagonists of the first drama become the authors of the second, who restrain its protagonist, Toad. Their dual role represents the primary pleasures of the idealized child-realm as compatible with socialization.

Sarah Gilead, "The Undoing of Idyll in *The Wind in the Willows*," *Children's Literature* 16 (1988): 148–49

NEIL PHILIP   *The Wind in the Willows* is a densely layered text fairly cluttered with second meanings (though not, as Grahame's phrase may imply, *double entendres*), but Grahame could not for his peace of mind afford to admit it. One of these second meanings, and one for which the book has come under considerable attack in recent years, is the political ethos. In chapter eleven, while Rat, Mole, Badger, and Toad prepare to storm Toad Hall, 'the bell rang for luncheon.' Grahame's 'character economy' enables him to evade the question 'who rings the bell?' For his animal heroes form a leisured class which implies for its continuation a servant class, whom we never see. Instead the rough, uncouth 'Wild Wooders' are built up into a class enemy, uncomfortably like the Victorian working class. ⟨. . .⟩

Yet though on one level the book encodes genteel Victorian paranoia about the mob, the anarchy Arnold and others felt heaving below the surface restraints of civilized society, to interpret the book in these simple political terms would be to read it perversely. For though the stoats and the weasels are on one level the beastly working class, they are also, more truly, the forces which for Grahame threaten and destroy the ideal life: the destructive part of human nature, and the inconvenient demands of human society. To consider the riverbank world as a working class economy is to misread Grahame's escape fantasy, and mistake its implications. For in its paean to the simple uncluttered pleasure of friendship, it works to warm, not chill, the reader. While class prejudices may impinge on the book, human feeling drives it. ⟨. . .⟩

'I love these little people,' said Grahame to the illustrator E. H. Shepard. 'Be kind to them.' That love communicates itself; in *The Wind in the Willows* Grahame created, out of thwarted and lonely imagination, one of the most companionable of all English classics: a book which enters and nourishes the mind, and whose plangent rhythms establish a resonance that enriches and enlivens one's sense of language, of landscape, of life.

> Neil Philip, "*The Wind in the Willows:* The Vitality of a Classic," *Children and Their Books*, ed. Gillian Avery and Julia Briggs (Oxford: Clarendon Press, 1989), pp. 303–5, 313–14

⊠ Bibliography

Pagan Papers. 1894.

The Golden Age. 1895.

Lullaby-Land: Songs of Childhood by Eugene Field (editor). 1897.

Dream Days. 1898.

The Headswoman. 1898.

The Wind in the Willows. 1908.

The Cambridge Book of Poetry for Children (editor). 1916, 1932.

The Grahame Day Book. Ed. Margery Coleman. 1937.

First Whisper of The Wind in the Willows. Ed. Elspeth Grahame. 1944.

The Penguin Kenneth Grahame. 1983.

H. Rider Haggard
1856–1925

HENRY RIDER HAGGARD was born on June 22, 1856, at Bradenham estate in Norfolk. He was educated at the Ipswich Grammar School. His parents did not wish to spend the money to send him to college, so he attempted to join the army, but he failed his army examination and went to London for private study. In 1875 he joined the staff of Sir Henry Bulwer in Natal, South Africa. Witnessing the conflict between the English and the Zulus had a powerful effect upon him, and for the rest of his life he remained ambivalent about the role of British imperialism. After the British annexation of the Transvaal in 1877, Haggard became clerk to the colonial secretary.

Before he had left for South Africa Haggard had struck up a romance with Mary Elizabeth Archer, but his father so strongly disapproved of the union that Haggard was forced to break it off, and she soon married someone else. Haggard brooded over this incident for the whole of his life; it led him to create many mysterious, tempting, but unreachable women in his novels. Haggard left South Africa in 1879 when the Zulu war flared up again. Returning to England, he married Louisa Margitson on August 11, 1880; they had one son and three daughters.

Haggard's first book, *Cetywayo and His White Neighbours* (1882), was a discussion of British policy in South Africa. His first novel was *Dawn* (1884). Haggard entered the bar in 1885, and shortly thereafter wrote *King Solomon's Mines*; its success allowed Haggard to retire from the bar and devote himself wholly to writing. *She* and *Allan Quatermain* followed in 1887. Haggard settled in an estate in Norfolk and met on Saturdays with Walter Besant, Edmund Gosse, Andrew Lang, and others at the Savile Club. Lang was particularly supportive of Haggard; he and Haggard co-wrote *The World's Desire* (1890). The critical establishment, however, scorned Haggard as a writer of popular romances.

In 1895 Haggard became co-editor of the *African Review* but resigned after nine months. During this time he devoted himself largely to agriculture, and his interests are recorded in *A Farmer's Year* (1898), *Rural England* (1902), and other volumes. These works gained for Haggard a reputation as an expert on environmental issues, and he was appointed to various commissions to investigate coastal and forest erosion in England.

Haggard was knighted in 1912. In 1914 he was sent to South Africa and Canada by the Dominions Royal Commission to examine agricultural conditions there, and began his "private diaries," which he continued until his death. Returning to England after the war, he joined Sir Reginald Hall's campaign to warn the nation of the dangers of Bolshevism. Sir Henry Rider Haggard died on May 14, 1925.

Haggard traveled widely—to Egypt, Iceland, Denmark, Mexico, Italy, Canada, the Middle East—and the impressions gained from his travels found their way into many of the nearly sixty fantasy-adventure novels he wrote. He carried on a long friendship with Rudyard Kipling, beginning in 1889. Haggard's novel *The Ghost Kings* (1908) was written from a plot devised in collaboration with Kipling. Among Haggard's other notable novels are the semi-autobiographical *Jess* (1887), *Montezuma's Daughter* (1893), *The People of the Mist* (1894), *Ayesha* (1905), and *Wisdom's Daughter* (1923).

◈ *Critical Extracts*

H. RIDER HAGGARD   There is indeed a refuge for the less ambitious among us, and it lies in the paths and calm retreats of pure imagination. Here we may weave our humble tale, and point our harmless moral without being mercilessly bound down to the prose of a somewhat dreary age. Here we may even—if we feel that our wings are strong enough to bear us in that thin air—cross the bounds of the known, and, hanging between earth and heaven, gaze with curious eyes into the great profound beyond. There are still subjects that may be handled *there* if the man can be found bold enough to handle them. And, although some there be who consider this a lower walk in the realms of fiction, and who would probably scorn to become a "mere writer of romances," it may be urged in defence of the school that many of the most lasting triumphs of literary art belong to the producers of purely romantic fiction, witness the *Arabian Nights*, *Gulliver's Travels*, *The Pilgrim's Progress*, *Robinson Crusoe*, and other immortal works. If the present writer may be allowed to hazard an opinion, it is that, when Naturalism has had its day, when Mr. Howells ceases to charm, and the Society novel is utterly played out, the kindly race of men in their latter as in their earlier developments will still take pleasure in those works of fancy which appeal, not to a class, or a nation, or even to an age, but to all time and humanity at large.

> H. Rider Haggard, "About Fiction," *Contemporary Review* 51, No. 2 (February 1887): 180

H. B.   Mr. Rider Haggard has the gift of invention to such a point as to be practically a man of genius. But he is not an artist; and the consequence is that when you read him you grudge him his genius, and wish (for art's sake) that he was only a man of talent. In *She,* his new romance, the invention is, to my thinking, admirable; but the writing, the taste, the treatment, are often beneath criticism. And the worst is, there is no hope of better. Mr. Haggard went out to Africa when he was very young; he returned to achieve success, almost at once, with *King Solomon's Mines.* He had far rather act his works than write them; and it is hardly to be doubted that he will go on writing ill and inventing well until he is exhausted. Of course you have read *She,* and of course you read it at a gasp. For my part, I couldn't put it down until I had finished it, and Ayesha, by the operation of the Rolling Pillar of Life, had been turned into a reminiscence of the Gagool of *King Solomon's Mines.* But I have it on my conscience to say, that I blessed and banned alternately, and in proportions very nearly equal, all through the book. I couldn't help wishing that Mr. Stevenson had invented it; I couldn't help regretting that Mr. Rider Haggard is not Mr. Stevenson, and has never taken seriously to heart the difficulties of his profession. When I came to the Fight in the Cave, and to the Vision of Ayesha cursing Amenartas (with that inspiration of the fire that follows her hands as they rise and fall in imprecation!), I could have hurrahed in my enthusiasm; and when I came to Ayesha coquetting with Holly, and making puns on his name, exactly as if she had read the works of the late H. J. Byron, I stopped short as before an open drain. I reflected that God sends meat and the devil cooks. That is incontrovertible, but that it should be so as regards the art of literature is a shame as well as a misfortune. Walter Scott wrote ill enough sometimes; but he wrote ill in another way than Mr. Haggard's; and, moreover, he picked himself up in his dialogue, and towered, and was Walter Scott; whereas Mr. Haggard—unless he is dealing with a noble savage like Ustane—is only Mr. Haggard, and deforms his situations with facetiousness, or flatulence, in a way that is really heart-breaking to witness.

> H. B., "London Letter," *Critic*, 12 February 1887, p. 78

C. S. LEWIS   If I ask myself why it is that I have more than once read *She* with enjoyment, I find that there is every reason why I should have done so. In the first place the story makes an excellent approach; the central theme is suffered, in the first chapters, to woo us across great distances of space and time. What we are presently to see at close quarters is seen at first, as it were, through the wrong end of the telescope. This is a fine exercise in the art of alluring—you may see the same thing at work in the opening of the *Utopia*, in the second act of *Prometheus Unbound*, and in the early books of the *Odyssey*. In the second place it is a quest story, which is an attractive thing. And the object of the quest combines two strong appeals—it is the 'fountain of youth' theme and the *princesse lointaine* in one. Finally, the withdrawal or conclusion, which is always the difficulty in quest stories, is effected by unexpected means which are nevertheless, on the author's suppositions, sufficiently plausible. In the conduct of the story the detail is mostly convincing. The characters who are meant to be amiable are amiable and those who are meant to be sinister are sinister. The goodness of *She* is grounded, as firmly as that of any book whatever, on the fundamental laws of the imagination. But there is badness as well as goodness. Two things deter us from regarding it as a quite satisfactory romance. One of them is the continuous poverty of the style, by which, of course, I do not mean any failure to conform to certain *a priori* rules, but rather a sloth or incompetence of writing whereby the author is content always with a vague approximation to the emotion, the reflection, or the image he intends, so that a certain smudging and banality is spread over all. The other fault is the shallowness and folly of the things put into the mouth of She herself and offered us for wisdom. That She, in her secular loneliness, should have become a sage, is very proper, and indeed essential to Haggard's story, but Haggard has not himself the wisdom wherewith to supply her. A poet of Dante's depth could have given her things really wise to say; a poet of Shakespeare's address would have made us believe in her wisdom without committing himself.

If my analysis is correct, *She* is not a 'good "bad" book' in the sense of being a good specimen of a bad kind; it is simply good and bad, like many other books, in the sense that it is good in some respects and bad in others.

And those who have read it with enjoyment have been enjoying real literary merits, and merits which it shares with the *Odyssey* or *The Life and Death of Jason*.

C. S. Lewis, "High and Low Brows," *Rehabilitations and Other Essays* (London: Oxford University Press, 1939), pp. 100–102

HENRY MILLER   The deathless beauty of Ayesha, her seeming immorality, her wisdom which is ageless, her powers of sorcery and enchantment, her dominion over life and death, as Rider Haggard slowly but deftly reveals this mysterious being to us ⟨in *She*⟩, might well serve as a description of the soul of Nature. That which sustains Ayesha, and at the same time consumes her, is the faith that she will eventually be reunited with her beloved. And what could the Beloved be but the holy Spirit? No less a gift than this could suffice a soul endowed with her matchless hunger, patience and fortitude. The love which alone can transform the soul of Nature is divine love. Time counts for naught when spirit and soul are divorced. The splendor of neither can be made manifest except through union. Man, the only creature possessed of a dual nature, remains a riddle unto himself, keeps revolving on the wheel of life and death, until he pierces the enigma of identity. The drama of love, which is the highest he may enact, carries within it the key to the mystery. One law, one being, one faith, one race of man. Aye! "To die means to be cut off, not to cease being." In his inability to surrender to life, man cuts himself off. Ayesha, seemingly deathless, had thus cut herself off by renouncing the spirit which was in her. The beloved Kallikrates, her twin soul, unable to bear the splendor of her soul when he gazes upon it for the first time, is killed by Ayesha's own will. The punishment for this incestuous murder is arrestation. Ayesha, invested with beauty, power, wisdom and youth, is doomed to wait until her Beloved assumes flesh once again. The generations of time which pass in the interval are like the period separating one incarnation from another. Ayesha's Devachan is the Caves of Kôr. There she is as remote from life as the soul in limbo. In this same dread place Kallikrates too, or rather the preserved shell of her immortal love, passes the interval. His image is with her constantly. Possessive in life, Ayesha is equally possessive in death. Jealousy, manifesting itself in a tyrannical will, in an insatiable love of power, burns in her with the brightness of a funeral pyre. She has all time, seemingly, in which to review her past, to weigh her deeds, her thoughts, her emotions. ⟨. . .⟩

To summarize thus briefly the salient features of this great romance, especially perhaps to offer interpretation of his theme, is to do an injustice to the author. But there is a duality in Rider Haggard which intrigues me enormously. An earth-bound individual, conventional in his ways, orthodox in his beliefs, though full of curiosity and tolerance, endowed with great vitality and practical wisdom, this man who is reticent and reserved, English to the core, one might say, reveals through his "romances" a hidden nature, a hidden being, a hidden lore which is amazing. His method of writing these romances—at full speed, hardly stopping to think, so to speak— enabled him to tap his unconscious with freedom and depth. It is as if, by virtue of this technique, he found the way to project the living plasm of previous incarnations. In spinning his tales he permits the narrator to philosophize in a loose way, thus permitting the reader to obtain glimpses and flashes of his true thoughts. His story-teller's gift, however, is too great for him to allow his deepest reflections to assume the cloying form and dimensions which would break the spell of the recital.

Henry Miller, "Rider Haggard," *The Books in My Life* (New York: New Directions, 1952), pp. 92–94

MORTON N. COHEN   The real protagonist ⟨in Haggard's novels⟩ is the narrator, an aging, experienced, wise gentleman who is more complex than his youthful companion. Between him and Rider Haggard there is always a very strong family resemblance. He is not the universal man. He is far better with a machete in the African bush than with a tea-cup in the English drawing-room; he has learned more from nature than from books; but if he is somewhat coarse, it is only because in pitting his wits against raw nature he has grown rough and rugged. No matter what his negative qualities, he is essentially an excellent person of unimpeachable honour and genuine feeling. And, despite modest disclaimers, he has a glittering eye and can tell a cracking good story. His superhuman strength is well concealed, but his power rescues him and his companions from certain death even when the Adonis's strength has failed. He is clear-minded in all situations, prudent, practical, strong-willed, decisive, humble, ingenious, resourceful, sporting, and a devoted friend, a kind master, and of course an expert rifleman. Though well on in years, Quatermain (who figures in the role more than any other Haggard hero) cuts quite a figure. He is tall, trim, with a head of scrubby hair and a neat Van Dyke. He takes an occasional drink and he smokes a pipe. But he possesses minor physical defects. He speaks with a 'curious little accent' and in later life he is slightly lame. He reads the Bible and the *Ingoldsby Legends;* but as a man of action he has no use for fiction. The emotions he displays are conventional. He knows fear and is capable of trembling when facing it—but it never unmans him; it only sharpens his faculties. Personal tragedy he keeps sealed within his heart: he rarely speaks of the death of his first wife or of his son. He gets on with most men very well, regardless of their colour or nationality, and although he was reared on the Dark Continent (he has learned Dutch and three or four Kaffir dialects perfectly), he is an Englishman staunch and steady, and England is his home. He is in fact the Englishman of Empire, the crusader who takes England's divine mission to heart and carries the white man's burden of spreading Christian love and Anglo-Saxon justice to the far corners of the world.

But Quatermain is more than the masked Haggard, the silent hero of the tales, and the model Englishman abroad—he is the Modern Man, and as such he lends verisimilitude to the Haggard adventure. Quatermain believes in scientific realism: all unusual phenomena must be proved before he will believe them. This is not a world of cock-and-bull ghost stories, of fairies and wraiths—this is a man's world, and science is man's tool for proving or disproving. From the outset Quatermain is a hard-headed cynic who has no use for humbug, will not tolerate magical hocus-pocus, and absolutely abhors superstition. He is a detached observer, a phlegmatic judge of the universe and its natural operation. He is the last man in the world to believe in subterranean cities, eternal goddesses, hidden civilizations, in any form of miracle, and he says so freely and frankly. He is, in a word, a sceptic, and since he usually is the teller of the tales, he tells them from a sceptical point of view.

> Morton N. Cohen, *Rider Haggard: His Life and Works* (New York: Walker, 1961), pp. 221–22

ALAN SANDISON   There are two words which are quite crucial to the vocabulary of any criticism of Haggard's work, words to which events of his age had added new and troublesome life. They are 'process' and 'purpose'. The first acknowledges Haggard's acute feeling of things being in a state of flux and change, the second relates to his lasting preoccupation with the question of design in nature, with whether or not there was a Providence which ordered events. The inter-dependence of these notions is obvious: the terms reflect two aspects of the same concern. Given the fact that things were in continuous process, in a state of Becoming, there were for Haggard three possibilities. These were firstly that there *was* a principle of order in the universe and that it was dictated by God; secondly, that there *was* a principle of order in the universe, but its determination was purely mechanical with accident as its first cause; thirdly, that there was *no* order inherent in the universe and chance dominated all. There is, occasionally, the merest hint of an interesting fourth possibility—that what order there is in nature has been put there by man.

It is towards the pessimistic end of this scale that Haggard undoubtedly inclines. More precisely, though the third seems at times to have a certain purchase, it is the second possibility which exercises the most powerful fascination over him: a fascination which, ideologically, owes much to his association with a certain evolutionary doctrine. At the same time, his desire to find justification for supporting the first possibility is inextinguishable and profound.

⟨. . .⟩ for Haggard as for Darwin the crucial issue was the accidental variation from which species developed. Though ⟨. . .⟩ Darwin was well aware of, and indeed troubled by, the moral implications of his theory, it is the novelist Haggard for whom these implications come to be of fundamental concern: hence his preoccupation with the notions of purpose and process. Pursuing this further, it can be shown clearly that Haggard's relationship to the imperial idea, as it emerges in the role assumed by the latter in his fiction, is dictated by an idea of nature rooted in his reaction to the evolutionary doctrine advanced by Charles Darwin. ⟨. . .⟩

⟨. . .⟩ it was the awareness of flux and change which gave Haggard his humanity and his humility, and in few places is this better displayed than in his African stories. On occasion he is, of course, to be found subscribing to a belief in Britain's imperial destiny. But there are very few traces of the familiar Victorian paternalism which contact with 'natives' normally elicited—far fewer than one might have expected from a man who had himself run up the flag in Pretoria on the annexation of the Transvaal. His consciousness of 'process', of 'the truth that it is impossible to isolate phenomena from their antecedents and their consequents' gave him a much wider perspective, and his own honesty both to himself and to a scientific accuracy of observation enabled him to escape the vice of racial prejudice to which so many of his contemporaries succumbed.

When one thinks of what someone like ⟨John⟩ Buchan would have made of the white man's presence in *King Solomon's Mines* one can appreciate Haggard's disengagement from the more vulgar presumptions of the imperial idea. In this book, as in every other he wrote on Africa, he repudiates without fuss the whole arrogant notion of the white man's burden. Physically the European remains supernumerary to the great sum of human tribulation which rises clamorously around him. For it is in the lives and destiny of the Zulus themselves that the main current of life in these novels makes itself manifest. The depiction of them caught in its grip is vivid and memorable, but above all it is their *consciousness* of their predicament which ensures that they are not mistaken merely for the colourful native background to the derring-do of a band of Victorian hearties. It is this which allows them— the native race—to hold their own in the centre of the stage with the white man who has strayed into their world. The spiritual reality of their existence may be equalled by that of the lives of the intruders, but it certainly is neither surpassed nor put to shame. Indeed it is Haggard's presentation of them as being under the same doom as the Europeans and sensitively aware of the fact that results in the remarkable degree of identification of native and European spiritual life.

> Alan Sandison, "Rider Haggard: 'Some Call It Evolution . . .,' " *The Wheel of Empire: A Study of the Imperial Idea in Some Late Nineteenth and Early Twentieth-Century Fiction* (London: Macmillan, 1967), pp. 25–26, 30–31

EVELYN J. HINZ   In his use of a kind of reverse metamorphosis to emphasize a journey back in time Haggard ⟨. . .⟩ begins to appear as a forerunner of Conrad. As the narrative ⟨of *She*⟩ progresses, the characters lose their Christian names and begin to be called by the names of the animals which they resemble. The Arab Mohamed becomes "the black goat"; the Christian Job becomes "the black pig"; the physical hero, Leo, becomes "the lion"; the intellectual narrator becomes "the baboon." But most important of all, Ayesha, the post-Darwinian female Faustus, turns back into the shape of what nineteenth-century science had announced as the origin of the human species—a monkey. For as in *Heart of Darkness*, Haggard's theme is that progress is an illusion. With Tennyson and Aldous Huxley, facing the problem of time, history, and the peculiar Western desire for personal immortality, he recognizes that "after many a summer dies the swan." But because Haggard's "heart of darkness" is a definitively mythological one, it is ultimately a positive feature; it is, as Lawrence suggests, a place "where one can always come to."

"The most wonderful history, as distinguished from romance, that [the world's] records can show," is the way the narrator describes his manuscript in the introduction. Unlike the nostalgia of the historical romancer or the escapist romantic whose interest in the past is based upon the premise that the past is past, Haggard's premise is the archetypal one, and possibly best expressed by Schopenhauer in his chapter, "On History." "The true philosophy of history consists in the insight that in all these endless changes and their confusion we have always before us only the same, even, unchanging nature. . . . The motto of history in general should run: *Eadem, sed aliter*. If one has read Herodotus, then in a philosophical regard one has studied history enough." In the case of *She*, ⟨. . .⟩ if one has examined the sherd of Amenartas one knows what is going to happen in the narrative at large. Instead of the principle of suspense, it is according to a theory of inevitability that the work is structured; and it is this sense of "a fate that never swerves" that makes *She* an archetypal rather than an ordinary "history of adventure."

On the other hand, it is Haggard's recognition of the difference between the present and the past that prevents *She* from becoming either an allegory or the fictive counterpart of the anthropological works of his "eminently respectable fossil friends at Cambridge." The past cannot be recovered artificially, only ritualistically. The artist is the only person capable of such a function, but he must be a true shaman—an evoker rather than an invoker of the mysteries. The popularity of *She*, in this sense, may be evidence of Haggard's power.

> Evelyn J. Hinz, "Rider Haggard's *She*: An Archetypal 'History of Adventure,' " *Studies in the Novel* 4, No. 3 (Fall 1972): 429–30

NORMAN ETHERINGTON   Haggard called his novel ⟨*She*⟩ a "romance," a label applied in the nineteenth century to works in a literary line of descent from Walter Scott and the "Gothic" novels of late eighteenth-century romanticism. The label will not do today because in the course of the twentieth century the genre has bifurcated. Some list makers include Haggard among the practitioners of science fiction. Others leave him out. Brian Aldiss states flatly that "Haggard himself never wrote science fiction." Robert Scholes and Eric Rabkin would exclude Haggard from science fiction proper because he does not use fantasy incidentally, like Jules Verne, but "centrally, exhaustively." They would consign him instead to the "sword and sorcery" subfamily of their category "space opera." Certainly Haggard made little use of the technology that is so important to most writers of science fiction. There is no need, however, to enter into this taxonomic discussion here. What is important is that certain themes of *She* have been widely acknowledged to have exerted a pervasive influence on the literary genres commonly called science fiction and fantasy. In particular, Haggard's ideas permeate that literature whose central theme is, in Aldiss's words, "descent from a 'natural world' to inferno or incarceration, where a protagonist goes, willingly or otherwise, in search of a secret, an identity, or a relationship."

Haggard's technique for inducing belief in the unbelievable is a variation on a trick used by many writers of fantasy and science fiction. H. G. Wells held that any writer of fantastic stories must help the reader "in every possible unobtrusive way to *domesticate* the impossible hypothesis." Whereas Wells employed "an ingenious use of scientific patter" about time and physics to undermine disbelief in his time machine, Haggard used archaeological and linguistic artifacts. Once the reader has plowed through the minute description of the Sherd of Amenartas and all its translations into other languages, he is prepared to have the impossible hypothesis confirmed by the appearance of the deathless queen. Horace Holly's long-winded accounts of geographical, zoological, and ethnographical particulars serve the same purpose by imitating the productions of late-Victorian scientific expeditions.

The secret valley where time stands still for savage peoples and ancient civilizations has been taken up and developed in works as diverse as Arthur Conan Doyle's *Lost World*, James Hilton's *Lost Horizon*, Edgar Wallace's concept for the motion picture *King Kong*, and Edgar Rice Burroughs's John Carter series of Martian adventures. In 1895 Wells introduced the world to time travel by machine, but many other writers of science fiction have stuck to Haggard's method, which is to move spatially into zones where creatures live as our ancestors did, or as our descendants may live in times to come. His invention of the lost civilization of Kôr—where, thousands of years before the rise of Pharaonic Egypt, awe-inspiring feats of science and engineering were accomplished—prefigures many a tale that ascribes to extraterrestrial beings of long ago superiority over the technical achievements of modern times.

Most of Haggard's striking fictional characters—Allan Quatermain, Umslopogaas, Henry Curtis—belong specifically to a colonial Africa that is fast slipping away from contemporary consciousness. How appropriate that Ayesha alone appears destined to exercise a deathless influence on writers of fantastic tales. Under various names she can be found, enthroned amid archaic architecture, exercising absolute dominion over barbarous kingdoms and adventurous hearts from one end of the fictional universe to the other. Buck Rogers met her in the caverns of other planets. So did Flash Gordon. And so have innumerable other intergalactic travelers. It is difficult to dissent from Henri Gougaud's prediction that she will always be there, waiting "at the edge of the farthest frontiers, femme fatale, the woman whose encounters direct destinies of life eternal or death, according to the stature of the heroes. She has a legion of sisters in Outer Space. . . . For the seeker of the absolute, She exists as a sort of Holy Grail on the highest tower of desire."

Norman Etherington, "Critical Introduction," *The Annotated She* (Bloomington: Indiana University Press, 1991), pp. xxxix–xl

◈ *Bibliography*

Cetywayo and His White Neighbours. 1882.

Dawn. 1884. 3 vols.

The Witch's Head. 1885. 3 vols.

King Solomon's Mines. 1885.

She: A History of Adventure. 1887.

Jess. 1887.

Allan Quatermain. 1887.

Maiwa's Revenge; or, The War of the Little Hand. 1888.

Mr. Meeson's Will. 1888.

Colonel Quaritch V.C. 1888. 3 vols.

Cleopatra. 1889.

Allan's Wife and Other Tales. 1889.

Beatrice. 1890.

The World's Desire (with Andrew Lang). 1890.

Eric Brighteyes. 1891.

Nada the Lily. 1892.

An Heroic Effort. 1893.

Montezuma's Daughter. 1893.

The People of the Mist. 1894.

Church and State: New Style: An Appeal to the Laity. 1895.

Joan Haste. 1895.

Heart of the World. 1896.

The Wizard. 1896.

A Visit to the Victoria Hospital. 1897.

Dr. Therne. 1898.

Swallow. 1899.

A Farmer's Year: Being His Commonplace Book for 1898. 1899.

The Last Boer War. 1899.

Black Heart and White Heart and Other Stories. 1900.

Lysbeth: A Tale of the Dutch. 1901.

A Winter Pilgrimage. 1901.

Rural England: Being an Account of Agricultural and Social Researches Carried Out in the Years 1901 & 1902. 1902. 2 vols.

Pearl-Maiden: A Tale of the Fall of Jerusalem. 1903.

Stella Fregelius: A Tale of Three Destinies. 1904.

The Brethren. 1904.

A Gardener's Year. 1905.

Report on Salvation Army Colonies in the United States and at Hadleigh, England. 1905, 1905 (as *The Poor and the Land*).

Ayesha: The Return of She. 1905.

The Way of the Spirit. 1906.

Benita: An African Romance. 1906.

Fair Margaret. 1907.

The Real Wealth of England. 1908.

The Ghost Kings. 1908.

The Yellow God: An Idol of Africa. 1909.

The Lady of Blossholme. 1909.

Morning Star. 1910.

Queen Sheba's Ring. 1910.

Regeneration: Being an Account of the Social Work of the Salvation Army in Great Britain. 1910.

Rural Denmark and Its Lessons. 1911.

Red Eve. 1911.

The Mahatma and the Hare: A Dream Story. 1911.

Marie. 1912.

Child of Storm. 1913.

The Wanderer's Necklace. 1914.

A Call to Arms: To the Men of East Anglia. 1914.

The Holy Flower. 1915.

The After-War Settlement & Employment of Ex-Service Men in the Overseas Dominions. 1916.

The Ivory Child. 1916.

Finished. 1917.

Love Eternal. 1918.

Moon of Israel: A Tale of the Exodus. 1918.

When the World Shook: Being an Account of the Great Adventure of Bastin, Bickley and Arbuthnot. 1919.

The Ancient Allan. 1920.

Smith and the Pharaohs and Other Tales. 1920.

She and Allan. 1921.

The Virgin of the Sun. 1922.

Wisdom's Daughter: The Life and Love Story of She-Who-Must-Be-Obeyed. 1923.

Heu-Heu; or, The Monster. 1924.

Queen of the Dawn: A Love Tale of Old Egypt. 1925.

The Days of My Life: An Autobiography. Ed. C. J. Longman. 1926. 2 vols.

The Treasure of the Lake. 1926.

Allan and the Ice Gods. 1927.

Mary of Marion Isle. 1929.

Belshazzar. 1930.

Private Diaries 1914–1925. Ed. D. S. Higgins. 1980.

Best Short Stories. Ed. Peter Haining. 1981.

Lafcadio Hearn
1850–1904

PATRICK LAFCADIO HEARN was born on the Ionian island of Lafcadio (Levkas) on June 27, 1850, of Irish-Greek parentage. When he was two he was taken to Dublin, where he lived for the next eleven years; his mother went insane when he was four, and he was made an informal ward of a great-aunt, Mrs. Brenane. Hearn was educated in England, where through an accident he lost the sight of his left eye. In 1869 he left for the United States, where he worked as a journalist in Cincinnati and New Orleans. While living in New Orleans (1877–87) Hearn also published sketches of Creole life and various translations from the French, including Flaubert's *Temptation of St. Anthony* (published 1910) and Gautier's *One of Cleopatra's Nights* (1882). Between 1887 and 1889 he lived in Martinique, an experience that produced *Two Years in the French West Indies* (1890) and a novel, *Youma* (1890).

In 1890 Hearn went to Japan, where he spent the rest of his life. He married a Japanese woman, Koizumi Setsu, daughter of an old Samurai family, wore Japanese dress, was naturalized, and was then adopted into the Koizumi family as Koizumi Yakumo. He taught at a school in Matsue, and from 1896 to 1903 lectured on English literature at the Imperial University in Tokyo. Although he never completely mastered the Japanese language, Hearn published a series of books on Japanese culture, including several collections of loosely translated folktales. Many of his lectures to Japanese students were published posthumously.

Hearn is nowadays perhaps best remembered for his supernatural fiction, collected in two volumes, *Fantastics* (1914), containing stories and sketches written between 1879 and 1884, and *Kwaidan* (1904). Also of note are the nonfiction volumes *Some Chinese Ghosts* (1887) and *In Ghostly Japan* (1899). Lafcadio Hearn died in Japan on September 26, 1904.

▨ *Critical Extracts*

LAFCADIO HEARN   Now let me speak to you about this word "ghostly"; it is a much bigger word, perhaps, than some of you imagine. The old English had no other word for "spiritual" or "supernatural"—which two terms, you know, are not English but Latin. Everything that religion today calls divine, holy, miraculous, was sufficiently explained for the old Anglo-Saxons by the term ghostly. They spoke of a man's ghost, instead of speaking of his spirit or soul; and everything relating to religious knowledge they called ghostly. In the modern formula of the Catholic confession, which has remained almost unchanged for nearly two thousand years, you will find that the priest is always called a "ghostly" father—which means that his business is to take care of the ghosts or souls of men as a father does. In addressing the priest, the penitent really calls him "Father of my ghost." You will see, therefore, that a very large meaning really attaches to the adjective. It means everything relating to the supernatural. It means to the Christian even God himself, for the Giver of Life is always called in English the Holy Ghost.

Accepting the evolutional philosophy which teaches that the modern idea of God as held by western nations is really but a development from the primitive belief in a shadow-soul, the term ghost in its reference to the Supreme Being certainly could not be found fault with. On the contrary, there is a weirdness about this use of the word which adds greatly to its solemnity. But whatever belief we have, or have not, as regards religious creeds, one thing that modern science has done for us, is to prove beyond all question that everything that we used to consider material and solid is essentially ghostly, as is any ghost. If we do not believe in old-fashioned stories and theories about ghosts, we are nevertheless obliged to recognize today that we are ghosts of ourselves—and utterly incomprehensible. The mystery of the universe is now weighing upon us, becoming heavier and heavier, more and more awful, as our knowledge expands, and it is especially a ghostly mystery. All great art reminds us in some way of this universal riddle; that is why I say that all great art has something ghostly in it. It touches something within us which relates to infinity. When you read a very great thought, when you see a wonderful picture or statue or building, and when you hear certain kinds of music, you feel a thrill in the heart and mind much like the thrill which in all times men felt when they thought they saw a ghost or a god. Only the modern thrill is incomparably larger and longer and deeper. And this is why, in spite of all knowledge, the world still finds pleasure in the literature of the supernatural, and will continue to find pleasure in it for hundreds of years to come. The ghostly represents always some shadow of truth, and no amount of disbelief in what used to be called ghosts can ever diminish human interest in what relates to that truth.

Lafcadio Hearn, "The Value of the Supernatural in Fiction" (c. 1900), cited in Jonathan Cott, *Wandering Ghost: The Odyssey of Lafcadio Hearn* (New York: Alfred A. Knopf, 1991), pp. 345–46

PAUL ELMER MORE   In his recent book, *Kotto,* as he calls it, Mr. Hearn has added another volume to the series of tales and essays in which he has attempted to interpret the illusive mystery of Oriental life through Western speech. The new venture rounds out what must be deemed one of the most extraordinary achievements of modern days. For it is as an art of strange subtlety that we must regard his literary work, an art that, like some sympathetic menstruum, has fused into one compound three elements never before associated together.

In the mere manner and method of this art there is, to be sure, nothing mysterious. One recognizes immediately throughout his writing that sense of restraint joined with a power of after suggestion, which he has described as appertaining to Japanese poetry, but which is no less his own by native right. There is a term, *ittakkiri,* it seems, meaning "all gone," or "entirely vanished," which is applied contemptuously by the Japanese to verse that tells all and trusts nothing to the reader's imagination. Their praise they reserve for compositions that leave in the mind the thrilling of a something unsaid. "Like the single stroke of a bell, the perfect poem should set murmuring and undulating, in the mind of the hearer, many a ghostly aftertone of long duration." Now these ghostly reverberations are precisely the property of the simplest of Mr. Hearn's pictures. Let him describe, for instance, the impression produced by walking down the deep canyon of Broadway, between those vast structures, beautiful but sinister, where one feels depressed by the mere sensation of enormous creative life without sympathy and of unresting power without pity,—let him describe this terror of Broadway, and with a few words he shall set ringing within you long pulsations of emotion which reach down to the depths of experience. Or, let him relate by mere allusion the story of hearing a girl say "Good-night" to someone parting from her in a London park, and there shall be awakened in your mind ghostly aftertones that bring back memories of the saddest separations and regrets of life. His art is the power of suggestion through perfect restraint.

But this self-restrained and suggestive style is merely the instrument, the manner so to speak, of his art. If we examine the actual substance of that art, we shall discover that it is borrowed from three perfectly distinct, in fact almost mutually destructive, philosophies, any one of which afford material for the genius of an ordinary writer. He stands and proclaims his mysteries at the meeting of three ways. To the religious instinct of India,—Buddhism in particular,—which history has engrafted on the aesthetic sense of Japan, Mr. Hearn brings the interpreting spirit of Occidental science; and these three traditions are fused by the peculiar sympathies of his mind into one rich and novel compound,—a compound so rare as to have introduced into literature a psychological sensation unknown before. More than any other living author he has added a new thrill to our intellectual experience.

Paul Elmer More, "Lafcadio Hearn: The Meeting of Three Ways," *Atlantic Monthly* 91, No. 2 (February 1903): 204–5

UNSIGNED   A new book by Lafcadio Hearn is a literary event, indeed. No living writer (not even Algernon Blackwood) has so great and fiery an imagination as had this quondam reporter of *The New Orleans Daily Item*; no living writer (except Alice Meynell) understands so thoroughly the art of putting together a few hundred words so as to form a structure of enduring loveliness. If Lafcadio Hearn were not already recognized as a great artist in prose, this little book ⟨*Fantastics and Other Fancies*⟩ would so establish him beyond question. ⟨. . .⟩

He was not always absolutely original, this obscure hack whose genius was one day to surprise and delight the world. Subconsciously, he remembered his spiritual brother, Edgar Allan Poe, when he wrote those tales of grotesque and arabesque, "The Black Cupid" and "The One Pill Box." Also there are echoes of Coleridge standing at his elbow when he wrote of those Parnassian Frenchmen whose methods and ideals Hearn always shared.

But no Frenchman of his time could match the tender humor of "The Post Office," nor were Poe or Coleridge standing at his elbow when he wrote "Hiouen-Thrang." These were written by Lafcadio Hearn himself, by that strange nomad who called no one race his own, who looked at life with huge and perilous curiosity, who gave to most un-English thoughts a splendidly English dress, who just missed being a poet, who just missed being a mystic, who just missed being happy.

Already, the *Fantastics* show, Hearn was hearing the Orient's alluring voice. New Orleans, that brave old bright-colored Latin city, struggling with the aftermath of war and pestilence, was just the place for a man with his exotic tastes. "I cannot say how fair and rich and beautiful this dead South is," he wrote. "It has fascinated me." But not the venerable splendors of New Orleans, not the picturesque shores of Grand Isle, could take the place of the radiant East, to which he continually referred, of which clairvoyantly he seemed to know himself already a citizen.

Unsigned, "Lafcadio Hearn's Fancies," *New York Times Review of Books*, 7 February 1915, p. 41

H. P. LOVECRAFT   Lafcadio Hearn, strange, wandering, and exotic, departs still farther from the realm of the real; and with the supreme artistry of a sensitive poet weaves phantasies impossible to an author of the solid roast-beef type. His *Fantastics*, written in America, contains some of the most impressive ghoulishness in all literature; whilst his *Kwaidan*, written in Japan, crystallises with matchless skill and delicacy the eerie lore and whispered legends of that richly colourful nation. Still more of Hearn's weird wizardry of language is shewn in some of his translations from the French, especially from Gautier and Flaubert. His version of the latter's *Temptation of St. Anthony* is a classic of fevered and riotous imagery clad in the magic of singing words.

H. P. Lovecraft, "Supernatural Horror in Literature" (1927), *Dagon and Other Macabre Tales*, ed. S. T. Joshi (Sauk City, WI: Arkham House, 1986), p. 413

MALCOLM COWLEY   It seems to us now that Hearn started by misestimating and underestimating his own gifts. "Knowing that I have nothing resembling genius," he said in a letter to Whitman's disciple, William D. O'Connor, "and that any ordinary talent must be supplemented with some sort of curious study in order to place it above the mediocre line, I am striving to woo the Muse of the Odd, and hope to succeed in thus attracting some little attention." In another letter to O'Connor he spoke of pledging himself to the worship of the Odd, the Queer, the Strange, the Exotic, the Monstrous. "It quite suits my temperament," he added mistakenly. The great weakness of his early sketches is that they aren't sufficiently odd or monstrous or differentiated from one another. The best of them are folk tales adapted from various foreign literatures. The others keep reverting to the same situation, that of a vaguely pictured hero in love with a dead woman or with her ghost (just as Hearn was in love with the memory of his mother, who disappeared from his life when he was seven years old). They are obsessive rather than exotic; and they are written in a style that suggests the scrollwork on the ceiling of an old-fashioned theater.

After his death, Hearn's reputation suffered from the collections that others made of his early newspaper work, most of which should have been allowed to sleep in the files of the Cincinnati and New Orleans press. Even the books he wrote in his later New Orleans years—*Stray Leaves from Strange Literatures*, *Some Chinese Ghosts*, and *Chita*—though they all contained fine things are not yet his mature writing. *Two Years in the French West Indies* (1890) is longer and richer and shows how Hearn could be carried out of himself by living among people with whom he sympathized. Still, it was not until after his first years in Japan that he really mastered a subject and a style.

He wrote to ⟨Basil Hall⟩ Chamberlain in 1893, "After for years studying poetical prose, I am forced now to study simplicity. After attempting my utmost at ornamentation, I am converted by my own mistakes. The great point is to touch with simple words." That is exactly what he did in the best of his later writing. Instead of using important-sounding words to describe events that were not always important in themselves, he depended upon the events to impress the reader and looked for works that would reveal them as through a clear glass. Here, for example, is a crucial paragraph from "The Story of Mimi-Nashi-Hoïchi," a Japanese legend retold in *Kwaidan*:

> At that instant Hoïchi felt his ears gripped by fingers of iron, and torn off! Great as the pain was, he gave no cry. The heavy footfalls receded along the verandah,—descended into the garden,—passed out to the roadway,—ceased. From either side of his head, the blind man felt a thick warm trickling; but he dared not lift his hands.

Today we don't like the exclamation point after the first sentence, or the commas followed by dashes in the third; but Hearn was following his own theories about punctuation as a guide to the reader's voice. Primarily he was writing for the ear, not the eye; and the passage in its context sounds exactly right when read aloud.

Malcolm Cowley, "Lafcadio Herun-san" (1949), *A Many-Windowed House* (Carbondale: Southern Illinois University Press, 1970), pp. 110–11

LEWIS LEARY Wandering through the Vieux Carré, listening to street cries and street brawls, "the melancholy, quavering beauty and weirdness of Negro chants," absorbing sights and sounds and odors, listening to and reading strange "traditions, superstitions, legends, fairy tales, goblin stories, impossible romances," blending them, he attempted a new form, based on brief impressions of scene fleetingly glimpsed or conversation overheard, and then painstakingly embellished—"moulded," he said, "and coloured by imagination alone." He called these writings *Fantastics*, and some thirty of them appeared through 1881, telling "of wonders and of marvels, of riches and rarities": in "Aphrodite and the King's Prisoners," of a captive kept in luxury, but alone only with an ebony statue of the Goddess of Love for company, until he kills himself at the foot of the statue in "Love which is brother to death", in "El Vómito," which celebrates beauty and death, and "The Name on the Stone," in which a Ligeia-like maiden returns from the grave to inform her lover that "Love is stronger than death"; or in "The Fountain of God," a parable of eternal youth and love and happiness secured in death and dream. ⟨. . .⟩

The tales are brief, and often bold; they speak of passion, especially the passion of love, and of wisdom which may, but does not always, bring comfort or calm. Weirdness is their keynote: spectral lovers and enchantress wives, and love which leads to death. "The Wise," he wrote in introduction to one tale, "will not attach themselves unto women; for women sport with the hearts of those who love them," and women die, even as love dies, so that memories are best, and sad, strange tales not shrouded in reality. He told of Polynesian lands "where garments are worn by none save the dead," of youth which might be eternal, and of dreams despoiled by phantoms, of intelligence greater than wisdom, and faith superior to truth.

Each tale is carefully chiseled, and meant to be enchanting. Each is frankly derivative, a retreat to ancient quietness. The language is honeyed with Biblical phrasing, cloyed sometimes with alliterative rhythm, as Hearn strove to attain what Baudelaire described as "le miracle d'une prose poétic." They were exercises done by a young man who trained for something beyond virtuosity; "veritable poems," Charles W. Coleman thought them, "heavy with the perfume and glamour of the East, delicate, fragrant, graceful."

Lewis Leary, "Lafcadio Hearn, 'One of Our Southern Writers'" (1967), *Southern Excursions: Essays on Mark Twain and Others* (Baton Rouge: Louisiana State University Press, 1971), pp. 148–51

ARTHUR E. KUNST   The reveries and imaginative fragments collected under the name of *Fantastics and Other Fantasies* are, to say the least, decadent. For Lafcadio Hearn, who thought the way to express his new found happiness with Louisiana was to call it "a dead face that asked for a kiss," decadence was a natural humor. Occasionally these selections are merely unsuccessful experiments; occasionally they pass over the line from decadence to sentimentality, as in the nauseating archness of "The Little Red Kitten." But other times, when by accident or design a sketch manages to hold back from the seductions of profundity, the decadence achieves that willful denial of reality that marks the dying century's flight toward the dream and the unconscious. At these moments, Hearn's "dreams of a tropical city" have all the unexplained and fixated beauty that no amount of invocations and cosmic metaphorings could otherwise provide. The heavy burden which figuration and eternities place on such brief narratives can be observed in "The Vision of the Dead Creole."

The leading sentence of the opening paragraph makes thoroughly consistent and satisfying decadence combine with metaphors which we must either find beyond the range of the narrator who is making his way onto the shore, or hold to be the blatherings of the dreariest kind of *poseur*: "The sea-ripples kissed the brown sands silently, as if afraid; faint breezes laden with odors of saffron and cinnamon and drowsy flowers came over the water;—the stars seemed vaster than in other nights;—the fires of the Southern Cross burned steadily without one diamond-twinkle;—I paused a moment in terror;—for it seemed I could hear the night breath—in long weird sighs."

One is distracted by the problem of those silent, fearful kisses on behalf of the sea-ripples: does it have something to do with sighs of the night air—is it because the sands are brown that the ripples are afraid? One worries over the phrase "diamond-twinkle": do we have a resentful reference to the bejeweled décor of some rococo faith—why should there be diamonds in a fire, especially twinkling ones? And why should his terror appear before he acknowledges that the night seems to be breathing?

Nothing, of course, is wrong with fiery stars or sighing nights. The difficulty tries in trying to reconcile the feeling of the narrator's terror with a simultaneous feeling that the author is blandly handicrafting the sentences before our eyes. Moreover, none of these possibilities lasts for long—we begin to perceive a deeper explanation for these distracting paradoxes, and then the story turns and leaves us with an expectation that goes nowhere. We have, for instance, the odd but incredible image of blood from his torn hands "dripping with a thick, dead sound, as of molten lead, upon the leaves" at his feet. Such a metaphysical conceit does not belong to a world where flowers open their hearts to the moon. The same world, presumably, cannot accommodate the woman who had smiled "when I flung myself like a worm before her to kiss her feet, and vainly shrieked to her to trample upon me, to spit upon me!" and her corpse, which murmurs sweetly, "I knew thou wouldst come back to me—howsoever long thou mightst wander under other skies and over other seas."

Although "All in White" uses the garrulous I-narrator device, it has one who is more direct, less "refined." "No," he starts, "I did not stay long in Havana." The body of the story is taken up with events so isolated and so insistently sketched that their conjunction maddeningly suggests some undetectable relevance: a narrow, walled street; an iron window behind which one can see the reclining body of a girl in white; the passing battalion of Spanish soldiers which presses him against the wall. Instead of these events for a plot, the story devotes itself to a frightened clarification of details: "candles were burning at her head and feet; and in the stillness of the hot air their yellow flames did not even tremble." But there is not so much clarification of details as to convey a sense of disinterest in the moment. There is some connection between the iron bars, the dead woman in the silent chamber, the swarthy thousand faces; and even the narrator suggests it: "and every eye looked at me as if I had been detected in some awful crime." But he, like us, has to be content with only raising questions.

The story, a nightmare, has the meaningfulness of one; with or without dream analysis, it characterizes the dreamer. The "Americano" does not survive to offer us his free associations; still, insofar as we can respond to these vivid symbols, the effects of association are left to us. Such a presentation of Lust and Death together is the main theme of the *Fantastics* (Hearn would say, Love and Death).

Arthur E. Kunst, *Lafcadio Hearn* (New York: Twayne, 1969), pp. 46–48

JON CHRISTOPHER HUGHES   ⟨. . .⟩ his most graphic and sensual writings ⟨in Cincinnati newspapers⟩ belong to what can be called the

gruesome. All senses are attacked with graphic scenes of the Stink Factory where dead animals are processed to be later made into candles, lard-oil and soap, and of autopsies, dissecting rooms, abortion houses, body-snatching and grave robbing (practiced by persons Hearn called "Resurrectionists"), slaughter houses with their blood drinkers, a hanging where the rope breaks and the person is hanged again, suicides, embalming, the police court, opium dens, and morphine abuse. The complete coverage by Hearn of the infamous Perkins and tanyard murders has recently been reprinted including the scene where Hearn examines the human remains with his fingers. There are sympathetic portraits of the poor in the Tallow District and Bucktown and of the city's rag-pickers. There is a fascinating account of a former slave who survived the slave-traders in the North and plantation life in the South prior to the Civil War. And Hearn could not neglect the preacher who owns property in the "Row." But there is also some fore-shadowing of Hearn's future literary interests with several ghost stories. ⟨. . .⟩

His best stories described the misfits, the outcasts, those on and over the fringe of society. He was comfortable in the dirty, often ugly underbelly of Cincinnati. Hearn pursued ghastly crimes, questionable professional practices, and injustices with lust and there was plenty for him to write about in the disorderly city. It was Hearn's first biographer, George M. Gould in *Concerning Lafcadio Hearn* (1909), who called this Hearn's "period of the gruesome."

Jon Christopher Hughes, "Period of the Gruesome," Lafcadio Hearn Journal 1, No. 1 (Spring 1991): 2–3

CARL DAWSON   His fascination with Japanese ghost stories (*kwaidan*, or *kaidan*) grew out of a lifelong interest in the supernatural, in the ways that ordinary experience intersects with a complex realm of indefinable forces and interrelationships.

To explore the psychology of the ghost stories meant exploring an unknown world, as if, like Urashima, Hearn submerged himself below the surface of an unplumbed sea. Ghost stories allowed a measure of control over personal doubt and desire, involving at once a lowering of boundaries of self and the erection of more concrete barriers. To reconstruct Japanese ghost stories was, to put this differently, a way of reaching the supernatural or uncanny, or both, through acceptable and often ancient accounts, in which the personal is both subordinate and paramount, its inmost fears realized with the least of risks. This is what Freud would soon be saying about writers and their daydreaming (reveries, as Hearn would say) and about the play of the unconscious in literary works. ⟨. . .⟩

Hearn remained throughout his adult life a passionate apologist for an early idol, Edgar Allan Poe, whose radical sensibilities seemed akin to his own. Poe represented a fictional world more profoundly interesting than that of other American writers, although Nathaniel Hawthorne's tales also appealed to him. ⟨. . .⟩ What he emphasizes in Poe is less the narrative skill than the emotional effects of the tales, or the psychological conditions in which they flourish. "A little of the element of fear enters into every great and noble emotion," he says, "and especially into the higher forms of aesthetic feeling." If Poe's "nightmare absolute," or his depiction of the "atrociously ugly," is singular in depth or intensity, all nightmares in literature, Poe's included, demand "a clever mixture of the playful and the terrible." ⟨. . .⟩

While Hearn rarely mentions British ghost stories—by Sheridan Le Fanu and other masters of the genre—he remained intrigued by any writing—literary, religious, or philosophical—that probed dangerous regions of the mind. ⟨. . .⟩

He makes this point directly in a piece titled "A Ghost," written for *Harper's Magazine* in 1889, shortly before his departure for Japan. Defining his own life and the consequences of its "nomadic" course, he sees a kind of elective affinity between a wanderer like himself and the ghosts he will meet:

> Perhaps the man who never wanders away from the place of his
> birth may pass all his life without knowing ghosts, but the
> nomad is more than likely to make their acquaintance. I refer
> to the civilized nomad, whose wanderings are not prompted
> by the hope of gain, nor determined by pleasure, but simply
> controlled by certain necessities of his being,—the man
> whose inner secret nature is totally at variance with the stable
> conditions of a society to which he belongs only by accident.

Carl Dawson, *Lafcadio Hearn and the Vision of Japan* (Baltimore: Johns Hopkins University Press, 1992), pp. 88–91

▣ *Bibliography*

Ye Giglampz. 1874. 9 nos.

One of Cleopatra's Nights and Other Fantastic Romances by Théophile Gautier (translator). 1882.

Stray Leaves from Strange Literature. 1884.

La Cuisine Créole (editor). 1885.

"*Gombo Zhèbes*": *Little Dictionary of Creole Proverbs* (translator). 1885.

Some Chinese Ghosts. 1887.

Chita: A Memory of Last Island. 1889.

The Crime of Sylvestre Bonnard by Anatole France (translator). 1890.

Two Years in the French West Indies. 1890.

Youma: The Story of a West-Indian Slave. 1890.

Glimpses of Unfamiliar Japan. 1894. 2 vols.

"*Out of the East*": *Reveries and Studies in New Japan.* 1895.

Kokoro: Hints and Echoes of Japanese Inner Life. 1896.

Gleanings in Buddha-Fields: Studies of Hand and Soul in the Far East. 1897.

The Boy Who Drew Cats (translator). 1898.

Exotics and Retrospectives. 1898.

The Goblin Spider (translator). 1899.

In Ghostly Japan. 1899.

Shadowings. 1900.

A Japanese Miscellany. 1901.

The Old Woman Who Lost Her Dumpling (translator). 1902.

Kotto: Being Japanese Curios, with Sundry Cobwebs (editor). 1902.

Chin Chin Kobakama (translator). 1903.

Kwaidan: Stories and Studies of Strange Things. 1904.

Japan: An Attempt at Interpretation. 1904.

The Romance of the Milky Way and Other Studies and Stories. 1905.

Letters from the Raven: Being the Correspondence of Lafcadio Hearn with Henry Watkin. Ed. Milton Bronner. 1907.

The Temptation of St. Anthony by Gustave Flaubert (translator). 1910.

Japanese Letters. Ed. Elizabeth Bisland. 1910.

Leaves from the Diary of an Impressionist: Early Writings. Ed. Ferris Greenslet. 1911.

Editorials from the Kobe Chronicle. 1913.

Fantastics and Other Fancies. Ed. Charles Woodward Hutson. 1914.

Japanese Lyrics. 1915.

Interpretations of Literature. Ed. John Erskine. 1915. 2 vols.

Appreciations of Poetry. Ed. John Erskine. 1916.

Life and Literature. Ed. John Erskine. 1917.

Japanese Fairy Tales (translator; with others). 1918.

Karma. Ed. Albert Mordell. 1918.

Letters from Tokyo. Ed. M. Otani. 1920.

Diaries and Letters. Ed. R. Tanabé. 1920.

Impressions of Japan. Ed. T. Ochiai. 1920.

Talks to Writers. Ed. John Erskine. 1920.

Books and Habits: From the Lectures of Lafcadio Hearn. Ed. John Erskine. 1921.

Insect Literature. Ed. M. Otani. 1921.

Pre-Raphaelite and Other Poets. Ed. John Erskine. 1922.

The Fountain of Youth (translator). 1922.

Writings. 1922. 16 vols.

Essays in European and Oriental Literature. Ed. Albert Mordell. 1923.

Creole Sketches. Ed. Charles Woodward Hutson. 1924.

An American Miscellany. Ed. Albert Mordell. 1924. 2 vols.

Saint Anthony and Other Stories by Guy de Maupassant (translator). Ed. Albert
        Mordell. 1924.

Stories and Sketches. Ed. R. Tanabé. 1925.

Lands and Seas. Ed. T. Ochiai. 1925.

Occidental Gleanings: Sketches and Essays. Ed. Albert Mordell. 1925. 2 vols.

Some New Letters and Writings. Ed. Sanki Ichikawa. 1925.

Editorials. Ed. Charles Woodward Hutson. 1926.

Insects and Greek Poetry. 1926.

A History of English Literature in a Series of Lectures. 1927 (2 vols.), 1930.

Some Strange English Literary Figures of the Eighteenth and Nineteenth Centuries.
        Ed. R. Tanabé. 1927.

Supplement to A History of English Literature. 1927.

Lectures on Shakespeare. Ed. Iwao Inagaki. 1928.

Japan and the Japanese. Ed. Teisaburo Ochiai. 1928.

Poets and Poems. Ed. R. Tanabé. 1928.

Facts and Fancies. Ed. R. Tanabé. 1929.

Essays on American Literature. Ed. Sanki Ichikawa. 1929.

Lectures on Prosody. Ed. Teisaburo Ochiai. 1929.

Insect-Musicians and Other Stories and Sketches. Ed. Jun Tanaka. 1929.

Victorian Philosophy. 1930.

The Adventures of Walter Schnaffs and Other Stories by Guy de Maupassant
        (translator). 1931.

Complete Lectures on Art, Literature and Philosophy. Ed. Ryuki Tanabé, Teisa-
        buro Ochiai, and Ichiro Nishizaki. 1932–34. 4 vols.

Letters to a Pagan. 1933.

Stories from Pierre Loti (translator). 1933.

Gibbeted. Ed. P. D. Perkins. 1933.

Spirit Photography. Ed. P. D. Perkins. 1933.

Letters from Shimane and Kyushu. 1934.

Sketches and Tales from the French. (translator). Ed. Albert Mordell. 1935.

Stories from Emile Zola (translator). Ed. Albert Mordell. 1935.

Barbarous Barbers and Other Stories. Ed. Ichiro Nishizaki. 1939.

Buying Christmas Toys and Other Essays. Ed. Ichiro Nishizaki. 1939.

Literary Essays. Ed. Ichiro Nishizaki. 1939.

The New Radiance and Other Scientific Sketches. Ed. Ichiro Nishizaki. 1939.

Oriental Articles. Ed. Ichiro Nishizaki. 1939.

Père Antoine's Date Palm. 1940.

Lectures on Tennyson. Ed. Shigetsugu Kishi. 1941.

An Orange Christmas. 1941.

Selected Writings. Ed. Henry Goodman. 1949.

Children of the Levee. Ed. O. W. Frost. 1957.

Articles on Literature and Other Writings from the Cincinnati Enquirer *1873*. Ed. Hojin Yano, Tadanobu Kawai, and Hiroyoshi Kishimoto. 1975.

Buddhist Writings. Ed. Kenneth Rexroth. 1977.

Writings from Japan: An Anthology. Ed. Francis King. 1984.

Period of the Gruesome: Selected Cincinnati Journalism. Ed. Jon Christopher Hughes. 1990.

Lafcadio Hearn, Japan's Great Interpreter: A New Anthology of His Writings 1894–1904. 1992.

Rudyard Kipling
1865–1936

RUDYARD KIPLING was born on December 30, 1865, in Bombay, India, where his father was a professor at the School of Art. His early years were happy, but he suffered greatly after being taken to England at the age of six and left by his parents in the charge of a stern disciplinarian. His schooldays ended in 1882, and he returned to India to work as a journalist for the *Civil and Military Gazette* in Lahore. Apart from news items, he contributed poems, collected in *Departmental Ditties* (1886), and short stories, published in *Plain Tales from the Hills* (1888), *The Phantom 'Rickshaw and Other Tales* (1888) (which contained most of his stories of supernatural horror), and many subsequent successful volumes. In 1887 he joined the *Pioneer* in Allahabad, and saw more of the country before leaving India in 1889 to travel via America to England.

Taking up residence in London, Kipling soon made an impact on the literary scene with the reissue of his Indian stories and the publication of *Life's Handicap* (1891). That year Kipling made an extended voyage for reasons of health, visiting India for the last time before returning to England to marry an American, Caroline Balestier, in 1892, and traveling with her to settle in Vermont. *Barrack-Room Ballads* appeared in 1892, the short stories *Many Inventions* in 1893, *The Jungle Book* in 1894, and its sequel in 1895, but these productive years in America ended when Kipling quarreled with his brother-in-law and returned to England in 1896.

After 1898 Kipling frequently wintered in South Africa, and he was outspoken in his support of England in the Boer War. He continued writing fantasy tales for children with *Just So Stories* (1902), *Puck of Pook's Hill* (1906), and *Rewards and Fairies* (1910). In later years he remained staunchly imperialist in outlook, harboring an idealistic vision of the white man's mission, though he declined the many honors offered him by the state, including knighthoods and the Order of Merit. He did accept the Nobel Prize for Literature in 1907 and various honorary degrees. After World War I, in which his son died, he felt increasingly isolated, though he enjoyed the respect and friendship of George V. He died a few days before the king on January 18, 1936, and was buried in Poet's Corner, Westminster Abbey.

▨ *Critical Extracts*

G. K. CHESTERTON   Mr. Rudyard Kipling is a most extraordinary and bewildering genius. Some of us have recently had reason to protest against certain phrases of his later development, and we protested because they were pert and cockney and cruel, and full of that precocious old age which is the worst thing in this difficult cosmos, a thing which combines the brutality of youth with the disillusionment of antiquity, which is old age without its charity and youth without its hope. This rapidly aging, rapidly cheapening force of modernity is everywhere and in all things, a veritable spiritual evil: it looks out of the starved faces of a million gutter-boys, and its name is Ortheris. And just as we are in the afterglow of a certain indignation against this stale, bitter modernity which had begun to appear in Mr. Kipling's work, we come upon this superb thing, the *Just So Stories*; a great chronicle of primal fables, which might have been told by Adam to Cain, before murder (that artistic and decadent pastime) was known in the world.

For the character of the *Just So Stories* is really unique. They are not fairy tales; they are legends. A fairy tale is a tale told in a morbid age to the only remaining sane person, a child. A legend is a fairy tale told to men when men were sane. We grant a child a fairy tale, just as some savage king might grant a missionary permission to wear clothes, not understanding what we give, not knowing that it would be infinitely valuable if we kept it to ourselves, but simply because we are too kind to refuse. The true man will not buy fairy tales because he is kind; he will buy them because he is selfish. If Uncle John who has just bought the *Just So Stories* for his niece were truly human (which of course Uncle John is not) it is doubtful whether the niece would ever see the book. One of the most lurid and awful marks of human degeneration that the mind can conceive is the fact that it is considered kind to play with children.

But the peculiar splendour, as I say, of these new Kipling stories is the fact that they do not read like fairy tales told to children by the modern fireside, so much as like fairy tales told to men in the morning of the world. They see animals, for instance, as primeval men saw them; not as types and numbers in an elaborate biological scheme of knowledge, but as walking portents, things marked by extravagant and peculiar features. An elephant is a monstrosity with his tail between his eyes; a rhinoceros is a monstrosity with his horn balanced on his nose; a camel, a zebra, a tortoise are fragments of a fantastic dream, to see which is not seeing a scientific species, but like seeing a man with three legs or a bird with three wings, or men as trees walking. The whole opens a very deep question, the question of the relations between the old wonder and the new wonder, between knowledge and science. The hump of the camel is very likely not so much his characteristic from a scientific point of view as the third bone in the joint of his leg, but to the eyes of the child and the poet it remains his feature. And it is more important in this sense that it is more direct and certain: there is a relation between the human soul and the hump of a camel, which there is not between the human soul and the bone in his hind leg. The hump still remains and the bone vanishes, if all of these physical phenomena are nothing but a grotesque shadow-show, constructed by a paternal deity to amuse an universe of children.

> G. K. Chesterton, [Review of *Just So Stories*], *Bookman* (London) No. 134 (November 1902): 57–58

RUDYARD KIPLING   I forget who started my notion of writing a series of Anglo-Indian tales, but I remember our council over the naming of the series. They were originally much longer than when they appeared, but the shortening of them, first to my own fancy after rapturous re-readings, and next to the space available, taught me that a tale from which pieces have been raked out is like a fire that has been poked. One does not know that the operation has been performed, but everyone feels the effect. Note, though, that the excised stuff must have been honestly written for inclusion. I found that when, to save trouble, I 'wrote short' *ab initio* much salt went out of the work. This supports the theory of the Chimaera which, having bombinated and been removed, *is* capable of producing secondary causes *in vacuo*.

This leads me to the Higher Editing. Take of well-ground Indian Ink as much as suffices and a camel-hair brush proportionate to the interspaces of your lines. In an auspicious hour, read your final draft and consider faithfully every paragraph, sentence and word, blacking out where requisite. Let it lie by to drain as long as possible. At the end of that time, re-read and you should find that it will bear a second shortening. Finally, read it aloud alone and at leisure. Maybe a shade more brushwork will then indicate or impose itself. If not, praise Allah and let it go, and 'when thou hast done, repent not.' The shorter the tale, the longer the brushwork and, normally, the shorter the lie-by. I have had tales by me for three or five years which shortened themselves almost yearly. The magic lies in the Brush and the Ink. For the Pen, when it is writing, can only scratch; and bottled ink is not to compare with the ground Chinese stick. *Experto crede.*

Rudyard Kipling, *Something of Myself: For My Friends Known and Unknown* (Garden City, NY: Doubleday, Doran, 1937), pp. 224–25

EDMUND WILSON   The packed detail, the automatic plot, the surfaces lacquered with dialect, the ever-tightening tension of form, are all a part of Kipling's effort to impose his scheme by main force. The strangest result of this effort is to be seen in a change in the subject matter itself. Kipling actually tends at this time to abandon human beings altogether. In that letter of Henry James in which he speaks of his former hope that Kipling might grow into an English Balzac, he goes on: 'But I have given that up in proportion as he has come steadily from the less simple in subject to the more simple—from the Anglo-Indians to the natives, from the natives to the Tommies, from the Tommies to the Quadrupeds, from the quadrupeds to the fish, and from the fish to the engines and screws.' This increasing addiction of Kipling to animals, insects and machines is evidently to be explained by his need to find characters which will yield themselves unresistingly to being presented as parts of a system. In the *Jungle Books*, the animal characters are each one all of a piece, though in their ensemble they still provide a variety, and they are dominated by a 'Law of the Jungle,' which lays down their duties and rights. The animals have organised the Jungle, and the Jungle is presided over by Mowgli in his function of forest ranger, so that it falls into its subsidiary place in the larger organization of the Empire.

Yet the *Jungle Books* (written in Vermont) are not artistically off the track; the element of obvious allegory is not out of place in such fairy tales. It is when Kipling takes to contriving these animal allegories for grown-ups that he brings up the reader's gorge. What is proved in regard to human beings by the fable called 'A Walking Delegate,' in which a pastureful of self-respecting horses turn and rend a yellow loafer from Kansas, who is attempting to incite them to rebellion against their master, Man? A labor leader and the men he is trying to organize are, after all, not horses but men. Does Kipling mean to imply that the ordinary workingman stands in the same relation to the employing and governing classes as that in which the horse stands to its owner? And what is proved by 'The Mother Hive,' in which an invasion of wax-moths that ruin the stock of the swarm represents the infiltration of socialism? (Compare these with that more humane fable of 1893, 'The Children of the Zodiac,' which deals with gods become men.) And, though the discipline of a military unit or of the crew of a ship or a plane may provide a certain human interest, it makes us a little uncomfortable to find Kipling taking up locomotives and representing '.007' instead of the engineer who drives it as the hero of the American railroad; and decending even to the mechanical parts, the rivets and planks of a ship, whose drama consists solely of being knocked into place by the elements so that it may function as a co-ordinated whole.

> Edmund Wilson, "The Kipling That Nobody Read," *The Wound and the Bow: Seven Studies in Literature* (Boston: Houghton Mifflin, 1941), pp. 153–54

J. M. S. TOMPKINS   There are not very many pages of strictly mythological imagination in *The Jungle Books*. There is Hathi's tradition of how Fear came, a more mysterious *Just So* story, told in the setting of the Water-Truce; there is Kotick's search for the shore where man has never come to destroy the seals—a combination of Leif Erikson's Wonder-Strands with the Islands of the Blest; and there is, in the later Mowgli tales, the majestic shadow of Adam, King of the Jungle. It is, however, only a shadow; for Mowgli moves in place and time, suffers the ill-temper of Buldeo and the stones of the man pack, lets Messua comb his hair, and speeds her to the unknown English at Kanhiwara. He has drawn the milk of a woman and a wolf. Messua thinks him a wood-god; but to children he is more like a boy who is helped by kindly beasts in a fairy-tale. He has a fairy-tale extension of power, and his communion with his foster-brothers, which makes old Muller of 'In the Rukh' describe him as before the Stone Age, is to the child another magic power. ⟨. . .⟩

The realm of wonder extends beyond the limits of myth. The magical distance and strangeness, of which there are hints in the *Just So Stories*, are here all around us. In the midst of the city there is a vast ruined city, and under it an abandoned treasure-house, where a sacred white cobra still guards the jewels; there are glades, too, where the axe of the little Gond hunter flies across the clearing like a dragon-fly. Up in the Arctic the pack-ice grinds and roars round the unseen shores, and the sorcerer sings charms in his snow-hut. The wise elephants, tame and wild, in the Assamese hills, meet at night to trample out their dancing ground. A Himalayan mountain-side is loosened by rain, and the animals sense the coming landslide and save the holy man who has shown them hospitality. And in all these places people live with strange skills and strange beliefs. Kotuko buckles himself into his belt for the long watch by the seal's breathing-hole; old Buldeo asserts that the Lame Tiger embodies the spirit of a dead money-lender; the seasonal round of a Himalayan village takes place at a great depth below the shrine where Purun Bhagat meditates. The refinement of human senses to meet special conditions and the intuitive knowledge of ancestral habit are often brought to notice. In the jungle Mowgli weaves little huts with sticks and creeper, like his forefathers the woodcutters, and knowledge comes to him, as to the beasts his brothers, though not so unerringly, by a taint in the air, a falling shadow, a movement of the grass, the faintest of sounds. All this wonder comes with vivid concrete detail. The world unfolds, unspeakably various and wild and old; and everywhere the family group keeps the child in touch with its own reality. Toomai's mother and Matkah the seal sing their lullabies; Big Toomai and Sea-Catch grumble; and Kotuko's little brother gnaws a nice nutty strip of blubber.

J. M. S. Tompkins, *The Art of Rudyard Kipling* (London: Methuen, 1959), pp. 68–70

NOEL ANNAN   *Puck of Pook's Hill* is a study in the dynamics of culture and its tales are deliberately arranged unchronologically to illustrate the connection between social order and civilisation. The main theme is that the Sword led men to the Treasure, and the Treasure gave the Law. The two symbols of Power are civilised by the Law. The Norman stories present a picture of England smitten by rebellion and riven between Norman and Saxon. How had order and civilisation collapsed? The Roman stories provide the answer: the Wall, the symbol of civilisation, was then about to fall because Rome had lost its genius for government. The Norman De Aquila by his cunning and political wisdom is trying to unite the country. He marries his young knights to the conquered and does not hang but uses the rebels Fulke and Gilbert. " 'I am too old to judge or to trust any man', he said . . . De Aquila was right. One should not judge men." And the theme is repeated in "Hal o' The Draft" where the shrewd J. P. lets the smugglers go scot free: he does not want civil war in Sussex and a lot of nonsense talked about traitors. The last story cuts back to Magna Carta, the formal pronouncement of the English Law. Here Kipling introduces the theme of the Jew who alone understands money, the dangerous solvent of society. When the Danes returned from Africa with the Gold, all except the landless Thorkild of Borkum were infected by its presence. "Gold changes men altogether." But the rootless Jew knows that Gold is stronger than the Sword and can make and break kings. "That is *our* God in our captivity. Power to use!" And Kadmeil uses it to benefit his race by getting the barons to include even Jews under the provisions of the Magna Carta.

Four orders of men appear; those like the Picts, slaves by Necessity, ground between the grindstones of Rome and the Winged Hats, and also slaves by nature, "too little to love or to hate"; the craftsmen of England, Hal the painter and Hobson the yeoman; the officers or administrators, Parnesius and Pertinax (the Ordes and Tallentires of yesterday) who know their province and their people; and Maximus and De Aquila, the politicians and governors. To test Parnesius' flexibility Maximus orders him to execute a soldier for trivial disobedience, he refuses, and Maximus tells him that he will never be a staff officer or rule a province for he lacks the will to please his superiors. Meanwhile the fairy theme illuminates a different order of reality. The fairies, gods of a bye-gone age who have come down in the world and learnt humility through misfortune, were worshiped in the days when man was the child of nature. But when he discovered iron and believed himself to be her master they fell, and when the Reformation turned Englishmen's religion into hate they flitted. Now they are gone— but Puck bestowed a gift upon the descendants of the widow who gave them her blessing and the means to flit: in each generation one of her family will be a simpleton blessed with the gift of insight into the ways of Nature to preserve the immemorial wisdom of the country and the rituals which descend from the runes on the sword and Mithraism through the religion of freemasonry.

The presence throughout of the children conveys the hope for the future. For beneath the solid trappings of Edwardian affluence Kipling scanned the future with anxious eyes. Would the Wall fall again before the democratic hordes of little men and the Prussian Winged Hats? Were not the young rulers, F. E. Smith and the renegade conservative Winston Churchill, tainted by the ambition of Maximus? Were not the financiers manipulating trade and industry to their own ends—were not luxury and wealth corrupting the ruling class and turning their children into flannelled fools at the wicket? What then was the fate of England—an England rent by class warfare and in a few years' time to be meditating civil war in Ireland? Critics have pointed out that other writers also scanned the future. *Heartbreak House*,

Howards End, and *Puck of Pook's Hill* are attempts by a socialist, a liberal, and a conservative to discern England's destiny.

Noel Annan, "Kipling's Place in the History of Ideas," *Victorian Studies* 3, No. 4 (June 1960): 339–40

KINGSLEY AMIS   One of the most famous (by name at any rate) of Kipling's volumes is *Puck of Pook's Hill* (1906), a linked series of tales told in the first person by characters from selected stages of our island story, of whom the best presented is a Roman centurion. Always one to fiddle with modes of presentation, Kipling has each of them in turn summoned in the flesh by the not unamiable sprite, Puck, for the benefit of two comparatively unrevolting Edwardian children—it is a children's book that has won much favor from adults. The structure has its drawbacks. There are constant interruptions at which questions are asked and hard bits cleared up. This helps to see to it that what should be romantic becomes businesslike and everyday. As Gillian Avery has acutely observed, the various narrators 'are not ghosts, there is no nimbus of mystery about them, and they seemed to me as a child like dressed-up figures from a pageant'. Puck would have been better advised to turn his time-machine round and send the children off to the past with no one to hold their hands. The tales themselves are often clever and vivid, but they are weighed down by the sense that the author's grasp of the sweep of British history is being not so much drawn upon as shown off.

Kingsley Amis, *Rudyard Kipling and His World* (New York: Charles Scribner's Sons, 1975), p. 95

W. W. ROBSON   Even when they are read only as fairytales, it is clear that the Mowgli stories are the expression of a powerful myth. They tell the story of how the baby abandoned in the jungle by his parents when the tiger attacks them is brought up by animals; (he is adopted by the wolves, a mighty people, and secures strong protectors, the head wolf Akela, the bear Baloo and the black panther Bagheera), and through a combination of what they have to teach him about the Jungle with his own innate capacities as a human being he becomes Master of the Jungle. The boy reader identifies with Mowgli and enjoys the transformation into joyful fantasy of the impulse to dominate. But at the same time the stories are carrying a message to him, which is only partly explicit. The explicit message is educational. Elliot L. Gilbert in *The Good Kipling* (1972) points out that the Mowgli stories are what he calls a *Bildungsroman*. In realistic fiction this genre is concerned with the struggle of a young man or woman to discover his or her 'identity', to discover as far as may be possible the truth about themselves. Gilbert shows how this kind of story is told in *The Jungle Books* in a fairytale, fabulous form. Mowgli spends his whole life among animals. But as he approaches manhood he begins to find that he is not like the animals. A central symbol for this is Mowgli's eyes. They are a source of his power over the beasts, who cannot meet his gaze. From the beginning they have been the sign that he is not one of the beasts: '. . . the look in [Mowgli's] eyes was always gentle. Even when he fought, his eyes never blazed as Bagheera's did. They only grew more and more interested and excited.' Mowgli has passed through a preliminary training which in many ways is like that suitable to animals. But a time comes when he must move beyond his animal 'brothers', and realize the truth about himself, and accept the responsibility of being a man, and the recognition that it sets him apart.

This theme of growing up, of becoming a new self, runs through much of *The Jungle Books*. Rikki-tikki-tavi, the mongoose, washed away from his parents by a summer flood, the White Seal discovering how to release his people from the threat of death, and finding himself at the end occupying on the new beach the position his father had held on the old, Purun Bhagat leaving the life of a westernized statesman to take up the totally different existence of an acetic hermit—all these stories, so different in setting and circumstances, are all exploring the theme of self-discovery and the realization that a new life has begun.

> W. W. Robson, "Introduction," *The Second Jungle Book* by Rudyard Kipling (New York: Oxford University Press, 1987), pp. xvii–xviii

---

SUKESHI KAMARA   In the preface to *Phantom Rickshaw and Other Tales*, Kipling states: "This is not exactly a book of downright ghost stories as the cover makes believe. It is rather a collection of facts that never quite explained themselves." Thus, the dividing line between empirical reality and the reality which defies definition, is deliberately blurred. The term "fact" itself is reduced to denoting mere external, incontrovertible phenomena, such as the fact that "one man insisted upon dying because he believed himself to be haunted; another man either made up a wonderful lie and stuck to it, or visited a very strange place; while the third man was indubitably crucified by some person or persons unknown and gave an extraordinary account of himself." It is with the vision, as it emerges from a study of these facts and experiences which take these characters to the twilight regions of the inexplicable, that this chapter is to be largely concerned. ⟨. . .⟩

In the Preface Kipling reveals the stance which the narrator takes in narrating the tales. In this selection, "facts" do not explain themselves because the narrator's growing interest in the twilight regions of the mind makes him narrate tales that delve deep into the minds of individuals tortured by memories of a horrifying past. This implies an implicit acceptance on the narrator's part as on Kipling's, that the battle ground on which the forces of light and dark, life and death struggle for supremacy is the mind of man. Therefore, the mind can make man divine, as in the case of Shelley's Prometheus, or demonic, as in the case of Marlowe's Faustus, or merely shadow, as with Eliot's hollow men. Since it is in the mind that the drama of conflict takes place, the reader is allowed to delve into the mind of the character and analyse, as the character himself does the torment of remembered experience. By doing so, both the narrator and the reader peer into the hell in which the tormented, alienated individuals who figure in *Phantom Rickshaw and Other Tales* know this desire is a dream made impossible to realize. The collection opens with an epigram which indicates the futility of cultivating "habits" that act as the "bulkhead" against despair. The epigram is in the form of a prayer to protect man from the already present darkness: "May no ill dream disturb my rest / Nor Powers of Darkness me molest." It is based on the awareness that the dark side of man's soul, inexplicable ill-dreams and the powers of darkness exist and must be believed to exist before they can be dealt with.

Sukeshi Kamara, *Kipling's Vision: A Study in His Short Stories* (New Delhi: Prestige Books, 1989), pp. 38–39

▨ Bibliography

Schoolboy Lyrics. 1881.
Echoes (with Alice Kipling). 1884.
Quartette (with others). 1885.
Departmental Ditties and Other Verses. 1886.
Plain Tales from the Hills. 1888.
Soldiers Three. 1888.

The Story of the Gadsbys: A Tale without a Plot. 1888.

In Black and White. 1888.

Under the Deodars. 1888.

The Phantom 'Rickshaw and Other Tales. 1888.

Wee Willie Winkie and Other Child Stories. 1888.

The Courting of Dinah Shadd and Other Stories. 1890.

The City of Dreadful Night and Other Sketches. 1890, 1891 (as *The City of Dreadful Night and Other Places*).

Departmental Ditties, Barrack-Room Ballads, and Other Verses. 1890.

The Light That Failed. 1890.

American Notes and The Bottle Imp. 1891.

The Smith Administration. 1891.

Letters of Marque. 1891.

Mine Own People. 1891.

Life's Handicap: Being Stories of Mine Own People. 1891.

The Naulahka: A Story of West and East (with Wolcott Balestier). 1892.

Barrack-Room Ballads and Other Verses. 1892.

Many Inventions. 1893.

The Jungle Book. 1894.

The Second Jungle Book. 1895.

Out of India. 1895.

The Seven Seas. 1896.

Soldier Tales. 1896.

The Kipling Birthday Book. Ed. Joseph Finn. 1896.

"Captains Courageous": A Story of the Grand Banks. 1897.

Recessional. 1897.

Departmental Ditties; The Vampire; etc. 1898.

An Almanac of Twelve Sports (with William Nicholson). 1898.

The Day's Work. 1898.

A Fleet in Being: Notes on Two Trips with the Channel Squadron. 1898.

Poems. Ed. Wallace Rice. 1899.

Stalky & Co. 1899, 1929 (as *The Complete Stalky & Co.*).

Departmental Ditties and Barrack-Room Ballads. 1899.

From Sea to Sea: Letters of Travel. 1899.

Recessional and Other Poems. 1899.

Works (Swastika Edition). 1899. 15 vols.

The Cornhill Booklet: Occasional Poems. 1899.

With Number Three, Surgical & Medical, and New Poems (with others). 1900.

Early Verse. 1900.

The Kipling Reader. 1900.

Kim. 1901.

Just So Stories for Little Children. 1902.

The Five Nations. 1903.

The Muse among the Motors. 1904.

Traffics and Discoveries. 1904.

Puck of Pook's Hill. 1906.

Collected Verse. 1907.

Letters to the Family. 1908.

Actions and Reactions. 1909.

Abaft the Funnel. 1909.

Kipling Stories and Poems Every Child Should Know. Ed. Mary E. Burt and W. T. Chapin. 1909.

Rewards and Fairies. 1910.

If. 1910.

A History of England (with C. R. L. Fletcher). 1911.

The Kipling Reader. 1912. 2 vols.

Songs from Books. 1912.

The New Army in Training. 1915.

A Call to the Nation. 1915.

France at War. 1915.

The Fringes of the Fleet. 1915.

Tales of "The Trade." 1916.

Sea Warfare. 1916.

A Diversity of Creatures. 1917.

The Eyes of Asia. 1918.

To Fighting Americans. 1918.

Twenty Poems. 1918.

The Graves of the Fallen. 1919.

The Years Between. 1919.

Verse: Inclusive Edition. 1919 (3 vols.), 1927, 1933, 1940.

Letters of Travel (1892–1913). 1920.

Q. Horatii Flacci Carminum Librum Quintum (translator; with others). 1920.

Selected Stories. Ed. William Lyon Phelps. 1921.

Kipling's Advice to "The Hat." 1922.

A Kipling Anthology: Verse. 1922.

A Kipling Anthology: Prose. 1922.

Kipling Calendar. 1923.

The Irish Guards in the Great War (editor). 1923. 2 vols.

Land and Sea Tales for Scouts and Guides. 1923.

The Two Jungle Books. 1924.

Songs for Youth. 1924.

A Choice of Songs. 1925.

"They" and The Brushwood Boy. 1925.

Works (Mandalay Edition). 1925–26. 26 vols.

Debits and Credits. 1926.

Sea and Sussex. 1926.

St. Andrews (with Walter de la Mare). 1926.

Songs of the Sea. 1927.

A Book of Words: Selections from Speeches and Addresses Delivered between 1906 and 1927. 1928.

The One Volume Kipling. 1928.

Poems 1886–1929. 1929. 3 vols.

Selected Stories. 1929.

Thy Servant a Dog: Told by Boots. 1930.

Selected Poems. 1931.

East of Suez: Being a Selection of Eastern Verses. 1931.

Humorous Tales. 1931.

Animal Stories. 1932.

Limits and Renewals. 1932.

Souvenirs of France. 1933.

All the Mowgli Stories. 1933.

Collected Dog Stories. 1934.

Ham and the Porcupine. 1935.

All the Puck Stories. 1935.

A Kipling Pageant. 1935.

Something of Myself: For My Friends Known and Unknown. 1937.

Complete Works (Sussex Edition). 1937–39. 35 vols.

Sixty Poems. 1939.

A Choice of Kipling's Verse. Ed. T. S. Eliot. 1941.

A Choice of Kipling's Prose. Ed. W. Somerset Maugham. 1952.

Best Short Stories. Ed. Randall Jarrell. 1961.

Letters from Japan. Ed. Donald Richie and Yoshimori Harashima. 1962.

Rudyard Kipling to Rider Haggard: The Record of a Friendship. Ed. Morton Cohen. 1965.

Stories and Poems. Ed. Roger Lancelyn Green. 1970.

Short Stories. Ed. Andrew Rutherford. 1970.

The Complete Barrack-Room Ballads. Ed. C. E. Carrington. 1973.

Tales of East and West. Ed. Bernard Bergonzi. 1973.

Kipling's English History: Poems. Ed. Marghanita Laski. 1974.

Selected Verse. Ed. James Cochrane. 1977.

Kipling's Horace (translator). Ed. Charles Carrington. 1978.

Proofs of Holy Writ. 1981.

"O Beloved Kids": Letters to His Children. Ed. Elliot L. Gilbert. 1983.

Early Verse 1879–1889. Ed. Andrew Rutherford. 1986.

A Choice of Kipling's Prose. Ed. Craig Raine. 1986.

Kipling's India: Uncollected Sketches 1884–1888. Ed. Thomas Pinney. 1986.

Kipling's Japan: Collected Writings. Ed. Hugh Cortazzi and George Webb. 1988.

Best Fiction. 1989.

Letters. Ed. Thomas Pinney. 1990- . 2 vols. (to date).

Something of Myself and Other Autobiographical Writings. Ed. Thomas Pinney. 1990.

Kipling's Science Fiction. Ed. John Brunner. 1992.

Andrew Lang
1844–1912

ANDREW LANG was born in Selkirk, Scotland, on March 31, 1844. Selkirk is in the Lowland or Border region of Scotland, close to England, and its history of warfare as well as its rich tradition of folklore profoundly shaped Lang's imagination. He was educated at St. Andrew's (1861–64), where he won a scholarship that allowed him to attend Oxford from 1865 until 1868, when he became a fellow. In 1875 Lang married Leonora Alleyne, resigned his fellowship, and moved to London, where he began working as a journalist.

His first published book, the verse collection *Ballads and Lyrics of Old France*, appeared in 1872 and was followed by more than 150 volumes. These included poetry (such as *Ballads in Blue China*, 1880–88; *Helen of Troy*, 1882; *Grass of Parnassus*, 1888); translations of the *Odyssey* (with S. H. Butcher, 1879) and the *Iliad* (with W. Leaf and E. Myers, 1883); three books on the Homeric question (*Homer and the Epic*, 1893; *Homer and His Age*, 1906; *The World of Homer*, 1910); a book on the Baconian controversy arguing in favor of Shakespearean authorship (*Shakespeare, Bacon and the Great Unknown*, 1912); and several works on folklore and religion, notably *Custom and Myth* (1884), *Myth, Ritual and Religion* (1887; rev. 1899), and *The Making of Religion* (1898). Lang also wrote literary reminiscences, imaginary letters and dialogues (such as *Letters to Dead Authors*, 1886), and historical monographs that were controversially supportive of the Stuarts (including *Pickle the Spy; or, The Incognito of Prince Charles*, 1896). Lang was a prolific and successful journalist as well who was notorious for being able to write articles while riding the train, watching a race, or engaging in conversation.

In addition to these other pursuits, Lang also wrote fiction. He published his first fairy tale for children, *The Princess Nobody: A Tale of Fairy Land*, in 1884, and four more original fairy tales followed: *The Gold of Fairnilee* (1888), *Prince Prigio* (1889), *Prince Ricardo of Pantouflia* (1893), and *Tales of a Fairy Court* (1907). Lang also collaborated with his friend H. Rider Haggard on an historical fantasy for adults, *The World's Desire* (1890). But he is best remembered today for a series of fairy tale collections that he

124

edited, in which each volume is named after a color, beginning with *The Blue Fairy Book*, published in 1889. Lang produced at least one new collection of stories for children every year for the next twenty years, most commonly editing stories collected and translated by his wife and other scholars. Still widely read today, the "color" fairy books did much to revive contemporary interest in fairy tales, despite objections to their violent content (which Lang vigorously rebutted). Lang died in Banchory, Scotland, on July 22, 1912.

Critical Extracts

J. M. BARRIE   Though written in the fine English of which Mr. Lang is a master, it is not probable that ⟨*The World's Desire*⟩ will repeat the success of Mr. Haggard's early stories. At first thought this seems surprising, for that one of these writers has a gift of story-telling is as certain as that the other has a delightful command of words. Mr. Haggard has no humour that is not better omitted from his pages, but he is dramatic; his writing is ungraceful but vigorous. Mr. Lang's humour is unfailing, but he is better at parodying writers whom he likes than at character drawing, so that he has not the dramatic faculty. His writing is always graceful. He is certainly one of our "Forty." Surely, then, the two in collaboration should produce a masterpiece. So it might be said, but *The World's Desire* is really not a work of great account, and probably for this very reason, that Mr. Haggard was to supply the matter and Mr. Lang the manner. He who puts style into Mr. Haggard's books must become their author, style being as much to a book as art to a picture. Collaboration in fiction, indeed, is a mistake, for the reason that two men cannot combine so as to be one. Now, though for convenience's sake we speak of the various qualities that go to the making of a great novelist as if they were distinct, yet they cannot be separated, nor may they be lent. The crowning misfortune of *The World's Desire* is that it is sometimes dull, a failing we should not find in any book written by Mr. Lang or Mr. Haggard alone. The characters do not interest as human beings, because the good ones are assisted by miracles from the gods above, while the bad ones can at any moment summon the gods from below. There is a lack of Mr. Haggard's realism and Mr. Lang's humour. The imitation of Homer is capital, but it wearies. It is as an allegory that the story is impressive, and though it is at times really striking when thus regarded, the public do not care for allegories. The slaughter is terrible, but hardly tragic. Yet it should be said that the story has one singularly beautiful moment: when Telegonous discovers that he has slain his father, Odysseus. This is most tragic, most pathetic, because the writing is so artistic. Throughout the story, too, there is scattered some very musical verse.

    J. M. Barrie, [Review of *The World's Desire*], *British Weekly*, 20 November 1890, p. 54

ANDREW LANG   It is a truism that the supernatural in fiction should, as a general rule, be left in the vague. In the creepiest tale I ever read, the horror lay in this—*there was no ghost!* You may describe a ghost with all the most hideous features that fancy can suggest—saucer eyes, red staring hair, a forked tail, and what you please—but the reader only laughs. It is wiser to make as if you were going to describe the spectre, and then break off, exclaiming, "But no! No pen can describe, no memory, thank Heaven, can recall, the horror of that hour!" So writers, as a rule, prefer to leave their terror (usually styled "The Thing") entirely in the dark, and to the frightened fancy of the student. ⟨. . .⟩

    ⟨. . .⟩ take the scene outside the closed door of the vanished Dr. Jekyll, in Mr. Stevenson's well-known apologue:

    They are waiting on the threshold of the chamber whence the doctor has disappeared—the chamber tenanted by what? A voice comes from the room. "Sir," said Poole, looking Mr. Utterson in the eyes, "was that my master's voice?"

    A friend, a man of affairs, and a person never accused of being fanciful, told me that he read through the book to that point in a lonely Highland chateau, at night, and that he did not think it well to finish the story till next morning, but rushed to bed. So the passage seems "well-found" and successful by dint of suggestion. On the other side, perhaps, only Scotsmen brought up in country places, familiar from childhood with the terrors of Cameronian myth, and from childhood apt to haunt the lonely churchyards, never stirred since the year of the great Plague choked the soil with the dead, perhaps *they* only know how much shudder may be found in Mr. Stevenson's "Thrawn Janet." The black smouldering heat in the hills and glens that are commonly so fresh, the aspect of Man, the Tempter of the Brethren, we know them, and we have enough of the old blood in us to be thrilled by that masterpiece of the described supernatural. It may be only a local success, it may not much affect the English reader, but it is of sure appeal to the Lowland Scot. The ancestral Covenanter within us awakens, and is terrified by his ancient fears.

Perhaps it may die out in a positive age—this power of learning to shudder. To us it descends from very long ago, from the far-off forefathers who dreaded the dark, and who, half starved and all untaught, saw spirits everywhere, and scarce discerned waking experience from dreams. When we are all perfect positivist philosophers, when a thousand generations of nurses that never heard of ghosts have educated the thousand and first generation of children, then the supernatural may fade out of fiction. But has it not grown and increased since Wordsworth wanted the "Ancient Mariner" to have "a profession and a character," since Southey called that poem a Dutch piece of work, since Lamb had to pretend to dislike its "miracles"? Why, as science becomes more cock-sure, have men and women become more and more fond of old follies, and more pleased with the stirring of ancient dread within their veins?

Andrew Lang, "The Supernatural in Fiction," *Adventures among Books* (London: Longmans, Green, 1905), pp. 273, 278–80.

ROGER LANCELYN GREEN   The mildly satirical fairy-story of the Thackeray tradition is a far easier form of literature to write than anything approaching the old folk-tales and legendary romances; and it was also a type of writing that came most easily to Lang of the gay mind, who confessed once that he was possessed by "the literary *follét* who delights in mild mischief." Yet in its essentials *Prince Prigio* goes contrary to Lang's own ideals, for it is a burlesque, however kindly, of the old tales. Of course, he was inventing no new *genre* when he wrote the Chronicles of Pantouflia, but merely carrying the methods of F. E. Paget, Thackeray and Tom Hood one step further, even as they had elaborated the methods of Madame d'Aulnoy and her followers. *The Gold of Fairnilee* should not be compared with *Prince Prigio*, any more than *Alice* with Grimm's tales. It is dangerous to make any very definite attempt to put fairy stories into precise categories, for most of them lie somewhere between the extremes of "primitive" (to which we would assign *Alice Learmont* and *The Gold of Fairnilee*) and "sophisticated" (to which *The Rose and the Ring* and *Prince Prigio* belong), and are best left scattered indeterminately between these extremes.

Thus, although it would be unfair to criticize one of Lang's tales by the standards of the other, we can go so far as to say that the Pantouflia stories belong to a lower and commoner form of art than *The Gold of Fairnilee*.

And yet, considered solely as books for children, one would be forced reluctantly to set *Prince Prigio* first. For lightness, humour, gay adventure have ever been the most popular with the majority of young readers. For every one child devoted to George MacDonald, there are a hundred whose faith is pledged to E. Nesbit, and the same distinction seems to hold good between Lang's two stories. The last twelve years have seen three new editions of *Prince Prigio*, but only one of *The Gold of Fairnilee*—and that has been exhausted for some time.

> Roger Lancelyn Green, *Andrew Lang: A Critical Biography* (Leicester: Edmund Ward, 1946), pp. 105–6

J. R. R. TOLKIEN   ⟨Lang's⟩ collections are largely a by-product of his adult study of mythology and folk-lore; but they were made into and presented as books for children. Some of the reasons that Lang gave are worth considering.

The introduction to the first of the series speaks of 'children to whom and for whom they are told'. 'They represent', he says, 'the young age of man true to his early loves, and have his unblunted edge of belief, a fresh appetite for marvels.' ' "Is it true?" ' he says, 'is the great question children ask.' ⟨. . .⟩

⟨. . .⟩ They do ask that question, I know; and it is not one to be rashly or idly answered. But that question is hardly evidence of 'unblunted belief', or even of the desire for it. Most often it proceeds from the child's desire to know which kind of literature he is faced with. Children's knowledge of the world is often so small that they cannot judge, off-hand and without help, between the fantastic, the strange (that is rare or remote facts), the nonsensical, and the merely 'grown-up' (that is ordinary things of their parents' world, much of which still remains unexplored). ⟨. . .⟩

Now I was one of the children whom Andrew Lang was addressing—I was born at about the same time as the *Green Fairy Book*—the children for whom he seemed to think that fairy-stories were the equivalent of the adult novel, and of whom he said: 'Their taste remains like the taste of their naked ancestors thousands of years ago; and they seem to like fairy-tales better than history, poetry, geography, or arithmetic.' But do we really know much about these 'naked ancestors', except that they were certainly not naked? Our fairy-stories, however old certain elements in them may be, are certainly not the same as theirs. Yet if it is assumed that we have fairy-stories because they did, then probably we have history, geography, poetry, and arithmetic because they liked these things too, as far as they could get them, and in so far as they had yet separated the many branches of their general interest in everything.

And as for children of the present day, Lang's description does not fit my own memories, or my experience of children. Lang may have been mistaken about the children he knew, but if he was not, then at any rate children differ considerably, even within the narrow borders of Britain, and such generalizations which treat them as a class (disregarding their individual talents, and the influences of the countryside they live in, and their upbringing) are delusory. I had no special 'wish to believe'. I wanted to know.

J. R. R. Tolkien, "On Fairy-Stories" (1947), *Tree and Leaf* (1964; rev. ed. Boston: Houghton Mifflin, 1989), pp. 36, 38–39

PERCY MUIR   The five columns listing ⟨Lang's⟩ work in the *Cambridge Bibliography of English Literature* are not exhaustive, although he is shown as poet, critic, parodist, historian, anthropologist, occultist, fisherman, golfer, and translator. He was one of the founders of the Society for Psychical Research, and contributed many papers to their Proceedings.

He was, in short, a versatile fellow; he delved below the surface of many subjects, and usually emerged with something that would serve for an essay or an article, if not a book. He was a scholar who could make a scholarly subject more palatable than caviare in general. The penalty of this, however, was that his scholarship never entirely deserted him, and even in his most popular fictional writings there is always a slight tang of midnight oil.

Thus in his collaboration with Haggard, *The World's Desire*, although the yarn is a good one, one is a little too conscious that one of the authors is closely familar with Icelandic saga. Similarly his own fairy-tales, excellent though some of them are, and even some of the collections, are not entirely freed from the anthropological background with which Lang himself was so familiar that he hardly detected its presence, or, if he did, thought it no matter.

Fairies had interested him since childhood. Not only had he been brought up on Perrault and Grimm, but he grew up in the Border country, where legends and tales of the "little people" abounded. Fairnilee, the locale of his best story, is Border country, and appears to be little more than a reconstruction of his own childhood adventures in search of fairy folk and fairy treasure.

Lang's two stories *Prince Prigio* (1889) and *Prince Ricardo* (1893) have recently been reprinted; but the immortality of his tales is tenuous. For us he is possibly more important as an influence, a background, than for what he wrote himself. He encouraged other romantic writers like Haggard and Stevenson, whom he recognised to be better at this particular job than he was himself; and in his writings and indefatigable collections he provided a valuable quarry for prospectors.

> Percy Muir, *English Children's Books: 1600 to 1900* (New York: Frederick A. Praeger, 1954), pp. 153–54

ELEANOR DE SELMS LANGSTAFF   In general, Lang moved from the known to the lesser known in his selection of tales—the tried and the true to the more experimental. In keeping with his concept of making manifest the universality of the human experience, he covered the world fairly well in each volume. Although *The Blue Fairy Book* ventured only as far afield as Asia Minor, *The Yellow Fairy Book* five years later presented three American Indian tales and one of the two Chinese tales in the series, as well as tales from Europe. *The Brown Fairy Book* of 1904 balanced its American Indian and African—both northern and southern—with Scandinavian, French, and Spanish tales. Where five countries had been represented in the first book of the series, from *The Yellow Fairy Book* of 1894 through *The Orange Fairy Book* of 1906 the number of countries represented averaged ten.

Lang was not the author of the Fairy Books; what therefore was his function? His prefaces bear witness to the fact that many had worked at retelling the stories—his wife, May Kendall, and a host of women who worked as translators of exotic languages and thus were particularly qualified to work on the tales. Lang identified the sources, worked with the illustrators—H. J. Ford, G. P. Jacomb Hood, and Lancelot Speed—and provided the reputation that made the series acceptable. ⟨Roger Lancelyn⟩ Green noted that, when *The Blue Fairy Book* first appeared, the trend in children's literature had been toward the realistic child's novel. "It would be no exaggeration to say that Lang was entirely responsible for this change in public taste . . . [from realism to fairy tale]," he stated.

There were three criteria by which Lang assessed the tales he chose. First, he had certain ideas about how a tale should be constructed, having written several literary fairy tales himself. He looked at these much as an artist might evaluate his materials—the clay or oil from which forms may emerge.

Second, he was familiar with the changes tales undergo through the centuries. He knew, and deplored, the technique of substituting a tinsel fairy for the traditional *deus ex machina,* as had been done in the French tales. Last, he felt that children should not be submitted to boredom or shoddy scholarship. Children enjoyed the toughness of folktales, "for children are innocent and love justice; while most of us are wicked and naturally prefer mercy," as ⟨G. K.⟩ Chesterton put it. Moreover he knew it was not the children who read prefaces, but adults who looked on childhood through a scrim of nostalgia. The versions of folktales Lang chose were given to children in a straightforward manner while disguising his scholarship as best he might in the reassuring prefaces.

Yet the scholarship is there. His anthropological studies created in him a strong awareness of basic plots and themes. Distortion of these themes would invalidate the transmission of the tale. After all, it was a tale, a piece of fiction, and overly scientific handling of the material could do as much harm as the French emendations did to theirs. Lang sought out a method by which the literary quality would be preserved and enhanced while at the same time the true text of the tale would be transmitted. In oral literature, the "text" does not have to match the same words to the same symbols as long as the concept is understood.

Eleanor De Selms Langstaff, *Andrew Lang* (Boston: Twayne, 1978), pp. 139–40

⊠ *Bibliography*

Ballads and Lyrics of Old France, with Other Poems. 1872.

The Odyssey of Homer: Book VI (translator). 1877.

Specimens of a Translation of Theocritus. 1879.

The Odyssey of Homer (translator; with S. H. Butcher). 1879.

Oxford: Brief Historical and Descriptive Notes. 1879, 1890.

Theocritus, Bion and Moschus (translator). 1880.

XXII Ballades in Blue China. 1880, 1881 (as *XXII* and *X: XXXII Ballades in Blue China*).

The Library (with others). 1881.

Notes on a Collection of Pictures by Mr. J. E. Millais. 1881.

The Black Thief. 1882.

Helen of Troy. 1882.

The Iliad of Homer (translator; with Walter Leaf and Ernest Myers). 1883.

Custom and Myth. 1884.

Much Darker Days. 1884.

Ballades and Verses Vain. Ed. Austin Dobson. 1884.

The Princess Nobody: A Tale of Fairy Land. 1884.

That Very Mab (with May Kendall). 1885.

Rhymes à la Mode. 1885.

Lines on the Inaugural Meeting of the Shelley Society. Ed. Thomas J. Wise. 1886.

The Politics of Aristotle: Introductory Essays. 1886.

The Mark of Cain. 1886.

In the Wrong Paradise and Other Stories. 1886.

Letters to Dead Authors. 1886, 1907 (as *New and Old Letters to Dead Authors*).

Books and Bookmen. 1886.

Myth, Ritual and Religion. 1887. 2 vols.

Johnny Nut and the Golden Goose by Charles Deulin (translator). 1887.

Almae Matres: St. Andrews 1862, Oxford 1865. 1887.

Aucassin and Nicolete (translator). 1887.

[*He* (with W. H. Pollock). 1887.]

Grass of Parnassus: Rhymes Old and New. 1888, 1892 (as *Grass of Parnassus: First and Last Rhymes*).

Euterpe: Being the Second Book of the Famous History of Herodotus, tr. Barnaby Rich (editor). 1888.

Perrault's Popular Tales (editor). 1888.

Ballads of Books (editor). 1888.

The Gold of Fairnilee. 1888.

Pictures at Play; or, Dialogues of the Galleries (with W. E. Henley). 1888.

Prince Prigio. 1889.

Letters on Literature. 1889.

Lost Leaders. Ed. William Pett Ridge. 1889.

The Blue Fairy Book (editor). 1889.

The Dead Leman and Other Tales from the French (translator; with Paul Sylvester). 1889.

Old Friends: Essays in Epistolary Parody. 1890.

The World's Desire (with H. Rider Haggard). 1890.

The Red Fairy Book (editor). 1890.

The Strife of Love in a Dream by Francesco Colonna (editor). 1890.

How to Fail in Literature. 1890.

Life, Letters, and Diaries of Sir Stafford Northcote, First Earl of Iddesleigh. 1890. 2 vols.

Angling Sketches. 1891.

Essays in Little. 1891.

The Blue Poetry Book (editor). 1891.

The Green Fairy Book (editor). 1892.

Prince Ricardo of Pantouflia: Being the Adventures of Prince Prigio's Son. 1893.

The Tercentenary of Izaak Walton. 1893.

The True Story Book (editor). 1893.

Homer and the Epic. 1893.

St. Andrews. 1893.

Ban and Arrière Ban: A Rally of Fugitive Rhymes. 1894.

Lyrics and Ballads by Sir Walter Scott (editor). 1894.

The Yellow Fairy Book (editor). 1894.

Cock Lane and Common-Sense. 1894.

The Voices of Jeanne d'Arc. 1895.

Border Ballads (editor). 1895.

My Own Fairy Book (editor). 1895.

Poetical Works by Sir Walter Scott (editor). 1895.

The Red True Story Book (editor). 1895.

A Monk of Fife (translator). 1895.

The Poems and Songs of Robert Burns (editor). 1896.

The Animal Story Book (editor). 1896.

The Compleat Angler by Izaak Walton (editor). 1896.

The Blue True Story Book (editor). 1896.

The Life and Letters of John Gibson Lockhart. 1897. 2 vols.

Modern Mythology. 1897.

Wordsworth (editor). 1897.

A Collection of Ballads (editor). 1897.

The Nursery Rhyme Book (editor). 1897.

The Pink Fairy Book (editor). 1897.

The Book of Dreams and Ghosts. 1897.

Pickle the Spy; or, The Incognito of Prince Charles. 1897.

The Miracles of Madame Saint Katherine of Fierbois (translator). 1897.

The Works of Charles Dickens (Gadshill Edition) (editor). 1897–1908. 36 vols.

The Making of Religion. 1898.

The Companions of Pickle: Being a Sequel to Pickle the Spy. 1898.

Coleridge (editor). 1898.

The Arabian Nights Entertainments (editor and translator). 1898.

Parson Kelly (with A. E. W. Mason). 1899.

The Homeric Hymns: A New Prose Translation, and Essays, Literary and Mythological. 1899.

The Red Book of Animal Stories (editor). 1899.

Prince Charles Edward. 1900.

A History of Scotland from the Roman Occupation. 1900–07. 4 vols.

Notes and Names in Books. 1900.

The Grey Fairy Book (editor). 1900.

The Mystery of Mary Stuart. 1901.

Alfred Tennyson. 1901.

The Violet Fairy Book (editor). 1901.

Magic and Religion. 1901.

Adventures among Books. 1901, 1905.

The Young Ruthven. 1902.

The Disentanglers. 1902.

James VI and the Gowrie Mystery. 1902.

The Gowrie Conspiracy by George Sprott (editor). 1902.

The Book of Romance (editor). 1902.

Social Origins (with *Primal Law* by J. J. Atkinson). 1903.

The Valet's Tragedy and Other Studies. 1903.

The Story of the Golden Fleece. 1903.

The Crimson Fairy Book (editor). 1903.

Historical Mysteries. 1904.

The Apology for William Maitland by James Maitland (editor). 1904.

The Brown Fairy Book (editor). 1904.

New Collected Rhymes. 1905.

The Puzzle of Dickens' Last Plot. 1905.

The Secret of the Totem. 1905.

The Clyde Mystery: A Study in Forgeries and Folklore. 1905.

John Knox and the Reformation. 1905.

Homer and His Age. 1906.

Sir Walter Scott. 1906.

The Story of Joan of Arc. 1906.

Portraits and Jewels of Mary Stuart. 1906.

The Orange Fairy Book (editor). 1906.

Aladdin and the Wonderful Lamp and Other Stories from the Blue, Brown, and Pink Fairy Books (editor). 1906.

The Elf Maiden and Other Stories from the Brown, Pink, and Yellow Fairy Books (editor). 1906.

The Golden Mermaid and Other Stories from the Pink, Green, and Crimson Fairy Books (editor). 1906.

The Magic King and Other Stories from the Yellow and Crimson Fairy Books (editor). 1906.

Pretty Goldilocks and Other Stories from the Brown, Blue, and Green Fairy Books (editor). 1906.

The Snow Queen and Other Stories from the Pink and Crimson Fairy Books (editor). 1906.

Trusty John and Other Stories from the Grey, Violet, Brown, and Blue Fairy Books (editor). 1906.

Tales of a Fairy Court. 1906.

[*Omar de Profundis.* 1906.]

Poet's Country (editor). 1907.

The Olive Fairy Book (editor). 1907.

Tales of Troy and Greece. 1907.

The King over the Water (with Alice Shield). 1907.

The Origins of Religion and Other Essays. 1908.

The Maid of France: Being the Story of the Life and Death of Jeanne d'Arc. 1908.

The Book of Princes and Princesses by Leonora B. Lang (editor). 1908.

Poems by Jean Ingelow (editor). 1908.

La Jeanne d'Arc de M. Anatole France. 1909.

Sir George Mackenzie, King's Advocate, of Rosehaugh: His Life and Times. 1909.

Beauty and the Beast and Other Stories from the Blue, Brown, Green, Violet, and Yellow Fairy Books (editor). 1909.

The Forty Thieves and Other Stories from the Blue, Crimson, Green, and Red Fairy Books (editor). 1909.

The Invisible Prince and Other Stories from the Brown, Yellow, and Grey Fairy Books (editor). 1909.

The Magician's Gifts and Other Stories from the Crimson, Green, and Brown Fairy Books (editor). 1909.

The Marvellous Musician and Other Stories from the Red, Crimson, Grey, and Violet Fairy Books (editor). 1909.

The Three Dwarfs and Other Stories from the Brown, Green, Red, and Yellow Fairy Books (editor). 1909.

The True History of Little Golden-Hood and Other Stories from the Red, Crimson, Blue, and Brown Fairy Books (editor). 1909.

The Twelve Huntsmen and Other Stories from the Green, Violet, Brown, and Blue Fairy Books (editor). 1909.

The Red Book of Heroes by Leonora B. Lang (editor). 1909.

The World of Homer. 1910.

Sir Walter Scott and the Border Minstrelsy. 1910.

The Lilac Fairy Book (editor). 1910.

Method in the Study of Totemism. 1911.

A Short History of Scotland. 1911.

Poems and Plays by Sir Walter Scott (editor). 1911.

Ballades and Rhymes: From Ballades in Blue China *and* Rhymes à la Mode.
      1911.

The All Sorts of Stories Book by Leonora B. Lang (editor). 1911.

Ode on a Distant Memory of Jane Eyre. Ed. Clement K. Shorter. 1912.

Shakespeare, Bacon, and the Great Unknown. 1912.

History of English Literature from Beowulf *to* Swinburne. 1912.

The Annesley Case (editor). 1912.

In Praise of Frugality by Pope Leo XIII (translator). 1912.

Ode to the Opening Century by Pope Leo XIII (translator). 1912.

The Book of Saints and Heroes by Leonora B. Lang (editor). 1912.

Highways and Byways in the Border (with John Lang). 1913.

The Strange Story Book by Leonora B. Lang (editor). 1913.

Bibliomania. 1914.

Poetical Works. Ed. Leonora B. Lang. 1923. 4 vols.

Tartan Tales from Andrew Lang. Ed. Bertha L. Gunterman. 1928.

The Andrew Lang Edition of the Rubaiyat. 1935.

Andrew Lang and St. Andrews: A Centenary Anthology. Ed. J. B. Salmond.
      1944.

The New Pygmalion. 1962.

Fifty Favourite Fairy Tales. Ed. Kathleen Lines. 1963.

The Gold of Fairnilee and Other Stories. Ed. Gillian Avery. 1967.

In College Gardens: Old Rhymes Written in 1871. 1972.

George MacDonald
1824–1905

GEORGE MACDONALD was born in Huntly, Aberdeenshire, Scotland, on December 10, 1824. In spite of the death of his mother when he was eight years old, his early years spent on his farm were idyllic, and autobiographical recollections of rural and pastoral life can be found throughout his work. Though his family was of limited means, MacDonald was awarded a scholarship that enabled him to study chemistry and physics at the University of Aberdeen from 1840 to 1845. His adjustment from rural to urban life was a rocky one, and, because of his free-spending ways, he had to leave the university for a time in 1842. In the summer of that year he stayed with his father in a castle in the far north of Scotland, where he avidly read many of the works—German Romanticism, early English poetry, and novels of romance—that would significantly influence his own writing.

After college MacDonald became a private tutor for three years in London, then decided to become a minister, attending Highbury College, a Congregationalist school of divinity in London, in 1848. In that same year he became engaged to Louisa Powell, whom he married in 1851 and with whom he had eleven children.

In 1850, while preparing to assume his first ministry in Arundel, Suffolk, MacDonald contracted tuberculosis and never fully recovered his health. He was interested in poetry and privately published a translation of *Twelve of the Spiritual Songs of Novalis* in 1851. MacDonald was dismissed from his position as pastor in 1853 on account of his pronounced heterodoxy; he was an ardent mystic with untraditional views on God, nature, epiphany, and the perfection of humankind. His dismissal from the ministry led him to turn to writing both as a way of making a living and as an alternate expression of the religious calling he still felt.

MacDonald's literary career began slowly, but he eventually became one of the most widely read authors of the period, and was a friend of both John Ruskin and C. L. Dodgson (Lewis Carroll), as well as many other Victorian intellectuals. During his lifetime his twenty-nine mainstream novels such as *David Elginbrod* (1863), *Alec Forbes of Howglen* (1865), and *Robert Falconer* (1868) were very successful. *England's Antiphon* (1868) is a significant treatise on poetry. His collected essays, *Orts*, appeared in 1882, and his *Poetical Works* was published in 1893. In 1872 he made a very successful lecture tour of the United States, and in 1877 Queen Victoria granted him a civil list pension of £100 a year. He purchased a residence at Bordighera on the Italian Riviera, where he spent winters for the sake of his health.

Today MacDonald is best remembered for his two symbolist fantasies, *Phantastes* (1858) and *Lilith* (1895), and for his stories for children, including *At the Back of the North Wind* (1871), *The Princess and the Goblin* (1872), and *The Princess and Curdie* (1883). Some of MacDonald's fairy tales— including "The Light Princess" and "The Golden Key"—appeared in *Good Words for the Young*, a children's magazine he edited early in his literary career, and were gathered in *Dealings with the Fairies* (1867) and other volumes.

In 1900 MacDonald suffered a stroke and lost the power of speech. His last few years were spent in increasing ill health until his death on September 18, 1905. His son Greville published an exhaustive and laudatory biography, *George MacDonald and His Wife*, in 1924. MacDonald's novels, with their heavy interlardings of didacticism and lowland Scots dialect, began to fall out of favor soon after his death, but his fantasy continues to be read, thanks in a large part to its influence on C. S. Lewis and J. R. R. Tolkien.

◈ *Critical Extracts*

UNSIGNED   In *Phantastes* Mr. MacDonald has attempted an allegory in prose, which reads as though it had been written after supping too plentifully on German romance, negative philosophy, and Shelley's *Alastor*, and then, instead of his having mounted Pegasus to ride it off, he seems to have been ridden himself by a nightmare. If we speak of this book in metaphors, we must be excused, for we cannot help it. Any one after reading it might set up a confusedly furnished second-hand symbol-shop. The author says on the title-page, "In good sooth, my masters, this is no door. Yet is it a little window, that looketh upon a great world." In good sooth, we have seen little through it save a wilderness of wilderment. Surely it is of ground glass. Or is there not a central crack which breaks every passing image with its fatal flaw?

Allegory shows us life moving with its shadow. This shadow may represent humanity in grotesque caricature, or as reaching to a loftier stature, but together they move—Life and Shadow—with their double existence and their double meaning, so perfectly that, according to binocular mind-vision, they may be seen as one. Now the great masters of allegory succeed by their firm grasp of reality, and they always give such a compelling interest to the life-figures that a man may and a child must follow them and their movements independently of the secondary meaning, which is shadowed on the background. We may read the *Faerie Queene*, and the allegory is quite optional. Without that inner meaning there is quite enough in the outer life of that marvelous tale of chivalry,—enough in the real men and women with which we are floated down an enchanted stream of poetry in their brave beauty and immortal strength. See also how Bunyan holds fast by the life as though he knew if that were true the shadow would be sure to fall right. By some happy naming of person or place he will thrust the very handle of his meaning into your hand. You may see the shadow, but he takes care to make you feel the reality. Mr. MacDonald has given us the shadow without the life which should cause it to him and account for it to us. Thus *Phantastes* is a riddle that will not be read. He has made his voyage into Dreamland with the phantom bark, but when he tries to bring it home to us and reveal something of the far wonder-world we cannot get on board. He has not anchored fast to the earth on which we stand.

Unsigned, [Review of *Phantastes*], *Athenaeum*, 6 November 1858, p. 580

C. S. LEWIS   If we define Literature as an art whose medium is words, then certainly MacDonald has no place in its first rank—perhaps not even in its second. There are indeed passages ⟨. . .⟩ where the wisdom and (I would dare to call it) the holiness that are in him triumph over and even burn away the baser elements in his style: the expression becomes precise, weighty, economic; acquires a cutting edge. But he does not maintain this level for long. The texture of his writing as a whole is undistinguished, at times fumbling. Bad pulpit traditions cling to it; there is sometimes a nonconformist verbosity, sometimes an old Scotch weakness for florid ornament (it runs right through them from Dunbar to the Waverley Novels), sometimes an over-sweetness picked up from Novalis. But this does not quite dispose of him even for the literary critic. What he does best is fantasy—fantasy that hovers between the allegorical and the mythopoeic. And this, in my opinion, he does better then any man. ⟨. . .⟩

It was in this mythopoeic art that MacDonald excelled. ⟨. . .⟩ The great works are *Phantastes*, the *Curdie* books, *The Golden Key*, *The Wise Woman*, and *Lilith*. From them, just because they are supremely good in their own kind, there is little to be extracted. The meaning, the suggestion, the radiance, is incarnate in the whole story: it is only by chance that you find any detachable merits. The novels, on the other hand, have yielded me a rich crop. This does not mean that they are good novels. Necessity made MacDonald a novelist, but few of his novels are good and none is very good. They are best when they depart most from the canons of novel writing, and that in two directions. Sometimes they depart in order to come nearer to fantasy, as in the whole character of the hero in *Sir Gibbie* or the opening chapters of *Wilfrid Cumbermede*. Sometimes they diverge into direct and prolonged preachments which would be intolerable if a man were reading for the story, but which are in fact welcome because the author, though a poor novelist, is a supreme preacher. Some of his best things are thus hidden in his dullest books: my task here has been almost one of exhumation. I am speaking so far of the novels as I think they would appear if judged by any reasonably objective standard. But it is, no doubt, true that any reader who loves holiness and loves MacDonald—yet perhaps he will need to love Scotland too—can find even in the worst of them something that disarms criticism and will come to feel a queer awkward charm in their very faults.

> C. S. Lewis, "Preface," *George MacDonald: An Anthology* (London: Geoffrey Bles, 1946), pp. 14, 17

DENIS DONOGHUE   So the motive for fairy tale is the motive for metaphor, the exhilaration of change. You like metaphor, Wallace Stevens says in an exemplary poem, when you want things to change, when you particularly want them to change to you, as if a cripple were to sing. The particular change that MacDonald wanted was a change of character, as he wanted people to be different by being better. This is the flow of feeling between his sermons, metaphors, novels, and fairy tales. Metaphor is the shortest way of getting out of Manchester, the quickest answer to the Industrial Revolution. Some of the evidence is contained in "A Manchester Poem," one of his most revealing compositions. "Slave engines utter again their ugly growl," he says, but every "marvellous imperfection" points ahead to "higher perfectness than heart can think." The strange feature of the poem is that it is so deeply committed to metaphor and change that Paradise itself, because it is the End, is deemed to be improper. To MacDonald it was far more important, because far more human, to travel hopefully than to arrive. He turns away from first and last things, preferring drama to eschatology. Value is embodied in action, striving, change; to arrive is to make metaphor redundant:

> Man seeks a better home than Paradise;
> Therefore high hope is more than deepest joy,
> A disappointment better than a feast,
> And the first daisy on a wind-swept lea
> Dearer than Eden-groves with rivers four.

The problem is to endow the Good Life with the right metaphors of action. In several stories we hear of "the place where the end of the rainbow stands," clearly the same place as "the back of the North Wind" and "the country from which the shadows come," but there is always a suggestion that this place is worthy because of the aspiration, the energy it engenders; and that its finality is its defect. Heaven is inferior to Nature, MacDonald goes to the brink of implying, because Heaven is changeless and Nature is always changing. His parishioners were right. MacDonald's sermons are short on doctrine. ⟨. . .⟩

⟨. . .⟩ In Emerson and in MacDonald Nature is ⟨. . .⟩ featured as discipline, because she contains and therefore presumably knows all the answers. Mac-Donald's *The Lost Princess* is often read as a moral tract, the point being that children should never be pampered. But its power as a story depends upon MacDonald's sense of natural forces working behind or beneath the maxim; forces far in excess of the moral occasion, but working on its behalf. North Wind has more business in hand than merely to push Diamond or Old Sal in the right direction. The point about Princess Rosamond and the shepherd-child Agnes in *The Lost Princess* is only incidentally that they are spoiled brats. Rather, it is that their young lives are perverse and unnatural, because deprived of the discipline of natural power. This is what the Wise Woman knows, so she takes the children away for their own good. Nature is a foster parent, better than the original. MacDonald's stories reach far and wide and deep because, especially in *The Golden Key* and the Curdie books, they imply a lively set of forces which can get out of hand, at least for a time.

Denis Donoghue, "The Other Country," *New York Review of Books*, 21 December 1967, p. 35

GLENN EDWARD SADLER   *Phantastes*, like most dream romances, is peopled by the disguised inhabitants of the imagination. Its title, taken from Canto vi of Phineas Fletcher's *Purple Island,* and the two lines which MacDonald extracts from it—

> Phantastes from "their fount" all shapes deriving,
>   In new habiliments can quickly dight

—hint at a seething array of semi-material beings, all of which "can quickly dight" themselves before us. We discover a colorful cosmology of talkative (sometimes ornery) garden flower-fairies, greedy and kind tree-spirits, a voluptuous marble maiden, dancing statues, a beautiful-wise old woman, an ominous Shadow, and other lively citizens of Faerie. The eye-catching power of *Phantastes* is derived, at the start, from the speed and smoothness of the transformation and from its teasing symbolism throughout. With wide sweep MacDonald crosses in Chapter i the "peach-colored" horizon of morning slumber and manages in three short pages in Chapter ii to skillfully shift Anodos ("pathless") from his Victorian bedroom, with its green marble washbasin and heavily carved black oak dresser, to the timeless "path into Fairy Land." Thus Anodos—followed by ⟨C. S.⟩ Lewis's John—leaves the land of Puritania. Both are overcome, however, like Novalis's Hyacinth, by the sickness of the young man's quest: " 'I must away to a foreign land!' he said: 'the strange old woman in the wood has told me what I must do to get well. . . .' "

MacDonald's infectious mentor was Novalis, to whom he paid repeated tribute. Commenting on an essay on biography by T. T. Lynch, MacDonald exclaimed: "It is, indeed, well with him who has found a friend whose spirit touches his own and illuminates it. . . . Shall I not one day, 'somewhere, somehow,' clasp the large hand of Novalis, and, gazing on his face, compare his features with those of Saint John?" The sudden loss of his adolescent Madonna, his mystic confidence in the prophetic worth of dreams, his emphasis on immortality and, above all, Novalis's peculiar belief in "magic idealism" (which became for him something more than metempsychosis) and his untimely death—these biographical facts influenced MacDonald to follow his German master closely.

> Glenn Edward Sadler, "The Fantastic Imagination in George MacDonald," *Imagination and the Spirit,* ed. Charles A. Huttar (Grand Rapids, MI: William B. Eerdmans, 1971), pp. 218–19

JACK ZIPES   *The Light Princess* (1864) like his tale *Little Daylight* (1867) is a parody of *Sleeping Beauty* and *Rapunzel,* and, for that matter, it reflects MacDonald's disrespectful attitude toward traditional folk and fairy tales. MacDonald realized that the symbolism of most of the traditional tales points to a dead end and prevents children from glimpsing their special relationship to the divine within and beyond them. It is striking that he does *not* see his point of departure for the fairy-tale discourse in the works of Grimm or Andersen but largely in those of the German romantics, particularly the fascinating stories of Novalis. Certainly the three tales in Novalis' *Heinrich von Ofterdingen* with their utopian motifs and religious-erotic development of young couples had a great impact on him. In *The Light Princess* MacDonald follows Novalis' tendency to turn an ordered world topsy-turvy so that the conventional social order and relations could be parodied and the possibility of creating new modes of behavior and values could be perceived and designated. ⟨. . .⟩

The irreverent tone of the story not only places the convention of traditional fairy tales in question but also the very style of aristocratic life. For instance, the king is a banal figure, a "little king with a great throne, like many other kings." The royal metaphysicians, Hum-Dru and Kopy-Keck, are fools. Even the typical prince is mocked. MacDonald winks his eye and debunks aristocratic language and codes, and yet, there is a serious side to the light comedy. From the beginning, after the bewitchment, the princess, court, and the implied reader of the tale are faced with a problem: how to provide gravity ⟨lost through a spell⟩ for the princess who does not have her feet on the ground and could cause continual havoc in the kingdom. The major theme of the tale concerns social integration, but—and this is significant—gravity (social responsibility and compassion) cannot be imposed or learned abstractly. It is gained through passion and experience, and it is also liberating. Once the princess touches water, she develops a veritable passion for it because she can control her own movements, and she can share her pleasure with the prince. Moreover, she overcomes her egocentrism by realizing her pleasure is not worth the death of a beloved human being. Through her relation to the prince, who is self-sacrificing and tender in the mold of traditional fairy-tale females, she develops social empathy, and her learning to walk after the spell is broken, though painful, can be equated to the difficult acceptance of social responsibility.

Of course, one could argue that MacDonald leaves the aristocratic social structure unchanged—a system which harbors authoritarianism—and that the princess seems to achieve her "gravity" or identity through the male hero. These were clearly his ideological preferences and weaknesses from a political point of view. It should be pointed out, however, that MacDonald was more interested in the reformation of social character and was convinced that all social change emanated from the development of personal integrity not necessarily through political restructuring and upheaval. This belief is why he stressed ethical choice and action through intense quests and experience. Moreover, in *The Light Princess*, his female protagonist does not become dependent on the prince, who is a "softy." Rather she gains certain qualities through her relationship with him just as he benefits from the encounter. There is more sensitive interaction between two unique individuals than traditional role-playing at the end of the tale, a special configuration which MacDonald was to develop in all his narrative.

> Jack Zipes, *Fairy Tales and the Art of Subversion: The Classical Genre for Children and the Process of Civilization* (New York: Wildman Press, 1983), pp. 105–7

HUMPHREY CARPENTER   *Phantastes* is nowadays best known as the book which introduced C. S. Lewis to MacDonald's writings, and set him on his own course as a writer of fantasy. Lewis's admirers, coming to it hopefully, are often puzzled by its extraordinary style and content. Lewis spoke of it as "baptising" his imagination, which implies that it is a holy book. It is actually very unholy, but reading it is rather like experiencing some sort of total immersion, so that the baptismal metaphor is not entirely inappropriate.

A modern reader may suppose the book to be largely about sexuality, and in fact *Phantastes*, unlike most of MacDonald's writings, may be interpreted almost entirely in sexual terms. The hero Anodos, whose name is Greek for "pathless," is on his twenty-first birthday initiated by a fairy mother- (or grandmother-) figure into a Fairyland whose features and events seem to stand for sexual experience and a child's or young man's reactions to it. He is menaced by the masculine, perhaps father-like, Ash tree, but is saved by the maternal Beech (" 'Why, you baby!' said she, and kissed me with the sweetest kiss of winds and odours"). The experience of lying in her arms leaves him feeling "as if new-born." But he is tricked into the arms of the Maid of the Alder, who he has been told "will smother you with her web of hair, if you let her near you at night"; and this and subsequent experiences with other female inhabitants of Fairyland give Anodos a sense of guilt and pollution which seem to be symbolic of a young man's guilty reaction to sexuality. Later he comes to a strange palace, where, in a library (the library-in-the-castle), he reads of a land where children are born without conception and there is not physical love between the sexes; he also reads of a young man who can only see the woman he loves by means of a mirror. In the palace he discovers a womblike hall to which he returns again and again;

later, he brings a female statue to life by chanting a startlingly erotic ballad to it, commanding each part of her body to come to life, from her feet gradually upwards:

> Rise the limbs, sedately sloping,
>   Strong and gentle, full and free;
> Soft and slow, like certain hoping,
>   Drawing nigh the broad firm knee . . .
> Temple columns, close combining
>   Lift a holy mystery . . .

The whole of *Phantastes,* indeed, may be interpreted as being about the "holy mystery" of sex—with the possible exception of the climactic scene, where Anodos dies in the act of exposing a false religion whose god devours its worshippers; this would appear to be autobiography of a different sort, and may refer to MacDonald's resignation from his Arundel ministry.

In fact *Phantastes* is many things, and an exclusively sexual interpretation ignores many other layers of meaning—or at least, layers of implied meaning, for MacDonald was not usually an allegorist. He denied that *Phantastes* was an allegory, called it simply a "fairy tale," and elsewhere asserted that fairy stories such as he wrote did not have one specific meaning. He continued: "Everyone, however, who feels the story, will read its meaning after his own nature and development. . . . A genuine work of art must mean many things; the truer its art, the more things it will mean." MacDonald, in other words, wished to be a myth-maker rather than an allegorist. C. S. Lewis judged him to have succeeded in this more than any other modern writer, and indeed it is hard to think of any other nineteenth or twentieth-century author who excelled him in sheer fertility of mythic imagination.

> Humphrey Carpenter, "George MacDonald and the Tender Grandmother," *Secret Gardens: A Study of the Golden Age of Children's Literature* (Boston: Houghton Mifflin, 1985), pp. 79–80

RODERICK McGILLIS   In several ways Vane ⟨of *Lilith*⟩ and Anodos ⟨of *Phantastes*⟩ are similar: both have scientific casts of mind; both are alone in the world; both have just graduated from Oxford; both have inherited a large estate; and neither has had to work for his daily bread. Both are Philistines: money and social position are criteria of social respectability. They are, in words which Mr. Raven applies to society in general, "childish" and "self-satisfied." Vane's first thoughts on finding himself in the strange land are concerned with economy, the getting of money and food: "I have never yet done anything to justify my existence; my former world was nothing the better for my sojourn in it: here, however, I must earn, or in some way find, my bread! But I reasoned that, as I was not to blame in being here, I might expect to be taken care of here as well as there! I had nothing to do with getting into the world I had just left, and in it I found myself heir to a large property!" Anodos too thinks of money early in the book, inspecting his purse to pay the woman in whose cottage he rests before embarking on his journey through fairy land. This interest in money and what it signifies—accumulation, possession, domination, power, desire, control, retention—diminishes as Anodos and Vane proceed on their journey.

If there is a difference between the two books, it is in the deepening of the books' imagery; *Phantastes* is a mid-century fantasy influenced by Pre-Raphaelite medievalism, and *Lilith* expresses the *fin de siècle* mood with its deeper uncertainty. *Phantastes* is self-consciously about poetry. Anodos is a poet, and MacDonald originally planned to make Vane a writer, but he changed his mind when he wrote the second version of *Lilith*. Although both books develop the themes of language and reading, *Lilith* does not deal directly with the poet and art; instead it deals with everyman's life-struggle against an evil that is as much external as it is psychological. The Fairy Palace in *Phantastes* represents the poet's imagination and its dancers are emblems of art. In *Lilith* this place appears as the castle overgrown with parasitic ivy, a hollow shell, and its dancers present a frightening vision of the predestined round which all men must take. ⟨. . .⟩

Phantastes, which MacDonald subtitles "*A Faerie Romance for Men and Women*," contains a genuine fairy land: it begins with the conventional fairy story motif that has the main character confronted by a fairy who will grant him a wish, and the animistic world of the tale contains humanized trees, enchanted gardens and woods, nasty goblins, old witches, and gallant knights. The plot is loose and diffuse like that of *The Faerie Queene*, and the prose is highly metaphoric. *Lilith*, on the other hand, has the haunting quality of a dream. The prose is much tougher, reflecting the barren landscape. The plot is concentrated and the whole more dramatic with a great deal of dialogue. Vane, unlike Anodos, is constantly asking questions and struggling to understand the world in which he finds himself. A greater sense of urgency pervades this book.

Roderick McGillis, "*Phantastes* and *Lilith*: Femininity and Freedom," *The Gold Thread: Essays on George MacDonald*, ed. William Raeper (Edinburgh: Edinburgh University Press, 1990), pp. 32–33

▥ *Bibliography*

Twelve of the Spiritual Songs of Novalis (translator). 1851.

Hymns and Sacred Songs (editor; with others). 1855.

Within and Without: A Dramatic Poem. 1855.

Poems. 1857.

Phantastes: A Faerie Romance for Men and Women. 1858.

David Elginbrod. 1863. 3 vols.

Adela Cathcart. 1864. 3 vols.

A Hidden Life and Other Poems. 1864.

The Portent: A Story of the Inner Vision of the Highlanders, Commonly Called the Second Sight. 1864.

Alec Forbes of Howglen. 1865. 3 vols.

Annals of a Quiet Neighbourhood. 1867. 3 vols.

Dealings with the Fairies. 1867.

The Disciple and Other Poems. 1867.

ʼΕπεα ʼΑπτερα: *Unspoken Sermons.* 1867, 1886, 1889. 3 vols.

Guild Court. 1868. 3 vols.

Robert Falconer. 1868. 3 vols.

England's Antiphon. 1868.

The Seaboard Parish. 1868. 3 vols.

The Miracles of Our Lord. 1870.

At the Back of the North Wind. 1871.

Ranald Bannerman's Boyhood. 1871.

Works of Fancy and Imagination. 1871. 10 vols.

The Princess and the Goblin. 1872.

The Vicar's Daughter: An Autobiographical Story ⟨*Wilfrid Cumbermede: An Autobiographical Story*⟩. 1872. 3 vols.

Gutta Percha Willie, the Working Genius. 1873.

Malcolm. 1875. 3 vols.

The Wise Woman: A Parable. 1875.

Exotics: A Translation of the Spiritual Songs of Novalis, the Hymn-Book of Luther, and Other Poems from the German and Italian. 1876.

Thomas Wingfold, Curate. 1876. 3 vols.

St. George and St. Michael. 1876. 3 vols.

The Marquis of Lossie. 1877. 3 vols.

Sir Gibbie. 1879. 3 vols.

Paul Faber, Surgeon. 1879. 3 vols.

A Book of Strife in the Form of the Diary of an Old Soul. 1880.

Cheerful Words from the Writings of George MacDonald. Ed. E. E. Brown. 1880.

Mary Marston. 1881.

Castle Warlock: A Homely Romance. 1882. 3 vols.

Orts. 1882, 1883 (as *The Imagination and Other Essays*).

Weighed and Wanting. 1882. 3 vols.

The Gifts of the Child Christ and Other Tales. 1882. 2 vols.

A Threefold Cord: Poems by Three Friends (with Greville E. Matheson and John Hill MacDonald). 1883.

Stephen Archer and Other Tales. 1883.

Donal Grant. 1883. 3 vols.

The Princess and Curdie. 1883.

The Tragedie of Hamlet, Prince of Denmark, with a Study of the Text of the Folio of 1623. 1885.

Selections from the Writings of George MacDonald; or, Helps for Weary Souls. Ed. J. Dewey. 1885.

An Old Story. 1886.

What's Mine's Mine. 1886. 3 vols.

Poems. Ed. V⟨ida⟩ D. S⟨cudder⟩ and C⟨lara⟩ F⟨rench⟩. 1887.

Home Again. 1887.

The Elect Lady. 1888.

A Rough Shaking. 1890.

A Cabinet of Gems by Sir Philip Sidney (editor). 1891.

There and Back. 1891. 3 vols.

The Flight of the Shadow. 1891.

Heather and Snow. 1893. 2 vols.

Poetical Works. 1893. 2 vols.

The Light Princess and Other Fairy Tales. 1893.

"Beautiful Thoughts" from George MacDonald. Ed. Elizabeth W. Dougall. 1894.

Lilith: A Romance. 1895.

Rampoli: Growths from a Long-Planted Root: Translations, New and Old, Chiefly from the German, Along with a Year's Diary of an Old Soul. 1897.

Salted with Fire. 1897.

Fairy Tales. Ed. Greville MacDonald. 1904 (5 vols.), 1924.

Daily Readings from George MacDonald. Ed. James Dobson. 1906.

The Pocket George MacDonald. Ed. Alfred H. Hyatt. 1906.

A Light to Live By: A Selection of Passages form the Unspoken Sermons. Ed. Frances M. Nicholson. 1909.

A Book of Life from the Works of George MacDonald. Ed. W. L. T. and S. M. T. 1913.

Short Stories. 1928.

Gathered Grace: A Short Selection of George MacDonald's Poems. Ed. Elizabeth
    Yates. 1938.

God's Troubadour: The Devotional Verse. Ed. Harry Escott. 1940.

In My Father's House: Selections from the Prose Writings. Ed. Harry Escott.
    1943.

George MacDonald: An Anthology. Ed. C. S. Lewis. 1946.

Visionary Novels: Lilith; Phantastes. Ed. Anne Fremantle. 1954.

The Light Princess and Other Tales: Being the Complete Fairy Stories. 1961.

Evenor. Ed. Lin Carter. 1972.

William Morris
1834–1896

WILLIAM MORRIS was born in Walthamstow, Essex, on March 24, 1834, the son of a successful London stockbroker. He was educated at the Malborough School, and in 1853 entered Exeter College, Cambridge, where he became friends with Edward Burne-Jones and other members of the Pre-Raphaelite circle, which met to read theology, medieval literature, Ruskin, and Tennyson, and to share aesthetic theories. After receiving his degree in 1855, Morris worked briefly in the office of the architect G. E. Street during 1856, and in that same year was one of the originators of the *Oxford and Cambridge Magazine*, to which he contributed poems, essays, and tales. During 1858 he worked with Dante Gabriel Rossetti, Burne-Jones, and others on the frescoes in the Oxford Union, and also published *The Defence of Guenevere and Other Poems*, which contains many of his most highly regarded verses, including "The Haystack in the Floods," "Concerning Geffray Teste Noire," "Shameful Death," and "Golden Wings."

In 1859, after marrying Jane Burden, Morris decided to build himself a house in which his own artistic ideals would be put into practice. The resulting home was the famous Red House at Upton, Kent, built from a design by architect Philip Webb and with furnishings designed and made by Morris and his friends. This experience led to the founding in 1861, with Burne-Jones, Webb, Ford Madox Brown, and others, of the firm of Morris, Marshall, Faulkner & Co., which produced furniture, printed textiles, tapestries, wallpaper, and stained glass. The firm did not succeed, as Morris had hoped, in introducing a new popular art based on craftsmanship rather than mass production, but it did help to bring about a profound change in Victorian taste.

In 1867 Morris published his poem *The Life and Death of Jason*, followed in 1868–70 by *The Earthly Paradise*, a collection of classical and medieval stories in verse that made him one of the most popular poets of the day. His poem *Love Is Enough*, based formally on the medieval morality play, appeared in 1872, and was followed by *The Story of Sigurd the Volsung* (1877), a long narrative poem inspired in part by a visit to Iceland in 1871.

In 1877 Morris founded the Society for the Protection of Ancient Monuments, and also became a member of the radical wing of the Liberal Party; from this time on he turned increasingly to political activity. He left London in 1878 for Merton Abbey, in Surrey, where he set up a carpet factory in 1881 and a printing press, the Kelmscott Press, in 1890. In 1883 he organized the Art Workers' Guild, and also joined the Social Democratic Federation. As the head of a group that had seceded from the Federation, Morris in 1884 founded the Socialist League, whose influential magazine, *Commonweal*, he also edited.

Morris's last volume of verse, *Poems by the Way*, appeared in 1891. It contained political and miscellaneous poems, including three sections of *The Pilgrims of Hope* (1885–86), a verse story about the Paris Commune, as well as some of the *Chants for Socialists* (1884–85). *A Dream of John Ball* (1888) and *News from Nowhere* (1890) are both prose fantasies about socialist utopias, while *The House of the Wolfings* (1889), *The Roots of the Mountains* (1890), *The Story of the Glittering Plain* (1890), *The Wood beyond the World* (1894), *The Well at the World's End* (1896), and *The Sundering Flood* (1898) are all historical romances set in the distant past of northern Europe, and are heavily influenced by Morris's admiration for the Middle Ages. All these romances, as well as other works by Morris, were published by his own Kelmscott Press, for which he designed typefaces, ornamental letters, and borders.

In 1892 Morris refused the opportunity of becoming Poet Laureate on the death of Tennyson, as he had earlier (1877) refused the offer of the professorship of poetry at Oxford. William Morris died at his home in Hammersmith on October 3, 1896. He was survived by his wife and two daughters, one of whom, May (b. 1862), later brought out Morris's collected works in twenty-four volumes (1910–15).

◈ *Critical Extracts*

THEODORE WATTS-DUNTON   ⟨. . .⟩ when, as in Mr. Morris's romances, the form of imaginative literature is imbued throughout with poetical colour rendered in a perfectly concrete diction—when the sentences (built on the simple method of poetry and not on the complex method of prose) have a cadence in which *recognized* metrical law has been abandoned, a cadence whose movement is born of the emotions which the words embody—may not such a form of literature be properly called poetry? ⟨. . .⟩

⟨. . .⟩ Intensely poetic and intensely dramatic ⟨. . .⟩ as are the Icelandic Sagas, they are lacking in one of the most delightful qualities of the unmetrical poems of Mr. Morris ⟨. . .⟩—that delicate sense of beauty in which the author of *The Earthly Paradise* has had no superior even in the epoch which has inaugurated the neo-romantic movement; and this last exquisite story of his ⟨*The Wood beyond the World*⟩ must be held to surpass the best of its predecessors in poetical feeling and poetical colour, and to equal them in poetical abundance. Here more abundantly than ever we get that marvellously youthful way of confronting the universe which is the special feature of Mr. Morris's genius. It is not easy to realize that it is other than a poet in the heyday of a glorious youth who tells with such gusto this wonderful story, how once upon a time, in the Land of Somewhere, young Golden Walter, on the eve of taking ship for foreign lands, saw a sight which at one moment seemed real and at another a dream ⟨. . .⟩

> Theodore Watts-Dunton, [Review of *The Wood beyond the World*], *Athenaeum*, 2 March 1895, p. 273

H. G. WELLS   It is Malory, enriched and chastened by the thought and learning of six centuries, this story of Ralph and his Quest of the Well at the World's End. It is Malory, with the glow of the dawn of the Twentieth Century warming his tapestries and beaten metal. It is Malory, but instead of the mystic Grail, the search for long life and the beauty of strength. And women as well as men go a questing. Tennyson, too, gave us Malory, but with the Grail—as remote and attenuated indeed as the creed of a Broad Churchman, but the Grail still, and for the simple souls of the future and the past, all the involved gentilities of the middle Victorian years. Morris is altogether more ancient and more modern.

Save that its spirit is living, the story does not seem to be coherently symbolical. Such analysis as a transient reviewer may give discovers no clue to a coherent construction. Life is too short for many admirable things— for chess, and the unravelling of the *Faerie Queen* and of such riddles as this. Ever and again the tale is certainly shot and enriched with allegory. But as we try to follow these glittering strands, they spread, twist, vanish, one after the other, in the texture of some purely decorative incident. In the tale of the upbringing of the girl, for instance, in the little house of the

Crofts, there are the strangest parallelisms with some of the deepest facts of life; and then, hither, thither leap the threads, and we are among sturdy knights and splintering spears under the greenwood tree ⟨. . .⟩

Symbolical, too, seems the Dry Tree and the Thirsty Desert across which the two seekers ride to the Well. And between the men of the Burgh and the Wheat Wearers is something dimly like our present discontents. ⟨. . .⟩

And free of all symbolic trammels is the naked beauty of the last three chapters in Book III.; chapters whose very headings are a cry of delight. "They came to the Ocean Sea," "Now they Drink of the Well at the World's End," and "Now have they Drunk and are Glad."

The book is to be read, not simply for pleasure. To those who write its pages will be a purification, it is full of clean strong sentences and sweet old words. "Quean" and "carle," "eme," "good sooth," "yeasay" and "naysay," we may never return to, nor ever again "seek *to*" a man, but "fain" and "lief" and "loth" and "sunder," and the like good honest words, will come all the readier after this reading.

And all the workmanship of the book is stout oaken stuff that must needs endure and preserve the memory of one of the stoutest, cleanest lives that has been lived in these latter days.

> H. G. Wells, [Review of *The Well at the World's End*], *Saturday Review* (London), 17 October 1896, pp. 414–15.

MARGARET R. GRENNAN   Unlike *A Dream of John Ball*, which began the period of prose romances, or *News from Nowhere*, the fourth in the series, the other eight were not written with a socialist audience in view. They were never intended to "delight the naive minds of the Victorian working classes." Indeed, if the typical British workingman could have found pleasure in them it would have argued one of Morris' dearest aims accomplished: the restoration to the ordinary man of the joy in the legendary past. The stories were intended, rather, to delight William Morris and those who could follow him in his knowledge of the romantic tradition. The pleasure in reading them arises not from an ignorant and naive wonder but from the recognition of old motifs in a new setting. ⟨. . .⟩

These romances were written during the most difficult years of Morris' life: when he was trying to share with men, to whom "the grey homes of their fathers had no story to tell," his vision of the new world to be born of the best traditions of the old. ⟨. . .⟩ the prose romances, the holiday work of the reformer weary of platform speaking, are like the opening of the flood gates. There is no need to convince, to persuade, or to clarify. The arid fields ploughed by party logic, with only here and there a green and flowery clearing formed by the large and more familiar patterns of the past, are now filled by a rush of memories. Seven volumes of the twenty-four in the complete works are devoted to this literature of "escape"—but it is escape to the poet's larger world. It is unthinkable that they should have little to tell of the man, written as they were during the years when he lived most intensely. ⟨. . .⟩

⟨. . .⟩ At the heart of these prose tales is an earthly paradise in which life is not "too short for the deed that dies not," where men and women, always experiencing to the full the joy of changing seasons and the pleasure in growing things, live happily, "knowing nothing that is too far off or too great for the affections." It is a vision of purely natural happiness and its creator, as Yeats recognized, would never be among those who "would have prayed in old times in some chapel of the star, but among those who would have prayed under the shadow of the green tree and on the wet stones of the well among the worshippers of natural abundance." The German student who solemnly listed the "flora and fauna" of the prose romances blundered close to the truth. There is a world here, real enough to have its flora and fauna catalogued and its cities described in some prophetic Baedeker. It encompasses what Morris thought good for man, realized in the best days of the past and coming again with the fulfillment of his "hope of the days to be."

Margaret R. Grennan, *William Morris: Medievalist and Revolutionary* (New York: King's Crown Press, 1945), pp. 106–8

NORTHROP FRYE   Of the famous utopias, the one which shows pastoral influence most consistently is William Morris' *News from Nowhere*. ⟨. . .⟩ It was an attempt to visualize the ultimate utopian goal of Communism after the classless society had been reached, and the reader is not asked whether he thinks the social conception practicable, but simply whether or not he likes the picture. The picture is considerably more anarchist than Communist: the local community is the sole source of a completely decentralized authority, and the centralizing economic tendencies have disappeared along with the political ones. There is, in other words, a minimum of industrial and factory production. Morris started out, not with the Marxist question, "Who are the workers?" but with the more deeply revolutionary question "What is work?" ⟨. . .⟩ Morris was influenced by

Carlyle, who, though he tended to imply that all work was good, and unpleasant work particularly beneficial to the moral fiber, still did succeed, in *Sartor Resartus*, in distinguishing work from drudgery as well as from idleness. Ruskin, though also with a good deal of dithering, followed this up, and established the principle that Morris never departed from: work is creative act, the expression of what is creative in the worker. Any work that falls short of this is drudgery, and drudgery is exploitation, producing only the mechanical, the ugly, and the useless. We notice that in Morris we need an esthetic, and hence imaginative, criterion to make any significant social judgment. According to Morris the pleasure in craftsmanship was what kept the medieval workers from revolution: this leads to the unexpected inference that, in an exploiting society, genuine work is the opiate of the people. In the society of the future, however, work has become a direct expression of the controlled energy of conscious life.

In Morris' state "manufacture" has become hand work, and the basis of production is in what are still called the minor or lesser arts, those that are directly related to living conditions. In terms of the societies we know, Morris' ideal is closer to the Scandinavian way of life than to the Russian or the American. To make craftsmanship the basis of industry implies an immense simplification of human wants—this is the pastoral element in Morris' vision. ⟨. . .⟩ The pastoral theme of the unity of man and physical nature is very prominent. Around the corner, perhaps, looms the specter of endless picnics and jolly community gatherings and similar forms of extroverted cheer; but the sense of this is hardly oppressive even to a cynical reader. There is a certain anti-intellectual quality, perhaps in the rather childlike inhabitants, their carefree ignorance of history and their neglect of the whole contemplative side of education. It is briefly suggested at the end that perhaps this society will need to mature sufficiently to take account of the more contemplative virtues if it is to escape the danger of losing its inheritance, as Adam did, through an uncritical perverseness of curiosity. In the meantime we are indebted to the most unreligious of the great English writers for one of the most convincing pictures of the state of innocence.

Northrop Frye, "Varieties of Literary Utopias," *Daedalus* 94, No. 2 (Spring 1965): 342–44.

PETER FAULKNER   Since the prose style of ⟨Morris's⟩ romances has been seriously criticised for its quaintness and archaism, said to be allied

to the escapist suggestions of the subject-matter, it is appropriate to examine
a passage near the opening of ⟨The Wood beyond the World⟩ in some detail:

> Now ye may well deem that such a youngling as this was looked
> upon by all as a lucky man without a lack; but there was this flaw
> in his lot, whereas he had fallen into the toils of love of a woman
> exceeding fair, and had taken her to wife, she nought
> unwilling as it seemed. But when they had been wedded some
> six months he found by manifest tokens, that his fairness
> was not so much to her but that she must seek to the foulness
> of one worser than he in all ways; wherefore his rest departed
> from him, whereas he hated her for her untruth and her hatred
> of him; yet would the sound of her voice, as she came and
> went in the house, make his heart beat; and the sight of her
> stirred desire within him, so that he longed for her to be
> sweet and kind with him, and deemed that, might it be so, he
> should forget all the evil gone by. But it was not so; for ever
> when she saw him, her face changed, and her hatred of him
> became manifest, and howsoever she were sweet with others,
> with him she was hard and sour.

Clearly Morris is using language in a very different way from Gissing, because
he wants to take the reader at once into an imaginative realm, rather than
to confront him with the world of ordinary experience. The diction—which
has excited so much criticism—is chosen for the end. In these paragraphs
the idiosyncratic elements are: ye may . . . deem; youngling; without a lack;
whereas (= because); exceeding fair; she nought unwilling; wedded; seek
to; worser; wherefore; untruth; howsoever. A consistent feature throughout
the romances is the use of the second person singular, especially in dialogue—
a common enough usage in authors aiming at a non-modern effect. The
diction is remarkable for the purity of its Old English emphasis. Morris
avoids words deriving from Latin or French when Teutonic equivalents are
available, and succeeds to a remarkable extent in demonstrating his version
of what R. C. Trench had envisaged in a chapter of his English, Past and
Present in 1855 entitled 'English as It Might Have Been' without the Norman
Conquest. None of the words used is obscure or difficult for the modern
reader, with the possible exception of 'whereas' used in the sense of because.
Some remind one of the Authorised Version of the Bible; a few, usually
those adapted from a familiar word, like 'youngling' and 'seek to', suggest
an extravagant determination to avoid conventional verbal forms. But it is
misleading to suggest that such elements predominate in the diction. ⟨. . .⟩
Some sentences are long, but these usually consist of a number of parallel
clauses rather than exhibiting complex syntax; semicolons are particularly

numerous, and relationships are usually expressed by the simple conjunctions (and, but yet) or relatives. This helps to create a sense of direct movement, in which the narrator is felt to be firmly in command of his material, which he presents in this clear and methodical way and in a mainly chronological sequence. Thus the reader who persists with the story after the first few paragraphs finds that there is a sustained thrust in the monosyllabic style which is appropriate to the succession of adventures of which the story consists. It is unfair to Morris's achievement in the romances to note the elements of archaism in the diction as if these superseded other elements of style.

> Peter Faulkner, *Against the Age: An Introduction to William Morris* (London: George Allen & Unwin, 1980), pp. 166–68

AMANDA HODGSON   An example of the romance protagonists' need to come to terms with their own past occurs in *The Water of the Wondrous Isles*. Birdalone, snatched from her home and her mother, is brought up by the witch whose control over the child parodies the care of a natural parent. From this tyranny Birdalone escapes with the aid of a second substitute mother, the wood-spirit Habundia, whose benevolence opposes the witch's cruelty. ⟨. . .⟩ Eventually ⟨. . .⟩ she meets her real mother and experiences a period of calm, contented life with her. When her mother dies Birdalone is drawn to retrace her steps. ⟨. . .⟩ At length she arrives, naked as she left, at the house of her witch-mistress—to find that powerful figure of her childhood dead at the door of their cottage ⟨. . .⟩ The cottage now becomes a place of love for Birdalone and Arthur. And there too Birdalone's new ascendancy over Habundia is demonstrated: when the spirit enters the cottage she immediately diminishes in size.

As in fairy-tales of the wicked stepmother, the several mother figures in this romance seem to embody ambivalent feelings in the child towards its parent. Feelings of frustration at the exercising of adult control are projected onto the witch; the need to trust a loving adult is related to Habundia. When Birdalone has set childhood behind her (and faced adult problems connected with her own sexuality) she meets her mother as an equal and friend, without the mediation of fantasy figures. Yet she does not fully escape from the emotional force of her own past until her mother dies, leaving Birdalone an autonomous human being. Then she is able to face her past and to discover that the witch-mother has no further power—while the spirit-mother, still benevolent, is less powerful than Birdalone herself. In her new adult selfhood, then, Birdalone can become a mature woman through sexual experience. Her feelings of contented security in the cottage express her integration with her past, which is no longer a source of remembered pain and fear. ⟨. . .⟩

Birdalone's progression to maturity involves her rejection of the power of the witch over her actions. As an adolescent (she is seventeen when she first meets Habundia) she begins to learn about the world, and with knowledge inevitably comes loss of innocence. When she goes back to her mistress after her first talk with Habundia, she discovers that 'in her heart now was some guile born to meet the witch's guile'. She finds a new courage, which enables her to stand up to her mistress's scoldings and threats, and the witch herself seems to realize that Birdalone has attained a degree of maturity. It is not enough, however, for the child to begin to assert itself against the controlling powers. It must at length take responsibility for its actions, and escape altogether from parental rule. Against Habundia's wishes, Birdalone eventually refuses to continue her life of deception in the witch's cottage. She tells her wood-mother:

> thy wisdom which thou hast set in my heart hath learned me
> that for these last months I have been meeting guile with
> guile and lies with lies. And now will I do so no more, lest I
> become a guileful woman.

She flees, naked, from the witch, and enters the world. Yet she is not free from the effects of her upbringing; ironically, her beauty and goodness do cause some of the misery and havoc which her mistress intended to provoke. She cannot find rest and fulfilled love ⟨. . .⟩ until she has returned to the cottage to face the wrath of her mistress. In other words, she must confront the power which ruled and tried to warp her childhood to prove that she has broken free from it.

Amanda Hodgson, *The Romances of William Morris* (Cambridge: Cambridge University Press, 1987), pp. 169–71, 173

CAROLE G. SILVER   In Morris's final romances erotic passion is itself informed by socialist thought. Relationships are interclass and free of economic considerations. Golden Walter, the son of a great merchant, weds the Maid, a thrall of unknown parentage. Ursula, the yeoman's daughter, is the bride of Ralph, son of a minor king. Birdalone, the child of a widow reduced to beggary, unites with a noble knight, Arthur, while her friend,

Aurea, a "lady of high degree," finds happiness with Robert Gerardson, a freeman's son. Only ignorant or evil characters question lineage and they are always silenced. When marriage occurs, it is often a voluntary private union that does not need the sanction of religion or law. Never is it the bourgeois institution that Engels condemned as an "official cloak of prostitution" and Morris denigrated as an arrangement designed to protect individual property and to resist such external forces as fellowship.

Since love is not tied to property and women ideally are not tokens of exchange, "free unions" among lovers meet with approval. In a conventional Victorian novel, the love of Ralph and the Lady of Abundance would be treated as adultery; in the terms established in a Morrisian romance, the relationship is acceptable because it is loving. Birdalone and Arthur simply make love to "wed" each other, while the nature of the union of Osberne and Elfhild, in *The Sundering Flood*, is never even discussed. Lovers love and unite and for Morris that union is enough.

In effect, Morris's last romances simply and undidactically praise lovers, workers, outlaws, and all who practice association and equality. Without overtly preaching, these works clearly proclaim the worth of joyful labor, cooperation, and mutual aid, and the possibility of harmonizing personal and communal needs. At the same time, they repudiate capitalist idealogy and the literary form that bears it. Like the works of literature Morris praised in his lecture on "The Society of the Future," his final prose fictions "tell their tales to our senses and leave them alone to moralize the tale so told." Through their internalized Marxism and direct sensory appeal, they constitute a new literary genre, the socialist romance.

> Carole G. Silver, "Socialism Internalized: The Last Romances of William Morris," *Socialism and the Literary Artistry of William Morris*, ed. Florence S. Boos and Carole G. Silver (Columbia: University of Missouri Press, 1990), pp. 125–26

▧ *Bibliography*

The Defence of Guenevere and Other Poems. 1858.

The Life and Death of Jason. 1867.

The Earthly Paradise. 1868–70. 3 vols.

Grettis Saga: The Story of Grettir the Strong (translator; with Eiríkr Magnússon). 1869.

Völsunga Saga: The Story of the Volsungs & Niblungs with Certain Songs from the Elder Edda (translator; with Eiríkr Magnússon). 1870.

Love Is Enough; or, The Freeing of Pharamond: A Morality. 1873.

Three Northern Love Stories, and Other Tales (translator; with Eiríkr Magnússon). 1875.

The Aeneids of Virgil Done into English Verse. 1876.

The Two Sides of the River, Hapless Love, and The First Foray of Aristomenes. 1876 ⟨or perhaps 1894?⟩.

The Story of Sigurd the Volsung and the Fall of the Niblungs. 1877.

Wake, London Lads! 1878.

The Decorative Arts: Their Relation to Modern Life and Progress: An Address Delivered before the Trades' Guild of Learning. 1878.

Address Delivered in the Town Hall, Birmingham. 1879.

Labour and Pleasure versus *Labour and Sorrow: An Address at Birmingham.* 1880.

Hopes and Fears for Art: Five Lectures Delivered in Birmingham, London, and Nottingham 1878–1881. 1882.

A Summary of the Principles of Socialism Written for the Democratic Federation (with H. M. Hyndman). 1884.

Art and Socialism: A Lecture; and Watchman: What of the Night? 1884.

Textile Fabrics: A Lecture Delivered in the Lecture Room of the International Health Exhibition. 1884.

Chants for Socialists: No. 1. The Day Is Coming. 1884.

The Voice of Toil, All for the Cause: Two Chants for Socialists. 1884.

The God of the Poor. 1885.

Chants for Socialists. 1885.

Socialists at Play: Prologue Spoken at the Entertainment of the Socialist League. 1885.

The Socialist League: Constitution and Rules Adopted at the General Conference. 1885.

Address to Trades' Unions (editor; with E. Belfort Bax). 1885.

The Manifesto of the Socialist League (with E. Belfort Bax). 1885.

Useful Work v. Useless Toil. 1885.

For Whom Shall We Vote? Addressed to the Working-men Electors of Great Britain. 1885.

What Socialists Want. 1885.

A Short Account of the Commune of Paris (with E. Belfort Bax and Victor Dave). 1886.

Socialism. 1886.

The Labour Question from the Socialist Standpoint. 1886, 1888 (as *True and False Society*).

The Pilgrims of Hope. 1886.

The Aims of Art. 1887.

The Tables Turned; or, Nupkins Awakened: A Socialist Interlude. 1887.

On the External Coverings of Roofs. 1887.

The Odyssey of Homer Done into English Verse. 1887. 2 vols.

Alfred Linnell, Killed at Trafalgar Square, November 20, 1887: A Death Song. 1887.

A Dream of John Ball and A King's Lesson. 1888.

Signs of Change: Seven Lectures Delivered on Various Occasions. 1888.

Atalanta's Race and Other Tales from The Earthly Paradise. Ed. Oscar Fay Adams. 1888.

A Tale of the House of the Wolfings and All the Kindreds of the Mark, Written in Prose and Verse. 1889.

The Roots of the Mountains: Wherein Is Told Somewhat of the Lives of the Men of Burgdale, Their Friends, Their Neighbours, Their Foemen, and Their Fellows in Arms. 1890.

Monopoly; or, How Labour Is Robbed. 1890.

Statement of Principles of the Hammersmith Socialist Society. 1890.

News from Nowhere; or, An Epoch of Rest: Being Some Chapters from a Utopian Romance. 1890, 1891.

The Socialist Ideal of Art. 1891.

The Story of the Glittering Plain Which Has Been Also Called the Land of Living Men or the Acre of the Undying. 1891.

Poems by the Way. 1891.

Address on the Collection of Paintings of the English Pre-Raphaelite School. 1891.

Under an Elm-Tree; or, Thoughts in the Country-side. 1891.

William Morris: Poet, Artist, Socialist: A Selection from His Writings. Ed. Francis Watts Lee. 1891.

The Saga Library (translator; with Eiríkr Magnússon). 1891–1905. 6 vols.

Manifesto of English Socialists (with H. M. Hyndman and George Bernard Shaw). 1893.

Arts and Crafts Essays (editor). 1893.

The Reward of Labour: A Dialogue. 1893.

The Tale of King Florus and the Fair Jehane (translator). 1893.

Concerning Westminster Abbey. 1893.

Socialism: Its Growth and Outcome (with E. Belfort Bax). 1893.

Help for the Miners: The Deeper Meaning of the Struggle. 1893.

Gothic Architecture: A Lecture for the Arts and Crafts Exhibition Society. 1893.

Of the Friendship of Amis and Amile (translator). 1894.

An Address Delivered at the Distribution of Prizes to Students of the Birmingham Municipal School of Art. 1894.

The Wood beyond the World. 1894.

Letters on Socialism. 1894.

The Tale of the Emperor Constans, and of Over Sea (translator). 1894.

The Why I Ams: Why I Am a Communist ⟨with Why I Am an Expropriationist by Louisa Sara Bevington⟩. 1894.

The Tale of Beowulf, Sometime King of the Folk of the Weder Geats (translator; with A. J. Wyatt). 1895.

Child Christopher and Goldilund the Fair. 1895. 2 vols.

The Legend of St. George and the Dragon (with Edward Burne-Jones). 1895.

Gossip about an Old House on the Upper Thames. 1895.

The Well at the World's End: A Tale. 1896.

Society for the Protection of Ancient Buildings. 1896.

Old French Romances (translator). 1896.

How I Became a Socialist. 1896.

Poetical Works. 1896. 10 vols.

The Water of the Wondrous Isles. 1897.

The Sundering Flood. Ed. May Morris. 1897.

A Note by William Morris on His Aims in Founding the Kelmscott Press. 1898.

Art and the Beauty of the Earth. 1898.

Some Hints on Pattern-Designing. 1899.

The Ideal Book: An Address. 1899.

Architecture and History, and Westminster Abbey. 1900.

Art and Its Producers, and The Arts & Crafts of Today: Two Addresses. 1901.

Architecture, Industry and Wealth: Collected Papers. 1902.

Communism: A Lecture. 1903.

The Hollow Land and Other Contributions to the Oxford and Cambridge Magazine (1856). 1903.

Collected Works. Ed. May Morris. 1910–15. 24 vols.

The Revolt of Ghent. 1911.

Prose and Poetry (1856–1870). 1913.

Selections from the Prose Works. Ed. A. H. R. Ball. 1931.

Stories in Prose, Stories in Verse, Shorter Poems, Lectures and Essays. Ed. G. D. H. Cole. 1934.

On Art and Socialism: Essays and Lectures. Ed. Holbrook Jackson. 1947.

Letters to His Family and Friends. Ed. Philip Henderson. 1950.

Unpublished Letters. Ed. R. Page Arnot. 1951.

Mr. Morris on Art Matters. 1961.

Selected Writings and Designs. Ed. Asa Briggs. 1962.

Icelandic Journals. Ed. James Morris. 1969.

A Choice of William Morris's Verse. Ed. Geoffrey Grigson. 1969.

Unpublished Lectures. Ed. Eugene D. LeMire. 1969.

Early Romances in Prose and Verse. Ed. Peter Faulkner. 1973.

Political Writings. Ed. A. L. Morton. 1973.

A Book of Verse: A Facsimile of the Manuscript Written in 1870. 1980.

The Ideal Book: Essays and Lectures on the Arts of the Book. Ed. William S. Peterson. 1982.

Juvenilia. Ed. Florence Boos. 1983.

Collected Letters. Ed. Norman Kelvin. 1984- . 3 vols. (to date).

William Morris by Himself: Designs and Writings. Ed. Gillian Naylor. 1988.

Beatrix Potter
1866–1943

HELEN BEATRIX POTTER, the only daughter in a wealthy family, was born on July 28, 1866. Although she was privately educated and spent most of her childhood in London, the Potters made regular trips to Scotland and to the Lake District. From an early age Potter showed a talent for drawing the plants and animals that she grew to love from her trips to the country. Her drawings of fungi resulted in her writing the unpublished *The Germination of the Spores of Agriculture*, which was presented to the Linnaean Society of London by a male friend (women were not allowed to attend meetings) in 1896. She also amused herself by including illustrated children's tales in letters to children she knew.

It was not until 1901, however, that she first wrote with a view to publication. Potter created *The Tale of Peter Rabbit* by rewriting and greatly expanding an eight-page illustrated letter written in 1893 to an invalid child of a friend (luckily the child, Noel Moore, saved the letter and returned it to her). It was rejected by several publishers but was a great success when Potter printed a private edition. After agreeing to revise *Peter Rabbit* and replace her black and white sketches with watercolor paintings Potter was able to get the book published by Frederick Warne & Company. From this time onward she produced a steady stream of illustrated books that became children's classics—among them *The Tailor of Gloucester* (1902), *The Tale of Squirrel Nutkin* (1903), *The Tale of Benjamin Bunny* (1904), *Mrs Tiggy-Winkle* (1905), and *The Tale of Jemima Puddle-Duck* (1908).

In 1905 Potter became engaged to one of her editors, Norman Warne. Her parents strongly objected to her marrying one who was engaged "in trade." (The elder Potters' obsession with class affected all their children; Beatrix's brother, Bertram, informed her in 1912 that he had been secretly married to a farmer's daughter for eleven years.) Their objection was needless, however, for Warne, never in good health, died later that year of acute anemia. In 1906, before Warne died, Potter bought the Hill Top farm at

Sawrey, the first of several Lancashire farms she would own and vacation in, and the setting for several of her books.

Her property was managed by a solicitor, William Heelis, whom Potter married (again over the objections of her parents) in 1913. Only at this point, at age forty-seven, did Potter move her residence from her parents' house to Lancashire. After her marriage she devoted herself largely to managing her household and farm and breeding pedigree sheep. She produced few books, and those she did were reworkings of older, unpublished material and are not considered the equal of her earlier work.

After her death on December 22, 1943, in Lancashire, several volumes of a journal from her early years were discovered. Written in a private code and in a microscopic hand, it baffled students of her life for many years. The code was broken in 1958, but it was not until the end of 1961 that the work of transcribing the journal was completed. It was published in 1966.

▨ *Critical Extracts*

UNSIGNED   If *The Tailor of Gloucester*, by Beatrix Potter, is not altogether so delightful as its dainty predecessors *Peter Rabbit* and *Squirrel Nutkin*, it still makes an excellent third to this pretty trio, and a pleasing contrast with many of the coarse and flaunting colour-schemes and inane letter-press that fill too many of this year's picture story-books. To no artist, not even the delicate draughtsmen of Japan, has been vouchsafed a more intimate expression of the charm of the "little and fubsy" than we find here. Miss Potter possesses a really extraordinary faculty for portraying little furry bright-eyed folk with a most poetic realism. The story itself harmonizes with the illustrations in its naïve simplicity, touched with quiet humour; and it were indeed a stony-hearted child who could remain indifferent to the tale of the kind tailor, his selfish cat, and the little brown mice whose fairy labours bring about a happy conclusion.

Unsigned, [Review of *The Tailor of Gloucester*], *Athenaeum*, 14 November 1903, p. 648

GRAHAM GREENE   Looking backward over the thirty years of Miss Potter's literary career, we see that the creation of Mr Puddle-Duck marked the beginning of a new period. At some time between 1907 and 1909 Miss Potter must have passed through an emotional ordeal which changed the character of her genius. It would be impertinent to inquire into the nature of the ordeal. Her case is curiously similar to that of Henry James. Something happened which shook their faith in appearance. From *The Portrait of a Lady* onwards, innocence deceived, the treachery of friends, became the theme of James's greatest stories. Mme Merle, Kate Croy, Mme de Vionnet, Charlotte Stant, these tortuous treacherous women are paralleled through the dark period of Miss Potter's art. 'A man can smile and smile and be a villain,' that, a little altered, was her recurrent message, expressed by her gallery of scoundrels: Mr Drake Puddle-Duck, the first and slightest, Mr Jackson, the least harmful with his passion for honey and his reiterated, 'No teeth. No teeth. No teeth', Samuel Whiskers, gross and brutal, and the 'gentleman with sandy whiskers' who may be identified with Mr Tod. With the publication of *Mr Tod* in 1912, Miss Potter's pessimism reached its climax. But for the nature of her audience *Mr Tod* would certainly have ended tragically. In *Jemima Puddle-Duck* the gentleman with sandy whiskers had at least a debonair impudence when he addressed his victim:

> 'Before you commence your tedious sitting, I intend to give you a treat. Let us have a dinner party all to ourselves!
> 'May I ask you to bring up some herbs from the farm garden to make a savoury omelette? Sage and thyme, and mint and two onions, and some parsley. I will provide lard for the stuff—lard for the omelette,' said the hospitable gentleman with sandy whiskers.

But no charm softens the brutality of Mr Tod and his enemy, the repulsive Tommy Brock. In her comedies Miss Potter had gracefully eliminated the emotions of love and death; it is the measure of her genius that when, in *The Tale of Mr Tod*, they broke the barrier, the form of her book, her ironic style, remained unshattered. When she could not keep death out she stretched her technique to include it. Benjamin and Peter had grown up and married, and Benjamin's babies were stolen by Brock; the immortal pair, one still neurotic, the other knowing and imperturbable, set off to the rescue, but the rescue, conducted in darkness, from a house, 'something between a cave, a prison, and a tumbledown pig-sty', compares grimly with an earlier rescue from Mr MacGregor's sunny vegetable garden ⟨. . .⟩ *Mr Tod* marked the distance which Miss Potter had travelled since the ingenuous romanticism of *The Tailor of Gloucester*.

Graham Greene, "Beatrix Potter" (1933), *Collected Essays* (New York: Viking Press, 1969), pp. 177–78

BEATRIX POTTER   I have been asked to tell again how Peter Rabbit came to be written. It seems a long time ago; and in another world. Though after all the world does not change much in the country, where the seasons follow their accustomed course—the green leaf and the sere— and where nature, though never consciously wicked, has always been ruthless.

In towns there is change. People begin to burrow underground like rabbits. The lame boy for whom Peter was invented more than forty years ago [Noel Moore] is now an air warden in a bombed London parish.

I have never quite understood the secret of Peter's perennial charm. Perhaps it is because he and his little friends keep on their way, busily absorbed with their own doings. They were always independant [sic]. Like Topsy—they just "grow'd". Their names especially seemed to be inevitable. I never knew a gardiner [sic] named "McGregor". Several bearded horticulturalists have resented the nick-name; but I do not know how it came about; nor why "Peter" was called "Peter". It is regrettable that a small boy once inquired audibly whether the Apostle was Peter Rabbit? There is great difficulty in finding, or inventing, names void of all possible embarassment [sic]. A few of the characters were harmless skits or cariacatures [sic]; but "Mr McGregor" was not one of them, and the backgrounds of Peter Rabbit are a mixture of locality.

"Squirrel Nutkin" lived on the shore of Derwentwater Lake near Keswick, and "Mrs Tiggy Winkle" in the nearby valley of Newlands. "Jemima Puddleduck", "Jeremy Fisher" and others lived at Sawrey in the southern part of the English Lake District.

The earlier books, including the later printed *Pig Robinson*, were written for real children in picture letters of scribbled pen and ink. I confess that afterward I painted most of the little pictures to please myself. The more spontaneous the pleasure—the more happy the result.

I do not remember a time when I did not try to invent pictures and make for myself a fairyland amongst the wild flowers, the animals, fungi, mosses, woods and streams, all the thousand objects of the countryside; that pleasant, unchanging world of realism and romance, which in our northern clime is stiffened by hard weather, a tough ancestry, and the strength that comes from the hills.

Beatrix Potter, Letter to Bertha Mahony Miller (25 November 1940), *Beatrix Potter's Letters*, ed. Judy Taylor (London: Frederick Warne, 1989), pp. 422–23

MARGARET LANE   Conveying truth by means of fantasy, enlarging our perception of life by poetic means, is one of the highest functions

of art, and it is not extravagant to say that in her small and special sphere
Beatrix Potter performed it.   She understood and loved the little animals
that she drew and painted, and perceiving—perhaps even without being
aware, for her response to imaginative stimulus was most innocent and
direct—perceiving that invisible thread of sympathy which runs through
the whole animal creation, including man, she interpreted her animals in
human terms. Displayed in the trappings of their human counterparts, they
reveal their own true natures by oblique methods, and we ever after know
more about them from having observed their behaviour in significant disguise. Mrs. Tiggy-Winkle, that 'scrupulously clean little animal', gets her
living by washing and ironing; Jemima Puddle-Duck, laying first in the rick-
yard, then under the rhubarb leaves, and finally, in desperation, in the foxy-
whiskered gentleman's wood-shed, raises the theme of frustrated maternity
almost to the level of a farmyard tragedy, and displays as well—as no
other story could better prove—the idiotic innocence of her kind. Mrs.
Tittlemouse, the 'woodmouse with a long tail', is exquisitely domesticated,
a 'most terribly tidy particular little mouse, always sweeping and dusting
the soft sandy floors' of her burrow, and though mops and brushes are not
seriously to be looked for in the holes of woodmice, Mrs. Tittlemouse,
inveterate nest-maker, typifies the beautifully observed fastidiousness of her
mouse nature.

In the same way Ginger the cat, serving behind the counter and doing
grocery accounts, is a figure of pure fantasy, yet his cat nature is thereby
delicately underlined. 'The shop was also patronized by mice—only the
mice were rather afraid of Ginger. Ginger usually requested Pickles to serve
them, because he said it made his mouth water. "I cannot bear," said he,
"to see them going out at the door carrying their little parcels." '

Even the clothes in which her animals are so unerringly dressed contribute
something, by however improbable a route, to our imaginative understanding
of their characters. Mrs. Tiggy-Winkle wears a print gown, a striped petticoat
and an apron—of course! one almost exclaims, what else would you
expect?—Mr. Jeremy Fisher is dressed, apart from his mackintosh and
galoshes, not unlike Mr. Pickwick, and the result is most suitable; and Mr.
Tod, as one would predict of that vindictive and sandy-whiskered person,
is something of a dandy. It is most interesting, too, to observe those situations
in which the animals appear without their clothes: it is never done by
accident, but always to stress and as it were recall their true natures—Mrs.
Tiggy-Winkle vanishing among the bracken at the end of the story; Jemima
Puddle-Duck without her ridiculous bonnet and shawl when she has achieved
the dignity of motherhood; most telling of all, the sandy-whiskered gentle-

man, unclothed, uncivilized, pure fox at last, turning over Jemima's eggs in the wood-shed.

Margaret Lane, "The Beatrix Potter Books," *The Tale of Beatrix Potter: A Biography* (London: Frederick Warne, 1946), pp. 119–20

MAURICE SENDAK   That gentleman in the audience contended that the people inhabiting "The world of children's books" had foisted *Peter Rabbit* onto the public. He, for one, resented that. He saw through the lie; he, in a word, saw nothing. What had that silly rabbit to do with the hard facts of life, or even the dream facts? Where was the imagination? Certainly, Peter does not perform any James Bondian feats of derring-do. Alas, I could not find the words to defend Peter to the gentleman in the audience. How does one defend the obvious? My only impulse was to smash him in the nose. *That* would be defending the honor of Beatrix Potter. Being aware, however, even from the platform, that his height and breadth were greater than my own, I quietly sulked instead. But here, in front of sympathetic, and no doubt true-blue Potterites, I can state my case, which is simply that *Peter Rabbit,* in its perfect tinyness, transcends all arbitrary categories. It is obviously no more a fact book about the habits of rabbits than it is a purely fantastical tale. It demonstrates that fantasy cannot be completely divorced from reality; that fantasy heightens, sometimes simplifies, and contributes new insights into that reality. 〈. . .〉

First, this gentle book vividly communicates a sense of life, and this, I believe, is achieved through an imaginative synthesis of factual and fantastical components. Amazingly, Peter is both endearing little boy and expertly drawn rabbit. In one picture he stands most unrabbitlike, crying pitifully when there seems no way out of his dilemma. In another he bounds, leaving jacket and shoes behind, in a superb rabbit bound, most unboylike, proving what we already know from her published sketchbooks: that Beatrix Potter drew from careful observation of her subject. And how she could draw!— a gift not all illustrators are endowed with.

This book, so apparently simple, smooth, straightforward, is to my eye beautifully textured and deepened by the intimate, humorous observations that Beatrix Potter makes in her pictures. Each one, with a deft and always subtle touch, expands the meaning of the words. Take the birds, for example, that emotionally mirror the action. Flopsy, Mopsy, and Cottontail, the good little bunnies, are accompanied by two chipper, pecking birds whose busyness seems to represent the perfect, down-to-earth safety of those cautious three.

One the other hand, the bird observing Peter on his dangerous mission has an air of still, sorrowful speculation. He represents, I imagine, the helplessness and concern we feel for Peter. He seems ancient and philosophic in his doomlike observation of Peter's shoe under the cabbage; I can almost see him shake his head. There is nothing chirpy about him; his movements are as quiet as the deadly atmosphere that hangs over Mr. McGregor's garden. But there is no mention of birds in the text until much later, when Peter, trapped in the gooseberry net, is implored by three sparrows "to exert himself." And what a brilliant threesome! There is such beauty in the drawing and it is so convincing, that their passionate outcry is almost audible—a miniature Greek chorus. Peter does exert himself, and escapes in the nick of time from Mr. McGregor's dreadful sieve; and the three sparrows, who surely could have flown off long before, have stopped with Peter up to the last moment, and all burst off to freedom together. They are apparently the same three who, near the end of the tale, anxiously watch Peter slip underneath the gate into the safety of the wood outside the garden; three birds who, in Peter's presence, behave almost like guiding spirits. Around Flopsy, Mopsy, and Cottontail, there are merely realistic, garden-variety birds.

> Maurice Sendak, "The Aliveness of Peter Rabbit," *Wilson Library Bulletin* 40, No. 4 (December 1965): 346–48

ROGER SALE   It is very much a rabbit who is doing these things ⟨in *Peter Rabbit*⟩, but, especially in the early going when Peter is dressed and walking on two legs, it is also very much a child, something much more faintly suggested in the original letter. It is a boyish Peter who wears a blue jacket, as opposed to the pink ones of his sisters, and a boyish Peter who knows the moment his mother tells him not to go to the garden that he must go there. What this means is that the story takes a real turn when Peter loses his clothes and goes about on all four legs. In the letter to Noel Moore the escape from the gooseberry net, which is on page 34 of the book, leads directly to the escape from the garden, which is on page 51 of the book; in that version, thus, the story is simply about being naughty and escaping, in which the punishment for naughtiness is not having bread, milk, and blackberries for supper. In the book Peter goes from the gooseberry net to the watering can in the tool shed; then he forlornly gets lost in the garden, sees the field mouse and the cat, then climbs the wheelbarrow, from which he can see the gate, far away across the garden. What this means is that as Peter "reverts" from clothes to no clothes, from boyish rabbit to rabbity rabbit, we move into a story where the trip to the garden becomes its own reward and punishment, and the sense of what Peter must endure becomes stronger, and the sense of Peter's mother as a dominating moral agent diminishes. Thus, when Peter collapses after returning home, the sense of exhaustion is paramount, and Potter's picture does everything she can to stress the exhaustion; Peter's mother is looking at him not as though he had been naughty, but as though she were perplexed and he were beyond the touch of any admonition. Peter's sisters get their berries, as why should they not, since they had gathered them, while Peter, put to bed with camomile tea, feels the consequences not just of his naughtiness but of his adventurousness and daring. Of course one would rather be Peter than his sisters, but that is no reason why they should not get their blackberries, just as Peter's silly courage is no reason why the world should suddenly be as he wants it to be. Mrs. Rabbit was right to warn her children about the garden, but of course we are glad Peter went, not because defiance is a virtue but because of all that Potter made him go through, wonderful but mostly miserable, while he was there.

Roger Sales, "Beatrix Potter," *Fairy Tales and After: From Snow White to E. B. White* (Cambridge, MA: Harvard University Press, 1978), pp. 140–41

RUTH K. MacDONALD   ⟨*The Tale of Mr. Tod*⟩ does have archetypical sources, however. Potter herself, in a preliminary letter about the book to her publisher, noted the similarity to the Uncle Remus stories. The primary debt of the former to the latter seems to be the presence of both rabbits and foxes in the story. But unlike the Uncle Remus stories, the rabbits here do not win by outsmarting either fox or badger.   In fact, it is only a stroke of luck that distracts both predators, leading to their mutual destruction and the happenstance that permits the rescue of the rabbit babies. The badger is not a typical character in the Uncle Remus stories, and here the fox does not seem particularly wily. In fact, he has not been successful in capturing his prey for the day, and he concocts an elaborate plan in order to do in Tommy Brock, one that seems bound to fail from the beginning. The badger is the smart animal in this story, but his easy accomplishment of the distracting of old Mr. Bouncer leads one to question whether this prey is really a sufficient match for his machinations. The climax features the happy ending of rabbit family reunited and safe at home, but the wily animals win nothing but the chance to fight again. The Uncle

Remus stories do tell of the triumph of the powerless over the powerful, and in that way *The Tale of Mr. Tod* is like the Uncle Remus tales, but the similarity ends there.

As Celia Catlett Anderson has noted, Beatrix Potter's fox stories owe more to the medieval stories of Reynard the Fox than they do to Uncle Remus. Mr. Tod, like the fox of *Jemima Puddle-Duck*, is a gentleman, as is Reynard. But in this story he does not have the opportunity for civil and suave persuasion that he does in *Jemima*. Here, his good breeding is evident in the fastidiousness of his housekeeping, with the neat kitchen, the table-cloth, and clean bed linens that Tommy Brock besmirches. He has a vast collection of crockery, some of it inherited from "his grandmother, old Vixen Tod," so that one can assume his table is properly appointed, at least until his fight with Tommy destroys every piece of china he might have inherited. Rather, it is Tommy Brock who is the smooth-talking gentleman, with the ingratiating manner capable of hoodwinking old Mr. Bouncer. But his housekeeping and personal hygiene are so deplorable that one does not associate elegant manners with the badger. ⟨. . .⟩

Finally, as Anderson notes, it is Potter's acknowledgment, without design to mute or disguise, of the disagreeable side of nature that most clearly ties *The Tale of Mr. Tod* to the Reynard stories. Animals have been eaten in this story, as evidenced by the presence of their bones in Mr. Tod's house. And Tommy Brock and Mr. Tod will both continue to exist, in order to harass the rabbits in the future. But like her frankness about the fate of Mr. Rabbit in Mrs. McGregor's pie in *Peter Rabbit*, Potter is unflinchingly truthful here, too. She describes the unpleasantness in detail, and the only time she judges her characters as less than honorable in their appetites is when she ironically comments on Tommy Brock's persiflage when he claims to eat baby rabbits only when he is otherwise deprived of sustenance, an eventuality that seems unlikely ever to happen, given his rotundity. Otherwise, her characters are simply living up to their animal nature in preying on each other. Mr. Tod is as justified as Mr. McGregor in chasing rabbits; it is simply the way of nature. It is the inevitability of such relationships, and Potter's willingness to explore them without reservation about the possible delicacy of her young audience, that makes her books seem all the more permanent and genuine to the child audience.

Ruth K. MacDonald, *Beatrix Potter* (Boston: Twayne, 1986), pp. 47–49

HUMPHREY CARPENTER   The 'voice' in the Beatrix Potter books would seem, at first encounter, to be a Victorian one. If you ask people what they chiefly remember about the stories, apart from the pictures, the answer is likely to be 'the long words'. ⟨. . .⟩ It seems to be an orgy of Victorian vocabulary. The present-day parent, attempting to explain these words to children, vaguely supposes that the original readers, in the first decade of this century, when the books were appearing, could take it all in their stride.

But could they? The years between *The Tale of Peter Rabbit* and *The Tale of Pigling Bland*, the first and last notable Potter stories, were 1901 to 1913, years in which Kenneth Grahame, J. M. Barrie, and E. Nesbit were writing for children in a variety of thoroughly un-Victorian styles; years when, to look at the wider world, Joyce, Eliot, and Pound were beginning their modernist experiments. Other picture-books for small children dating from the early 1900s ⟨. . .⟩ are quite without the Victorianisms of the Potter books. What is going on? Was Beatrix Potter a stranded survivor of the Victorian age, unable to jettison the diction of her parents' world, or was she consciously imitating the manners of an earlier age, and if so, why?

If you look at them carefully, her so-called Victorianisms reveal themselves as not Victorian at all. Victorians did not write that way, certainly not for children and usually not for adults. Victorian English tends to be very wordy; the Potter archaisms, or what we might call antiquities of style, are strikingly crisp. ⟨. . .⟩ If Beatrix Potter ⟨. . .⟩ is looking back stylistically, her glance seems to have travelled beyond the Victorian age, back to an earlier period when written English was an instrument capable of greater precision.

Humphrey Carpenter, "Excessively Impertinent Bunnies: The Subversive Element in Beatrix Potter," *Children and Their Books: A Celebration of the Work of Iona and Peter Opie*, ed. Gillian Avery and Julia Briggs (Oxford: Clarendon Press, 1989), pp. 280–83

◫ *Bibliography*

The Tale of Peter Rabbit. 1902.

The Tale of Squirrel Nutkin. 1903.

The Tailor of Gloucester. 1903.

The Tale of Benjamin Bunny. 1904.

The Tale of Two Bad Mice. 1904.

The Tale of Mrs. Tiggy-Winkle. 1905.

The Pie and the Patty-Pan. 1905.

The Tale of Mr. Jeremy Fisher. 1906.

The Story of a Fierce Bad Rabbit. 1906.
The Story of Miss Moppet. 1906.
The Tale of Tom Kitten. 1907.
The Tale of Jemima Puddle-Duck. 1908.
The Roly-Poly Pudding. 1908.
The Tale of the Flopsy Bunnies. 1909.
Ginger and Pickles. 1909.
The Tale of Mrs. Tittlemouse. 1910.
The Tale of Timmy Tiptoes. 1911.
The Tale of Mr. Tod. 1912.
The Tale of Pigling Bland. 1913.
Appley Dapply's Nursery Rhymes. 1917.
The Tale of Johnny Town-Mouse. 1918.
Cecily Parsley's Nursery Rhymes. 1922.
The Fairy Caravan. 1929.
The Tale of Little Pig Robinson. 1930.
Sister Anne. 1932.
Wag-by-Wall. 1944.
The Art of Beatrix Potter. 1955.
The Tale of the Faithful Dove. 1955.
Journal 1881–1897. Ed. Leslie Linder. 1966.
Beatrix Potter's Americans: Selected Letters. Ed. Jane Crowell Morse. 1982.
Beatrix Potter's Art: Paintings and Drawings. Ed. Anne Stevenson Hobbs. 1989.
Letters. Ed. Judy Taylor. 1989.

Oscar Wilde
1854–1900

OSCAR FINGAL O'FLAHERTIE WILLS WILDE was born in Dublin on October 16, 1854, the son of Dr. William (later Sir William) Wilde, a surgeon, and Jane Francesca Elgee, well known under the pseudonym "Speranza." Wilde studied classics with great success at Trinity College, Dublin (1871–74), and then at Magdalen College, Oxford (1874–78), where in 1878 he won the Newdigate Prize for his poem *Ravenna*. In 1881 Wilde published *Poems*, a volume that was successful enough to lead to a lecture tour in the United States during 1882. In all his public appearances Wilde, who proclaimed himself a disciple of Walter Pater, displayed a flamboyant aestheticism that did much to increase his notoriety.

Wilde returned to America in 1883 in order to attend an unsuccessful New York production of his play *Vera*, written three years before. In 1884, after moving to London, he married Constance Lloyd, although shortly afterward he began to assert his repressed homosexuality. *The Happy Prince and Other Tales*, a volume of fairy tales written for his two sons, appeared in 1888.

The year 1891 was distinguished by the publication of several important works by Wilde, including the book publication of his only novel, *The Picture of Dorian Gray* (it had appeared in *Lippincott's Magazine* in 1890); the essay "The Soul of Man Under Socialism," a plea for artistic freedom, in the *Fortnightly Review; Lord Arthur Savile's Crime and Other Stories* (which includes "The Canterville Ghost," a humorous ghost story); another collection of fairy tales, *The House of Pomegranates;* and the essay collection *Intentions*, containing the critical dialogues "The Decay of Lying" and "The Critic as Artist." These works helped to establish "art for art's sake" as the dominant aesthetic credo of the avant-garde. Also in 1891 Wilde's play *The Duchess of Padua* was anonymously produced in New York under another title, without much success.

Wilde first found theatrical success with his play *Lady Windermere's Fan* (produced 1892), which combined social observation with a witty, epigrammatic style. This formula was pursued successfully in the plays that followed, including *A Woman of No Importance* (produced 1893), *An Ideal Husband* (produced 1895), and *The Importance of Being Earnest* (produced 1895). *Salomé*, published in French in 1893, was translated into English by Lord Alfred Douglas in 1894 and performed in Paris by Sarah Bernhardt in 1896, after being denied a license in England. Lord Alfred, whom Wilde had first met in 1891, was Wilde's homosexual lover, a relationship that so disturbed the Marquess of Queensberry, Lord Alfred's father, that he publicly insulted Wilde on several occasions, beginning in 1894. This prompted Wilde to bring a charge of criminal libel against Lord Queensberry, but the suit misfired and Wilde himself was imprisoned for homosexual offenses in 1895. In prison, where he remained for two years, Wilde wrote a letter to Lord Alfred that was partially published in 1905 as *De Profundis*; it contained his own justification for his conduct.

After his release in 1897 Wilde went to France, where he published *The Ballad of Reading Gaol* (1898), inspired by his prison experiences. In exile he adopted the name Sebastian Melmoth, taken from the Gothic romance *Melmoth the Wanderer* by Charles Robert Maturin, to whom Wilde was related. In 1902 a translation of Petronius' *Satyricon* and of Jules Barbey d'Aurevilly's *What Never Dies* appeared under this pseudonym, but they are now believed to be apocryphal. Oscar Wilde died in Paris on November 30, 1900. His *Collected Works* was edited by Robert Ross (1908; 15 vols.). His *Letters*, edited by Rupert Hart-Davis, appeared in 1962; a supplementary volume was published in 1985.

Critical Extracts

OSCAR WILDE   Dear Mr. Kersley, I am very pleased that you like my stories ⟨*The Happy Prince*⟩. They are studies in prose, put for Romance's sake into a fanciful form: meant partly for children, and partly for those who have kept the childlike faculties of wonder and joy, and who find in simplicity a subtle strangeness.

Oscar Wilde, Letter to George Herbert Kersley (15 June 1888), cited in Rupert Hart-Davis, ed., *The Letters of Oscar Wilde* (New York: Harcourt, Brace & World, 1962), p. 219

ALEXANDER GALT ROSS   One of the chief functions of the
true fairy story is to excite sympathy. Whether they are princes, peasants,
or inanimate objects (Was the immortal tin soldier an inanimate object?),
the joys and sorrows of the heroes and heroines of fairyland will always be
real to those persons, whatever their age may be, who love the fairy story,
and regard it as the most delightful form of romance. Mr. Oscar Wilde, no
doubt for excellent reasons, has chosen to present his fables in the form of
fairy tales to a public which, though it should count among its numbers
most persons who can appreciate delicate humour and an artistic literary
manner, will assuredly not be composed of children. No child will sympathize
at all with Mr. Wilde's *Happy Prince* when he is melted down by order of
the Mayor and Corporation in obedience to the dictum of the art professor
at the University that, since "he is no longer beautiful, he is no longer
useful." Children do not care for satire, and the dominant spirit of these
stories is satire—a bitter satire differing widely from that of Hans Andersen,
whom Mr. Wilde's literary manner so constantly recalls to us. This quality
of bitterness, however, does not repel the reader (except in the story of the
"Devoted Friend," which is at once the cleverest and least agreeable in the
volume), inasmuch as Mr. Wilde always contrives to leave us at the end of
every tale with a very pleasant sensation of the humorous.

> Alexander Galt Ross, [Review of *The Happy Prince and Other Tales*], *Saturday Review*
> (London), 20 October 1888, p. 472

WALTER PATER   Dorian himself ⟨in *The Picture of Dorian Gray*⟩,
though certainly a quite unsuccessful experiment in Epicureanism, in life
as a fine art, is (till his inward spoiling takes visible effect suddenly, and in
a moment, at the end of his story) a beautiful creation. But his story is also
a vivid, though carefully considered, exposure of the corruption of a soul,
with a very plain moral, pushed home, to the effect that vice and crime
make people coarse and ugly. General readers, nevertheless, will probably
care less for this moral, less for the fine, varied, largely appreciative culture
of the writer, in evidence from page to page, than for the story itself, with
its adroitly managed supernatural incidents, its almost equally wonderful
applications of natural science; impossible, surely, in fact, but plausible
enough in fiction. Its interest turns on that very old theme, old because
based on some inherent experience or fancy of the human brain, of a double
life: of Döppelgänger—not of two *persons*, in this case, but of the man and
his portrait; the latter of which, as we hinted above, changes, decays, is

spoiled, while the former, through a long course of corruption, remains, to the outward eye, unchanged, still in all the beauty of a seemingly immaculate youth—"the devil's bargain." But it would be a pity to spoil the reader's enjoyment by further detail. We need only emphasise, once more, the skill, the real subtlety of art, the ease and fluidity withal of one telling a story by word of mouth, with which the consciousness of the supernatural is introduced into, and maintained amid, the elaborately conventional, sophisticated, disabused world Mr. Wilde depicts so cleverly, so mercilessly. The special fascination of the piece is, of course, just there—at that point of contrast. Mr. Wilde's work may fairly claim to go with that of Edgar Poe, and with some good French work of the same kind, done, probably, in more or less conscious imitation of it.

> Walter Pater, "A Novel by Mr. Oscar Wilde" (1891), *Sketches and Reviews* (New York: Boni & Liveright, 1919), pp. 132–33

ARTHUR RANSOME   *The Happy Prince and Other Tales*, published in 1888, with pictures by Jacomb Hood and Walter Crane, are very married stories. In reading them, I cannot help feeling that Wilde wrote one of them as an experiment, to show, I suppose, that he could have been Hans Andersen if he had liked, and his wife importuned him to make a book of things so charming, so good, and so true. He made the book, and there is one beautiful thing in it, 'The Happy Prince,' which was, I suspect, the first he wrote. The rest, except, perhaps, 'The Selfish Giant,' a delightful essay in Christian legend, are tales whose morals are a little too obvious even for grown-up people. Children are less willing to be made good. Wilde was himself perfectly aware of his danger, and, no doubt, got some pleasure out of saying so, at the end of the story called 'The Devoted Friend': " 'I am rather afraid that I have annoyed him,' answered the Linnet. 'The fact is, that I told him a story with a moral.' 'Ah! that is always a very dangerous thing to do,' said the Duck. And I quite agree with her." There is a moral in 'The Happy Prince,' but there is this difference between that story and the others, that it is quite clear that Wilde wanted to write it. It is Andersen, treated exactly as Wilde treated Milton in the volume of 1881, only with more assurance, and a greater certainty about his own contribution. We recognize Wilde by the decorative effects that are scattered throughout the book. He preferred a lyrical pattern to a prosaic perspective, and, even more than his wit, his love of decoration is the distinguishing quality of his work. Andersen might well have invented the story of the swallow who died to repay the statue for jewelled eyes and gold-leaf mail given to the poor of the town of which he had once been the Happy and unseeing Prince, but he would never have let the swallow say: "The King is there in his painted coffin. He is wrapped in yellow linen and embalmed in spices. Round his neck is a chain of pale green jade, and his hands are withered leaves." And only a swallow belonging to the author of *The Sphinx* would have said, "To-morrow my friends will fly up to the second Cataract. The river horse couches there among the bulrushes, and on a great granite throne sits the God Memnon. All night long he watches the stars, and when the morning star shines he utters one cry of joy, and then he is silent. At noon the yellow lions come down to the water's edge to drink. They have eyes like green beryls, and their roar is louder than the roar of the Cataract."

Arthur Ransome, *Oscar Wilde: A Critical Study* (London: Martin Secker, 1912), pp. 91–94

HESKETH PEARSON   In May 1888 *The Happy Prince and Other Tales* was published, and Oscar Wilde was seen in a fresh character: as a writer of fairy stories. He revelled in it, and in November '91 gave a more ornate representation in *A House of Pomegranates*. Although he frequently declared that technically speaking all his works were equally perfect, until his imprisonment he expressed a preference for the story of "The Young King" in his second volume of fairy tales. After his release he thoroughly disliked all his works, saying that they were inadequate expressions of his genius. "The Happy Prince" and "The Young King" are sermons in practical Christianity, and are, on the whole, the two most effective stories in the collection.   But to the biographer there are four interesting points about these tales which bear on the nature of their author. The first is that Wilde was becoming extremely interested in the personality of Jesus Christ, an interest that increased every year until at length he almost identified himself with Christ and often spoke in parables. The second point to notice is Wilde's sympathy with the poor and the downtrodden, which eventually found direct expression in *The Soul of Man Under Socialism*, an essay that aroused the secret enmity of the rich and powerful classes at whose house-parties he was an invaluable entertainer. Next we observe his growing addiction to the use of words merely for the sake of their sounds. Two stories, "The Birthday of the Infanta" and "The Fisherman and His Soul," are full of descriptions of jewels, flowers, clothes, furniture, fruits, embroider-ies, and so on. He took a sensuous pleasure in all this; but the queer thing

is that he seemed to think he was producing literature, possibly because
Pater and Flaubert had done something of the sort; and at his worst and
weakest he resembled them. In style he thought "The Birthday of the
Infanta" his best story, and he gravely told some friends that he had conceived
it "in black and silver," but that, when translated into French, it had come
out "pink and blue," which had taught him that there were certain colour-
forces in English, a power of rendering gloom, which were not in French.
In the nineties another school of writers laboured under the same misappre-
hension that it was producing literature by cataloguing machine parts; and
the best we can say for Wilde is that his tapestries and jewels are at least
more picturesque and therefore nearer to literature than Kipling's nuts and
bolts. There was also no scientific humbug about Wilde, who said that it
was "better to take pleasure in a rose than to put its root under a microscope."
The last personal point to note in connection with Wilde's fairy tales is
the fact that he should have written fairy tales at all. ⟨. . .⟩ Like all who have
expressed themselves in stories or plays for children, from Hans Andersen to
James Barrie, he was emotionally undeveloped. Even Dean Swift, who must
have been revolving in his grave ever since Gulliver became a favourite in the
nursery, was strangely immature in that respect and has delighted children for
two centuries in spite of himself. Wilde answered a critic of his second book
of fairy tales with the words "I had about as much intention of pleasing the
British child as I had of pleasing the British public." True; but he had
thoroughly pleased an Irish child: himself.

Hesketh Pearson, *Oscar Wilde: His Life and Wit* (New York: Harper & Brothers,
1946), pp. 120–21

CHRISTOPHER S. NASSAAR   If one reads Wilde's fairy tales
in the order of their composition, one notices that the demonic element
in them grows steadily more sinister until it threatens to break out of the
fairy-tale mold and destroy it. The movement from "Lord Arthur Savile's
Crime" through *The Happy Prince and Other Tales* to the tales of *A House
of Pomegranates* is toward an increasing awareness of the demonic and a
corresponding inability to control and contain it. In the earlier tales, Wilde
usually presents the demonic in a light-hearted way. ⟨. . .⟩

In the later fairy tales ⟨. . .⟩ it is not enough to become aware of the
demonic element—one must incorporate it within an all-inclusive framework of love. This becomes especially clear when we compare "Lord Arthur
Savile's Crime" and "The Fisherman and His Soul." ⟨. . .⟩ in the earlier tale

Arthur becomes aware of Podgers but tosses him into the Thames and attains a state of higher innocence by loving and marrying Sybil; he never feels any love or pity for Podgers. In the later tale, however, the fisherman attains the higher innocence only when his heart becomes large enough to include both the beautiful mermaid and his own demonic soul. Podgers and his fallen world are destroyed, but the soul and its evil, agonized world of dry land are loved and purified. These two tales stand at opposite ends of the spectrum, but a movement is discernible in the fairy tales away from Arthur's inability to love and pity the demonic.

The early "The Canterville Ghost"—written very shortly after "Lord Arthur Savile's Crime"—may be seen as transitional in this respect: the ghost, though sent to its grave, is pitied and loved by Virginia. This movement is again inextricable from the growing concern with the demonic in the fairy tales. As the demonic element becomes more sinister and difficult to control, it can no longer be flipped into the Thames or sent to its grave, but has to be dealt with more realistically.

Christopher S. Nassaar, "The Fairy Tales," *Into the Demon Universe: A Literary Exploration of Oscar Wilde* (New Haven: Yale University Press, 1974), pp. 30, 33–34

RODNEY SHEWAN   Parody or not, ⟨"The Canterville Ghost: A Hylo-Idealistic Romance"⟩ is relentlessly topical. 'Innocents Abroad', glib reminiscences of New World life, 'an entirely new and original ghost', and a Romantic virgin-heroine are combined in an entertainment which starts out as a high-class spoof of spooks (Wilde gleefully gives the pedigree of one of the Ghost's choicest victims) and ends up as an allegory of reconciliation between guilt and innocence, old world and new.

After the establishment of the Society for Psychical Research in 1882, interest quickly grew in the possibility of demonstrating 'the objective existence of phantasmata', and Wilde uses this interest, or lack of it, as the basis for his characterisation of the old and the new worlds. The established cultural prejudice and superstition of an ancient family is contrasted with the skepticism affected by practical republicans and members of the 'Free American Reformed Episcopalian Church'. Thus Canterville Chase becomes a kind of preposterous parallel to ⟨Jane Austen's⟩ Northanger Abbey. Instead of a ghost too few there is one too many; instead of too much 'sensibility' there is too little. Whereas Catherine Morland does all she can to discover a non-existent horror by exercising her imagination, the Otis family sets out at first to disbelieve in all ghosts, then to treat the resident ghost as a

tiresomely disorganised lodger. As the Ghost puts it, they are 'evidently
people on a low, material plane of existence, and quite incapable of appreciat-
ing the symbolic value of sensuous phenomena'.

In 1891 came the intellectualising subtitle which draws attention to this
aspect of the ploy. The 'hylo-idealist' is the heroine, Virginia, who rescues
the Ghost from his purgatory by believing in him and retaining that belief
until he can find death. The idea can be paralleled by such fairy tales as
"The Frog Prince", and Virginia has a fairy-tale innocence combined with
a forthright ignorance reminiscent of Isabel Archer or Carroll's Alice. ⟨. . .⟩
Her status as redemptive heroine becomes clear when she stands resolute
before the Ghost's interpretation of the prophecy in the library window:
'you must weep for me for my sins, because I have no tears, and pray with
me for my soul, because I have no faith, and then, if you have always been
sweet, and good, and gentle, the Angel of Death will have mercy on me.
You will see fearful shapes in darkness, and wicked voices will whisper in
your ear, but they will not harm you, for against the purity of a little child
the powers of Hell cannot prevail.' There is an unexpected sexual substratum
in this which the inappropriate reference to 'a little child' (Virginia is of
marriageable age) does nothing to dissipate. However, at Virginia's reappear-
ance it is soon forgotten. ⟨. . .⟩ Virginia takes the family to look at the
skeleton in the wainscot, and, as she kneels beside it in prayer, they see
the fulfillment of the prophecy: the old almond tree has blossomed in the
moonlight (marking the start of a sequence of sympathetically blooming
flora in Wilde's prose tales).

> 'God has forgiven him,' said Virginia gravely, as she rose to
> her feet, and a beautiful light seemed to illuminate her face.
> 'What an angel you are,' cried the young Duke, and he put
> his arm round her neck and kissed her.

The pun defines the extent of this ideal, ironic, and ultimately patronising
relationship. Virginia's vocabulary is basically moral, the Duke's basically
social. The happy ending, with its sentimental mercenary marriage, is perfected by the Ghost's gift of a casket of jewels—an old-world dowry which
may be financial or moral, depending upon one's view of the story—and
by her receiving 'the coronet, the reward of all good little American girls'.
Rodney Shewan, *Oscar Wilde: Art and Egotism* (London: Macmillan, 1977), pp. 32–34

ISOBEL MURRAY   Modern critics have searched out dark psychological motives for ⟨*The Happy Prince and Other Tales*⟩. Clearly it is possible

to consider all these stories as the work of 'the Wilde who had succumbed to the homosexual impulse and had become interested in sin and crime'. But it may seem more sane and realistic to follow actress Ellen Terry, who wrote to Wilde on the publication of The Happy Prince: 'They are quite beautiful dear Oscar, and I thank you for them from the best bit of my heart. I think I love "The Nightingale and the Rose" the best. . . . I should like to read one of them some day to NICE people—or even NOT nice people, and MAKE 'em nice.'

Wilde himself wrote to a friend that these stories were 'an attempt to mirror modern life in a form remote from reality—to deal with modern problems in a mode that is ideal and not imitative'. For once, he seems fairly accurately to describe his own work: the gently Christian-Socialist tone of 'The Happy Prince'—and of 'The Young King', written shortly after, and the quasi-biblical language do combine the fairy-tale mode with the shattering problems of Victorian poverty, privilege, and art, as Tennyson had most schematically outlined these in The Palace of Art.

Moreover, fairy-tales were popular and gave scope for invention: Wilde's mother and Yeats had both published collections of Irish folk-tales, and Andrew Lang, ever an acute judge of his market, began his series of multi-coloured 'fairy books' in 1889. Hans Andersen had established the fairy-tale, and there is no doubt that Wilde saturated himself in Andersen before producing The Happy Prince—and also A House of Pomegranates, although more and different impulses are at work there. ⟨. . .⟩

Themes that recur in Andersen certainly occur in Wilde. 'The Nightingale' is a parable about nature, art, and artifice which was bound to appeal to Wilde, and 'The Neighbouring Families' is similar in appeal. And Wilde probably learned from Andersen the witty, deflating touches which grace the stories, but never, even in 'The Selfish Giant', is he betrayed into such depths of sentimentality as Anderson. He takes over witty talking animals and objects and uses them as frames for stories, as in 'The Devoted Friend', but he avoids Andersen's cloying moments, and generally transcends him. Andersen wrote far, far more fairy-tales than Wilde; he did not write more that survive.

Isobel Murray, "Introduction," Complete Shorter Fiction by Oscar Wilde, ed. Isobel Murray (Oxford: Oxford University Press, 1979), pp. 9–10

RICHARD ELLMANN   Both in its magazine form and in its form as a separate novel, Dorian Gray has faults. Parts of it are wooden, padded, self-indulgent. No one could mistake it for a workmanlike job: our hacks can do that for us. But its continual fascination teaches us to judge it by new standards. Wilde made it elegantly casual, as if writing a novel were a diversion rather than 'a painful duty' (as he characterized Henry James's manner). The underlying legend, of trying to elicit more from life than life can give, arouses deep and criminal yearnings. These contrast with the polish of English civilization at its verbal peak, and create a tension beyond what the plot appears to hold. Wilde put into the book a negative version of what he had been brooding about for fourteen years and, under a veil, what he had been doing sexually for four. He could have taken a positive view of reconsidered aestheticism, as he would in 'The Critic as Artist' and 'The Soul of Man Under Socialism,' as he had already done in 'The Decay of Lying.' Instead, *Dorian Gray* is the aesthetic novel *par excellence,* not in espousing the doctrine, but in exhibiting its dangers. Pater's refurbishing of aestheticism in the late 1860s and early 1870s had been followed by a series of attacks upon it: by James in *Roderick Hudson,* 1876; by ⟨W. H.⟩ Mallock in *The New Republic,* 1877; by Gilbert and Sullivan in *Patience,* 1881; and by *Punch* and many others. In 1890 it would have been old hat for Wilde to offer an unequivocal defense. What he did instead was to write the tragedy of aestheticism. It was also premonitory of his own tragedy, for Dorian has, like Wilde, experimented with two forms of sexuality, love of women and of men. Through his hero Wilde was able to open a window into his own recent experience. The life of mere sensation is uncovered as anarchic and self-destructive. Dorian Gray is a test case. He fails. Life cannot be lived on such terms. Self-indulgence leads him to vandalize his own portrait, but this act is a reversal of what he intends and he discloses his better self, though only in death. Wilde's hero has pushed through to the point where extremes meet. By unintentional suicide, Dorian becomes aestheticism's first martyr. The text: Drift beautifully on the surface, and you will die unbeautifully in the depths.   In response to critical abuse, Wilde added the preface, which flaunted the aestheticism that the book would indict. *Dorian Gray* is reflexive in the most cunning way, like its central image.

Dorian progresses, or regresses, to art and back to life. Everything in the book has an aesthetic and a clandestine quotient, in terms of which it can eventually be measured. The portrait of Dorian is executed by Basil Hallward just at the moment when Lord Henry is fishing for Dorian's soul. Although Wilde states in the book's preface, 'To reveal art and conceal the artist is art's aim,' Hallward fears that the portrait is too revealing of his love for Dorian, as Dorian later fears that it is too revealing of himself. Wilde the preface-writer and Wilde the novelist deconstruct each other. Dorian offers a Faustian pact (with no visible devil) that he will exchange places with his portrait, to preserve himself as a work of art.

Richard Ellmann, *Oscar Wilde* (New York: Knopf, 1988), pp. 314–15

TERRY EAGLETON   *Dorian Gray* does indeed represent, in Freud's terms, the 'return of the repressed'—a ghastly, uncannily powerful exposer of the dangers of the hedonistic creed, which in the heartless Dorian now takes the form of driving a young girl to suicide. Sibyl Vane symbolizes that side of her author who emerges in his fairy tales for children: she is an image of vulnerable innocence, and bears witness to that tender, compassionate side of Wilde which his cavalier wit kept firmly under control but which was well in evidence in his personal life. The children's stories show a commitment to the lowly and dispossessed, and most of them are in their oblique way radical political tracts. But *Dorian Gray*, guilt-ridden and tormented though it may be, is in no simple sense Wilde's 'recantation'. For one thing, its sumptuous, hothouse style colludes with the very aestheticism the book officially questions. For another thing, Wilde finds it impossible to keep an entirely straight face even in this more 'earnest' of his works, strewn as it is with wisecracks which seem to have floated in from the drawing-room comedies, and which are sometimes tactfully ascribed to Lord Henry Wotton so as to keep them at arm's length from the author. More important, however, is the fact that Dorian's callow ideology of pleasure is something of a travesty of his creator's own philosophy. For Wilde, self-cultivation is the absolute goal of human life, but it involves an all-round, 'Hellenistic' development of the personality, not just the pursuit of perverse sensations. The true aesthete can sympathize imaginatively with any state of being, and so feels a Christlike solidarity with the suffering and oppressed which is far from Gray's emotionally retarded egoism. The cynical, corrupt Lord Henry is a caricature of his author, furnished with Wilde's hedonistic ethic and glib wit but entirely bereft of his sense of fun and generosity of spirit. He is, so to speak, Wilde shorn of his more Irish virtues, and thus a deliberately distorted version of his maker. The novel testifies to the dangers of a partial, superficial Epicureanism, rather than reneges on the philosophy of self-fulfillment; indeed that philosophy is still defended in the most penitent of all of Wilde's works, *De Profundis*. It is just that self-realization is a more complex affair than either Wotton or Gray will admit, and one, in Wilde's view, entirely compatible with sympathy and love. He is not out to promote the claims of egoism, but to unmask what he sees as the specious altruism of Victorian society—an altruism which is hand-in-glove with a sentimental paternalism towards the poor, and thus the enemy of the kind of radical social change which would really benefit them. Like William Blake, Wilde knew that pity and dutiful self-sacrifice are merely the other faces of exploitation; and he insisted instead, in his creed of Individualism, that those who did not strive to become rich, fully rounded human beings in their own right were unlikely to be of much use to others.

> Terry Eagleton, "Introduction," *Oscar Wilde: Plays, Prose Writings and Poems*, ed. Terry Eagleton (New York: Knopf, 1991), pp. xiv–xv

◈ Bibliography

Ravenna (Newdigate Prize Poem). 1878.

Vera; or, The Nihilists. 1880.

Poems. 1881.

The Duchess of Padua: A Tragedy of the XVI Century. 1883.

The Happy Prince and Other Tales. 1888.

The Picture of Dorian Gray. 1891.

Intentions. 1891.

Lord Arthur Savile's Crime and Other Stories. 1891.

A House of Pomegranates. 1891.

Salomé. 1893 (in French), 1894 (tr. Lord Alfred Douglas).

Lady Windermere's Fan: A Play about a Good Woman. 1893.

The Sphinx. 1894.

A Woman of No Importance. 1894.

Oscariana: Epigrams. 1895.

The Soul of Man (Under Socialism). 1895.

The Ballad of Reading Gaol. 1898.

Children in Prison and Other Cruelties of Prison Life. 1898.

The Importance of Being Earnest: A Trivial Comedy for Serious People. 1899.

An Ideal Husband. 1899.

[*The Satyricon* by Petronius (translator). 1902.]

[*What Never Dies: A Romance* by Jules Barbey d'Aurevilly (translator). 1902.]

Sebastian Melmoth. 1904.

De Profundis. 1905.

The Rise of Historical Criticism. 1905.

Four Letters Which Were Not Included in the English Edition of De Profundis.
   1906.

Wilde v. Whistler: Being an Acrimonious Correspondence on Art between Oscar
   Wilde and James A. McNeill Whistler. 1906.

Works. Ed. Robert Ross. 1908. 15 vols.

The Suppressed Portion of De Profundis. Ed. Robert Ross. 1913.

Resurgam: Unpublished Letters. Ed. Clement K. Shorter. 1917.

After Reading: Letters to Robert Ross. 1921.

After Berneval: Letters to Robert Ross. 1922.

For Love of the King: A Burmese Masque. 1922.

Selected Works with Twelve Unpublished Letters. Ed. Richard Aldington. 1946.

Complete Works. Ed. Vyvyan Holland. 1948.

Essays. Ed. Hesketh Pearson. 1950.

Five Famous Plays. Ed. Alan Harris. 1952.

Selected Writings. Ed. Richard Ellmann. 1961.

Letters. Ed. Rupert Hart-Davis. 1962.

The Artist as Critic: Critical Writings. Ed. Richard Ellmann. 1969.

Complete Shorter Fiction. Ed. Isobel Murray. 1979.

The Annotated Oscar Wilde. Ed. H. Montgomery Hyde. 1982.

More Letters. Ed. Rupert Hart-Davis. 1985.

The Definitive Four-Act Version of The Importance of Being Earnest. Ed. Ruth
   Berggren. 1987.

Oscar Wilde's Annotated Notebooks: A Portrait of Mind in the Making. Ed. Philip
   E. Smith II and Michael S. Helfand. 1989.

Aristotle at Afternoon Tea: The Rare Oscar Wilde. Ed. John Wyse Jackson.
   1991.